All Aboard!
The Complete North American Train Travel Guide

Jim Loomis

PRIMA PUBLISHING

Library of Congress Cataloging-in-Publication Data

Loomis, Jim.
    All aboard! : the complete North American train travel guide / Jim Loomis.
    p   cm.
    Includes index.
    ISBN 0-7615-0000-6 (pbk.)
    1. United States—Guidebooks.   2. Canada—Guidebooks.   3. Railroad
travel—United States—Guidebooks.   4. Railroad travel—Canada—
Guidebooks.   I. Title.
E158.L59 1995
917.304'929—dc20   95-3849
                                                                         CIP

95 96 97 98 99 AA 10 9 8 7 6 5 4 3 2 1
Printed in the United States of America

How to Order
Single copies may be ordered from Prima Publishing, P.O. Box 1260BK, Rocklin, CA 95677; telephone (916) 632-4400. Quantity discounts are also available. On your letterhead, include information concerning the intended use of the books and the number of books you wish to purchase.

Contents

Acknowledgments

This book was a big project—much more so than I ever dreamed at the outset—and it could never have been completed without the help and encouragement of many people.

My initial contact at Amtrak, the extremely competent Debbie Hare, proved a steady source of assistance. So, too, did many of her dedicated colleagues, including Rob Borella, Jim Brysnyski, Jeff Lowe, John Miller, Bill O'Dea, Tom Pape, Don Skinner, Peter Welsh, and others. Thanks especially to Craig Willett and Bob Kolkman, who made me feel welcome in the cab of Amtrak locomotive No. 343 for five informative and unforgettable hours as the *Empire Builder* rolled along between Milwaukee, Wisconsin, and Winona, Minnesota. I'm particularly grateful to the many on-board employees of both Amtrak and VIA Rail who took time from their grueling days and nights to tell me about themselves and their jobs.

Thanks to Terry Ross, former Burlington Northern engineer, who took the time to provide a running commentary on railroad operations as we rode the *Zephyr* together from Omaha, Nebraska, to Galesburg, Illinois, . . . then took even more time to review what I'd written and gently correct what I'd gotten wrong.

Finally, thanks to my brother, Pete, who knows more about all this than I ever will and who kept up a steady flow of ideas and suggestions; to my wife, Paula, for urging me to write this book even if it turned out to be just for me; and to Wif, because she likes riding trains almost as much as her dad.

Rediscovering the Train

When I was a youngster, back in the late 1940s and early 1950s, our family would take an annual train trip from our home in Connecticut to either St. Louis or Florida, where a set of grandparents would be waiting.

Those train rides were great adventures. I remember standing on the platform of the Hartford railroad station, waiting for the train to arrive. I would crane my neck for the first glimpse, all the while being careful to keep behind the yellow warning line. According to my father, anyone standing across that line as the train rolled into the station ran the risk of being "sucked under the wheels."

The anticipation was almost unbearable. Finally, a rasping monotone would blare out over the public address system: "Your attention, please. Now arriving on Track Two. . . ."

The platform came alive with that announcement—baggage carts rattled past, last-minute passengers ran up the stairs from the waiting room, mothers anxiously corralled their kids.

The general confusion quickly subsided and then thirty or forty people were craning their necks. Still we saw nothing, just the tracks curving away beyond our line of sight. Then a black steam locomotive suddenly materialized, bearing down on us, even appearing to accelerate as it loomed larger and larger. It was always so much bigger than I had remembered. And noisier, although the locomotive's bell, clang-clanging slightly out of rhythm, was somehow clearly heard above the din as the train rumbled past.

A train ride is still a great adventure for me. I'm always anxious to board; always reluctant to get off. There is obvious irony, of course, in the fact that someone who loves rail travel has spent the last thirty years living in Hawaii, over 2,000 miles from the nearest long-distance train. Strangely, it was for this very reason that my love of train travel was revived after so many years.

Several years ago, my family was organizing a reunion in Florida around my parents' 50th wedding anniversary. While discussing plans to attend the event, I realized that neither my wife nor my daughter had really seen America. Both had been born and raised in the Islands and, typical of most Hawaii residents, almost everything they knew of "the mainland" was what they had seen from 30,000 feet.

Not even sure it was possible, I suggested flying straight to Florida for the reunion, then taking the train back to the west coast before flying home to Honolulu. My wife thought I was crazy, and said so. Our daughter was six at the time, and Paula had visions of trying to occupy an active youngster in cramped quarters for hours upon end. Eventually, I worked out an itinerary that included overnight stops in Williamsburg, Virginia; Washington, D.C.; Chicago; the Colorado Rockies; the Sierras in California; and, finally, San Francisco. My wife still wasn't completely convinced, but agreed to give Amtrak a try.

We had a wonderful trip. Williamsburg was charming, Washington was inspiring (and delightfully cool for June), the Rockies and the Sierras were spectacular. Just as important, our train experience was all I had hoped.

Since then, the train has become the preferred means of long-distance travel for our family. My daughter, in particular, has become a train enthusiast. A few summers ago, she and I combined two passions into a wonderful three-week excursion, logging several thousand miles on Amtrak as we followed the Boston Red Sox on one of their west coast road trips: Oakland, Seattle, Chicago, and, finally, "home" to Boston. Neither of us will ever forget it. We had a priceless opportunity for a special father-daughter time together. The scenery was magnificent, the Red Sox won six of seven games with us in the stands . . . and we did it all by train.

This book grew from those experiences. It is written for the person who is naturally inquisitive, who notices and finds delight in little things, who knows that those who hurry miss a lot. My hope is that this book will significantly add to the experience of every train ride for such a person, and I take a great deal of pleasure in that thought.

You get a real feeling of this country
and the people in it
when you're on a train.

HARRY TRUMAN

CHAPTER 1

Why Take a Train?

Sophie Tucker once said, "I've been rich and I've been poor . . . and rich is better." With apologies to the late Miss Tucker, in my many travels I've been comfortable and I've been uncomfortable . . . and comfortable is better. A lot better. In a nutshell, that's why I take the train.

There are many societal and environmental reasons for being pro-rail, which we'll talk about in another chapter; but for long-distance travel, the train is the only civilized option left for us. You think not? Consider the other choices.

See America Through a Windshield?

Forget it. Droning great distances across the country by car or—I shudder at the very thought—by bus is, for the most part, a monumental waste of time and energy. If you're the driver, it's tiring. If you're a passenger, it's boring. And either way it's confining and uncomfortable.

In his delightful book *On the Road,* Charles Kuralt says, "Thanks to the interstate highway system, it is now possible to travel across the country coast to coast without seeing anything."

Kuralt's hyperbole can be forgiven. Unless or until you leave the interstate highways, you won't come close to much of the real America. When we build super highways in this country, we level everything, carving a swath across the land hundreds of yards wide from horizon to horizon. When we're through, there's nothing much left to see. The only conceivable reason for traveling long distances by car is to save money and that, I'll argue, is only possible when the cost is amortized over a number of passengers.

Flying Really Is for the Birds

Perhaps it's because of deregulation and the lack of competition that resulted. Maybe it's just the shifting economic conditions. But for the ordinary traveler, flying is no longer a pleasurable experience.

Unless you have the money, the frequent flyer mileage, or the connections to fly first class, you're forced to spend hours crammed into a narrow seat with virtually no leg room. Once, on a flight to Los Angeles, I sat next to a rather large woman. She was only moderately overweight, but the seats were so narrow I was forced to eat my meal left-handed. Add jet lag into the mix with the cramped conditions, and a cross-country trip is exhausting. Everyone has a horror story about the routine discomforts and inconveniences of flying, yet we have come to tolerate these conditions as an acceptable trade-off for getting somewhere quickly.

Flying isn't all bad, of course. It's quite true, for instance, that occasionally—*if* you are flying during daylight hours and *if* you can arrange a window seat and *if* there is no cloud cover—you can see some pretty spectacular things from a jetliner. Once, on a flight out of Ft. Myers, Florida, I had a ringside seat for a space shuttle launch. No doubt about it, that was something to see from 20,000 feet.

But how exciting is it when the captain says, "That city off to the left of our aircraft is Wichita, Kansas"? Assuming you have a window seat on the left side, Wichita looks a lot like Topeka . . . or Boise or Duluth or Portland (Oregon or Maine, take your choice). The fact is, you don't see much of America from a plane.

Finally, the technology of modern aviation is incomprehensible to ordinary people. Instead of entering through that long, mechanized tunnel, have you ever boarded a Boeing 747 from ground level? It's unnerving. You stand on the tarmac looking up at that monstrous machine and you know intellectually that it will not, cannot possibly, fly! Only God Himself understands how something that big actually gets off the ground. And only blind faith gets me aboard. I only know one thing for certain about a plane trip: the sooner we land, the better I like it.

A Simple Attitude Adjustment

Long-distance train travel isn't the best choice for everyone on every occasion. If you have to get somewhere fast, an airplane is admittedly the only practical answer. And some people simply can't gear down sufficiently to enjoy the train whether they're in a hurry or not.

For most people, though, all it takes to enjoy a long-distance train trip is a simple attitude adjustment before starting out. Just remember that the train should be an important part of your vacation experience; the plane is nothing more than the fastest way to get there.

On the *Coast Starlight,* en route from Los Angeles to Seattle . . . (By the way, you'll notice that long distance trains are traditionally given names as well as numbers. A nice touch, don't you think?) Anyway, on the *Coast Starlight,* you roll almost silently through the Cascade Mountains of Oregon on a single track cut through the wilderness. Heading east out of Seattle on the *Empire Builder,* you fall asleep in the Cascades and wake up the next morning in the Rockies as the train skirts Glacier National Park. The *Lake Shore Limited* takes you along the banks of Lake Erie and Lake Ontario; the *Adirondack* follows the Hudson River into

New York City; and if you want to gaze on some of the prettiest country anywhere, ride the *Cardinal* across West Virginia and Kentucky.

Just out of El Paso on the *Sunset Limited,* you pass an Indian boy sitting bareback on his pony and wonder if he's as curious about you as you are about him. From the *California Zephyr,* you see a man and a woman sitting with their arms around each other on a tractor in a field of corn that stretches to the horizon. She waves as you pass. On the *City of New Orleans,* you pass a man putting tar paper on the roof of a shack and, as he straightens and stares, you can tell that his back hurts. As you roll slowly through a South Carolina town on the *Silver Meteor,* you see an elderly woman tending a small vegetable garden in her backyard. Her tomatoes are ripe.

Twenty-four hours on a train will yield a thousand mental snapshots of America and her people . . . and the time to savor them.

More than anything, your train ride should be relaxing. That doesn't come automatically to everyone. You may have to work a bit at making that mental adjustment. Some people just can't do it. My sister once talked her husband into taking the train from Denver to Los Angeles. He enjoyed the spectacular scenery as they wound their way through the Rockies west of Denver, but somewhere in Nevada the next morning, as they were rolling along beside a highway, he suddenly sat straight up in his seat. "Good God! Those cars are moving faster than we are! They'll get to Los Angeles before we do!" Not true, of course, but he never could explain why that should matter anyway, but he was agitated and impatient for the rest of the trip.

Why travel by train? Because compared to the alternatives, it's comfortable and relaxing. Because it's *civilized*. And most of all, because it will broaden and elevate your appreciation and understanding of our country and its people. That's the United States of America out there, passing by right outside your living-room window.

CHAPTER 2

How It All Began

Railroads have been around for a long time. As far back as the sixteenth century they were used to haul coal out of mines in England and Wales. Actually, those were hardly what we would call railroads—just horses and mules pulling wagons along crude tracks—but they had the same fundamental advantage that modern railroads offer. By reducing friction, more weight could be moved with less energy. The people who ran those coal mines understood that concept in even simpler terms: the easier it was for a horse to pull one of their carts, the more coal they could put into it.

The potential of steam power had been understood for a long time and, in fact, steam engines had been used for years to pump water out of those same coal mines. The big breakthrough came about 1803 when Richard Trevithick, an English mining engineer, figured out how to mount a steam engine on a movable platform. Within a few years, the very first steam locomotives were used to haul that coal from the mines to seaports, from where it was shipped all over the world. In 1825, the first rail passenger service was begun, and the news of this new means of transportation started spreading beyond England's shores. It found fertile ground in America.

It's hard to think of another new technology that had a greater impact on our country—or the modern world, for that matter—than the railroad. The railroads caused this country to *be* . . . it's that simple.

A Mobile Society Is Created

America's first railroad was the Baltimore & Ohio, which started service in 1830 and immediately captured the imagination of the country. That's hardly surprising. Up to that time, no human had ever traveled faster than a horse could run. Now, almost overnight, ordinary people were traveling for greater distances at higher speeds than had ever been dreamed possible. Other railroads followed on the B&O's heels.

For the average American of the early-to-middle 1800s, it all took some getting used to. Of necessity, families and communities had always been virtually self-sufficient. The railroads changed all of that in a matter of a few years, first by linking towns, then states, and finally the entire continent. Suddenly Americans had mobility; almost anyone could go almost anywhere. It's an interesting paradox that while railroads were bringing Americans together as one people, they also made it possible for the country itself to expand.

By the middle of the nineteenth century, people were heading west by the thousands, chasing after gold that had been discovered in California in 1848 or looking for some land of their own. But however efficiently the railroads may have linked north and south and east, they could only take people halfway into the Great American West—just as far as Omaha.

The Biggest Construction Project Ever

There had been talk about extending the railroad to the west coast for some time, but the men who proposed it were largely written off as fools. It was indeed a huge, daunting project, arguably one of the largest and most ambitious engineering projects ever attempted. Furthermore, not everyone thought California was the promised land even if the transcontinental railroad did prove feasible. Probably the best-known nay-sayer of the time was Daniel Webster, who described the west as a "region of savages and wild beasts, of deserts of shifting sands and whirlwinds of dust, of cactus and prairie dogs."

Nevertheless, President Abraham Lincoln decided to move ahead with the transcontinental railroad and signed the Pacific Railroad Act in 1862. Although there may have been a fair amount of foresight and vision involved, the main reason for the decision was a very real concern that California, which had become our 31st state in 1850, would use the Civil War as an excuse to leave the Union and become a separate nation. Then, too, with the Gold Rush in full swing, there was always the threat of attack by a foreign power, and without a transcontinental railroad the United States could never get troops or supplies to California in time to deal with the problem.

When the work finally began, it was certainly in earnest and in spite of the fact that the Civil War had begun. The Union Pacific headed west from Omaha, Nebraska, while the Central Pacific Railroad started east from Sacramento, California. The CP had problems from the outset. Most of the able-bodied men were busily mining gold and those who were recruited proved to be largely unreliable. Finally, and as what they thought was a last resort, the railroad hired Chinese as laborers. As it turned out, they were much better workers. During the six-plus years of construction, the Central Pacific used a total of 10,000 workers, of which nine of ten were Chinese.

It was tough, dangerous work over terribly difficult terrain. In some areas laborers were suspended from cliffs by ropes in order to hack the roadbed out of the mountainside. While digging the Summit Tunnel in the Sierras, work crews had to blast through 1,600 feet of such hard granite that in spots they were able to progress just one foot a day. A new explosive, nitroglycerin, speeded the work, but was extremely unstable in its early form—always dangerous and frequently fatal. Nevertheless, work went on from both ends and, when the crews finally met, the two holes were only few inches off. After five years of prodigious effort, the CP crews had laid just 100 miles of track.

The Union Pacific didn't have the awful terrain to deal with and made much faster progress heading west across the Great Plains. There were still problems aplenty—finding wood from which to fashion cross ties, for instance, since there were no trees on the Nebraska prairie. To fill this obvious need, the railroad contracted with men, called tie hacks, to cut ties from trees in the western mountains, then haul the ties to meet the railroad.

The Union Pacific paid its railroad workers $1 per day, and all of them lived in rail cars which followed them as track was laid. Many were immigrants of Irish and German descent, and a good many had seen service in the Civil War. As the railroad moved farther west, it entered Sioux territory. While the Indians had largely ignored the occasional wagon train, this was clearly a serious threat to their way of life. Attacks became more frequent and progress slowed as the ex-soldiers were diverted into armed units assigned to protect the remaining work crews. Through it all, fueled by relatively high wages and visions of huge profits, the work went on at a feverish pace. In fact, one Union Pacific crew laid just over ten miles of track in one day—an astonishing feat considering the backbreaking nature of the work and the lack of any kind of power equipment.

The transcontinental link finally occurred on May 10, 1869, when the two railroads met near Promontory, Utah. Sorry, but it was an ordinary iron spike, not a golden one, that was driven into the last cross tie. For that matter, the event itself didn't really occur at Promontory itself, but at a site about 30 miles away. The famous photo of the event is actually of a reenactment. One other item of questionable relevance, but possible interest: America's transcontinental railroad and the Suez Canal were both completed in 1869, a coincidence which prompted Jules Verne to write *Around the World in 80 Days*.

The Stream Becomes a Flood

It's hard for us to imagine the impact on the country when the cross-country rail line was finally opened. For a quarter of a century it had taken a full six months to reach California or Oregon by wagon train from one of the several jump-off points in the midwest, and one of every ten pioneers died during the crossing. Then, quite suddenly, you could travel in relative safety and comfort all the way from New York City to Sacramento in a little over six and a half days. And people started to do so, by the thousands upon thousands.

If the western movement of people was a stream, then the mail they sent and received soon became a flood. Before the transcontinental link, mail was either carried by stagecoach or, if coast-to-coast, around the Horn by sailing ship—a matter of several months. Suddenly trains had the capacity to carry large quantities of mail at low cost and at unheard of speed: coast to coast in less than a week. Mail was sorted en route in mail cars. Speed was everything. Bags of mail were thrown from trains or snatched from trackside poles as trains sped through small towns all across America without stopping. There was glamour attached to speedy mail service and the railroads gave it top priority. Trains brought news for the masses, too—more of it and faster than ever before. Newspapers printed in major cities were delivered by train to subscribers in small-town America within hours.

America Starts Moving by Rail

By 1865, when the Civil War ended, some 30,000 miles of track crossed the country. During the next 25 years, steel rails spider-webbed out all over America until, by 1890, well over 200,000 miles of track ran from sea to shining sea.

The federal government encouraged the spread of the railroads by giving them land—not just rights of way on which to lay their tracks, but land adjacent to the tracks, too—millions of acres. The railroads sold this land at very low prices—actually gave it away in some cases. Railroads hired "colonization agents" to recruit families from the industrial east coast. Many railroads actually operated what were called immigrant trains, which carried entire families, including personal belongings and even livestock, from the eastern United States into the newly opened areas. Thousands took advantage of this new opportunity and, as word spread across the Atlantic, European immigrants joined the flood of new settlers.

The railroads were eager, almost desperate, to encourage this resettlement because they needed people—*lots* of people—wherever they laid their tracks if the railroad itself was to succeed. It worked, too, because the supplies these settlers needed to start and sustain their new lives on the American frontier were brought to them by the railroads. And, of course, as they became established farmers and ranchers, they sent their wheat and corn and cattle to eastern markets—also by rail.

In less than a quarter of a century, the railroads were prospering and so were the cities and towns they served. Chicago became a thriving center of business and trade, not coincidentally because the eleven different railroads serving that city made it the busiest railroad center in the world. New factories full of new employees sprang up to process the cattle, grain, lumber, and other raw materials being delivered to Chicago by rail from the west. And, naturally, the goods produced by these factories were then shipped by rail to consumers in every area of the country, including back to those people living in the now-prosperous western towns.

It was certainly a time for people with new ideas. No doubt Richard Sears and Alvah Roebuck had a good one when they started their catalog business in 1887, but it was the railroads and their efficient handling of letters and packages that made it all possible. In fact, it's hardly a coincidence that Richard Sears, the partner who first realized the potential of the mail-order business, began his working career as a railroad agent in Minnesota. In reality, the Sears tower that dominates the Chicago skyline today is as much a monument to the American railroad as to those two far-sighted entrepreneurs.

Bigger, Better, Faster Trains

As the country grew, so did the railroads. More trains were going to more places and getting there faster. And in greater safety, too. Air brakes had been developed by George Westinghouse and were in general use on most trains by the 1880s. About that same time, a simple but significant improvement in the design of passenger cars occurred when an elastic diaphragm was added to each end of every car. These diaphragms connected when the cars were coupled together and, just like that, the passageway between cars became enclosed. Until this improvement took place, the business of crossing from one lurching car to another was not for the young, the old, or the faint-hearted. Once it became easy and safe for passengers to pass between moving railway cars, the modern version of the dining car suddenly became feasible.

The first regular on-board food service had begun in 1842, with credit again going to the Baltimore & Ohio. The food was prepared elsewhere, brought aboard the trains, and served cold to the passengers. Then, in 1867, George

Pullman introduced a very early version of what we would come to recognize as a dining car. Actually, he called it a "hotel car," and for good reason: Since passengers didn't move back and forth between rail cars, this one car contained cooking facilities, a dining area, and sleeping accommodations for as many as 40 passengers.

George Pullman may have had a good idea with his hotel car, but he really hit it big when his Pullman Palace Car Company in Chicago began turning out luxury sleeping cars, which before long came to be known simply as "Pullmans." Not many people know that the railroads hauling George Pullman's sleeping cars around the country didn't actually own them. The Pullman Company retained ownership of the cars and merely leased them to the various railroads. Even the conductors and porters were Pullman employees. Pullman's "turn key operation" was several decades ahead of its time. In fact, for many years it was said that on any given night, more people were sleeping in Pullman car berths than in the beds of the largest hotel chains in the world.

George Pullman went so far as to build a small town for his workers adjacent to the Chicago plant where his rail cars were built. At its peak, some 12,000 workers lived in the community created by their employer—working in his factory, living in his houses, buying from his stores. Pullman was less a visionary than a relentless businessman, for the reality was that he made a profit on almost everything his employees bought, including the rent they paid for their homes.

Pullman's little empire began to come undone in 1893 when the country slid into a depression. As business declined and profits fell, Pullman reduced the wages he paid his employees. He did not, however, see a corresponding need to reduce the rents they paid for their housing. As the depression deepened, unrest among Pullman Company employees grew, and in 1894 they walked off their jobs in protest. Things turned ugly in short order, and in an ensuing riot, thirty-four people were killed at the Pullman plant. The U.S. Army was sent in and restored order by arresting the union leaders and tossing them in jail.

Government Regulation

For a number of years George Pullman had been regarded as an enlightened and respected businessman, but that image changed quickly after the strike. He soon found himself the object of severe criticism from many quarters. Pullman wasn't alone, either. Sharing the spotlight of harsh public opinion were a number of men who had made millions from railroads: Cornelius Vanderbilt, J. P. Morgan, James J. Hill, Jay Gould, and others.

These men were portrayed as greedy robber barons and, in truth, many of them richly deserved the label. These were, after all, the days before government controls, and many railroad tycoons took full advantage of that lack of regulation through shady stock deals and shameless gouging. In many areas of the west, for instance, farmers and ranchers were at the mercy of the railroads that carried their cattle or grain to eastern markets. The railroads regularly increased their rates and were soon making huge profits while their customers continued to struggle for survival. In 1887, the federal government finally reacted, and the Interstate Commerce Commission was created by Congress to regulate the railroads, specifically to set the rates that could be charged for hauling freight.

The Unions Appear

Railroading in these early days was notoriously dangerous work. The combination of bigger, faster trains and the lack of anything approaching modern safety standards took a terrible toll. Brakemen worked on top of moving rail cars in all weather. Bad track (usually laid in haste) often caused derailments. Locomotive boiler explosions were not uncommon and were always fatal to the head-end crew. It's estimated that in the 30 years leading up to World War I, railroad workers were killed on the job at the rate of some 2,500 a year, or an average of seven deaths every single day. Millions more were injured. Even everyday working conditions were often appalling. Temperatures in the locomotive cab could reach 30 below zero in winter and 150–160 degrees in summer. Not surprisingly, these were the years when railroad unions were formed and began to gain acceptance. Gradually, the lives of railroad workers began to improve.

Storm Clouds on the Railroads' Horizon

The pendulum began swinging the other way when the country's railroads were nationalized during World War I, and the government agreed to major concessions to the unions. Many of the new rules made sense at the time. For instance, an eight-hour day was established as standard for railroad employees, but at the same time, the government also agreed that a distance of 100 miles would constitute a full day's work for a train's operating crew. In those early days, that was realistic. Operating one of those early steam locomotives was exhausting work and, with stops along the route for watering and coaling, it could easily take a full eight hours to travel a hundred miles. But by the 1920s, long after the railroads had been returned to private ownership, the technology of steam locomotives had become more efficient and trains were being run at much higher speeds. The railroads were not able to change or get rid of the old union rules so they often found themselves giving a train crew four days' pay for eight hours' work because their train had covered four hundred miles during that time.

Then trucks appeared. Actually, the value of hauling supplies by truck had become apparent in Europe during

World War I, when the U.S. Army used fleets of vehicles to haul supplies and ammunition to the doughboys at the front. From that experience, it was easy to see that trucks had considerable potential for peacetime application. In 1919, a convoy of trucks set out to cross the country from Washington, D.C., to San Francisco. It took *three months* at an average speed of less than six miles per hour, but they did it—and it was suddenly clear that the truck needed only one thing to become a new mode of transportation: a decent road.

To provide jobs for the unemployed after the stock market crash of 1929, the government started building roads—the beginnings of our interstate highway system. As soon as new roads were finished, trucks began hauling freight over them. Instead of traveling city to city in a railroad boxcar, goods were traveling door to door in a truck. Then came buses—Greyhound and Trailways and a host of small-time carriers—and the railroads started losing passenger business, too. Right behind the buses came private passenger cars. Thanks to Henry Ford and mass production, ordinary people could now pile into the family car and visit friends or relatives several hundred miles away. As if competition from trucks and buses and cars wasn't bad enough for the railroads, a few visionaries talked about airplane travel becoming feasible for large numbers of people within 20 years. To top it all off, in some parts of the country, railroads were even competing against each other for both freight and passenger business.

The Way to a Passenger's Heart

Whatever their other faults, the railroad entrepreneurs were not quitters and they finally began to fight for their share of the passenger business. They competed by claiming faster trains, more comfortable routes, and more service amenities. But many railroads had come to realize that what passengers remembered most about their train trip was the *dining* experience. That's what they talked about with their friends and, as we all know, word of mouth is the most effective form of advertising. Soon, to the joy of rail passengers everywhere, competition between railroads had extended into the dining car.

During the 1930s, 1940s, and 1950s—the exception being an interruption for World War II—it wasn't unusual to have more than a dozen entrees, including fresh fish and wild game, on a dining car menu, plus a lavish selection of desserts. Many railroads became known for specific dishes served in their dining cars. Diners on the Great Northern, for instance, featured rainbow trout that was caught, handed aboard the moving train, cooked, and served in the space of just a few hours.

The railroads did their best to regain passenger business after World War II by promoting rail travel to the west. In addition to traditional forms of advertising, many of the crack trains were given what easterners would perceive to be Indian names: *Chief, Super Chief, Scout, Hiawatha,* and a few others.

Comes the Golden Age

Beginning around 1890 and continuing until the outbreak of World War II, Americans with the means were able to travel in real style from coast to coast and between many major cities throughout the country. It was a time that's come to be known as the *belle époque*—the golden age of train travel—as dozens of railroads vied for passenger business with crack trains that featured every manner of luxury and service.

The very, very rich—investment bankers, industrialists, the railroad tycoons themselves, and others of that ilk—traveled in their own private rail cars, but until the railroads themselves actually got into the business of providing it, luxury rail travel was simply not available—not even to the merely wealthy. Then, in the fall of 1911, the Santa Fe began offering once-a-week service between Chicago and Los Angeles with a train appropriately called the *de Luxe*. And indeed it was. Passengers slept in real brass beds. There were maids and a manicurist for female passengers, a barber for the men. The latest books and magazines could be found in an on-board library. Newspapers and the latest stock reports were put aboard at regular stops en route. In promoting the *de Luxe,* the railroad boasted that passengers would stay comfortable regardless of the outside temperature, thanks to a technological breakthrough the company described as an "air washing device"—a primitive form of air-conditioning.

As the years passed and passenger demand grew, the Santa Fe added more luxury trains to its popular Chicago–Los Angeles route. The *Chief* made its debut in 1926 and soon became the choice of movie stars traveling between coasts—a fact the railroad promoted relentlessly with publicity photos of the stars waving from the observation platform on the rear car. The lounge car featured a barber, a hairdresser, a manicurist, and a hostess. In the *Chief*'s dining car, the menu offered a dizzying variety, expertly prepared and served with a flourish. There was even a private dining room where Hollywood moguls could dine and make their blockbuster deals in private.

The *Chief* proved very popular. To meet the additional demand and broaden its passenger base, the Santa Fe added other new trains to the route. The *Scout* wasn't as fancy as the *Chief,* but it catered to middle-income families traveling on a budget and helped bring long-distance train travel to a whole new market. The *El Capitan* was an all-coach train, and the *California Limited* served only first-class passengers. Finally, in 1936, Santa Fe introduced the *Super Chief,* which soon became a standard in its own right. Gradually the traditional Pullman cars gave way to gleaming stainless steel consists (any combination of locomotives and cars making up the entire train) with the now-classic bullet-shaped observation/lounge car bringing up the rear. Even after auto and air travel forced rail passenger service into serious decline, the Santa Fe steadfastly maintained its standards of quality and service to the very last.

Competition for passengers among railroads themselves was probably fiercest on the routes between Chicago and New York City. A number of railroads served those cities, but most of the competition was between the Pennsylvania Railroad's *Broadway Limited* and the pride of the New York Central System, the famous *20th Century Limited.* Both trains ran at high speeds, both offered fine dining and many service amenities and, for a time anyway, both left Chicago heading east at about the same time. Old-time Chicago train watchers tell of waiting at any one of several vantage points in the suburbs to see which train would be leading as they came thundering past, still running on parallel tracks at that point.

Other railroads were also contributing to the lore and legacy of the American luxury long-distance train. The Baltimore & Ohio operated a number of excellent trains, but probably considered the *Capitol Limited,* running between Washington, D.C., and Chicago, to be its flagship. One of the Great Northern's best was the *Oriental Limited,* so named by the railroad's founder, James J. Hill, because he thought that his northern route from Chicago to Puget Sound would open the way for a vast amount of trade between the United States and Asian markets.

The Wabash Railroad's *Cannon Ball* began providing daylight service between St. Louis and Detroit in 1946. Curiously, even though the famous song had been around for decades, there's no record of any train with that name before the Wabash got around to using the title.

During this so-called *belle époque,* dozens of railroads operated literally hundreds of trains. Many developed their own identity and reputation—for speed, service, color

scheme, a special dish in the dining car, or just its own pecu-
liar *élan*. And, of course, in that wonderful railroad tradition,
they were all given names. Some were clearly regional
(*Connecticut Yankee, Southern Belle*), while others touted destinations (*Dixie Express, Texas Eagle*). Some trains were
named for people, both real and fictional (*Commodore
Vanderbilt, Pocahontas, Rip Van Winkle*). Some names were
highly evocative (*Black Diamond, Flying Cloud, North Wind*),
and at the other end of the spectrum, some tried to be clever
(*Silent Knight*) or cute (*Seven O'Klocker*).

Many of us actually remember riding some of those
trains, and they certainly were wonderful—maybe even as
luxurious as we remember them. Still, it's important to keep
things in perspective. The fact is that, during all those so-
called glory years of rail travel, most Americans rode on
trains that were quite ordinary—slow and probably neither
very clean nor very comfortable. Then as now, luxury was
for the fortunate few.

First It Rained, Then It Poured

When trouble came for the passenger trains, it came from
many directions at once, and it wasn't pretty. Trucks by the
hundreds of thousands began hauling commodities of all
kinds over a new system of interstate highways. Mom and
Dad and their 2.5 kids traveled wherever they wanted to go,
coast-to-coast over that same highway system in a family
car that ran on gasoline costing 25 cents a gallon. Airplanes
became larger and faster, which meant they carried more
people farther, faster, and cheaper than ever. With all those
fast, new jets flying everywhere, the U.S. Post Office
decreed that *all* first-class mail would henceforth travel by
air. (Remember? We used to pay one rate for letters sent by
surface and a higher rate for air mail.) Revenue from first-
class mail carried on fast passenger trains had been an

important source of income for the railroads. Any one of those factors would have hurt; all together they were fatal.

Some railroads had seen it coming and tried to fight back, but one after another they all came to realize that it was a losing battle. At that point, the problem became how to get out of the passenger business. It wasn't easy in those days before deregulation. The same Interstate Commerce Commission that had been created in the late 1800s was now a way of bureaucratic life for the railroads. The Commission approved requests for routes and reviewed and approved the fares the railroads charged. Unfortunately, from the railroads' perspective, the Commission also had to approve whenever a railroad wanted to cut out passenger service. Usually, approval would only be given if the railroad could demonstrate that there was little if any demand for the service.

And so the game began. Railroads allowed both their equipment and their service to deteriorate in the hope that train travel would become such an unpleasant experience that passengers would turn elsewhere for their transportation. Certainly a lot did, but for many unlucky souls, the train was the only way to get where they had to go. (By the way, that's still the case today in many rural communities, where an Amtrak train is literally the only way in or out of town.)

Gradually it settled into a standoff between the federal government and the railroads. The government refused to let the railroads stop providing passenger service; the railroads refused to provide more than the most basic service. The traditional dining car soon gave way to dirty lounge cars where vending machines dispensed stale packaged food. Sleeping cars on overnight trains were replaced with coaches, forcing passengers to sit up all night—even those willing and able to pay for first-class accommodations. It was a frustrating, maddening situation that went on for years. And everyone knew that sooner or later, it could end only one way.

The Railroad in Everyday Language

Some are obvious, others are obscure, but many expressions we all use in our daily lives have origins that can be traced to the railroad. These are but a few.

blocked   Today it means to prevent something from moving forward, but originally the word described a train prevented from entering a stretch of track, which is called a "block."

flag someone down   This refers to the railroad practice of signaling to a train with colored flags. Radios are now used to signal the engineer to stop for passengers at remote stations, but they're still called "flag stops."

highballing down the road   Early signals were given to a moving train by hoisting colored balls onto a pole; a ball at the top of the pole meant "all clear."

something is sidetracked   A reference to diverting a train onto a siding until another can pass.

a full head of steam   This expression originally referred to a steam engine with maximum pressure in its boiler.

staying on track; being off the track   A railroad track is the obvious origin of these expressions.

a light at the end of the tunnel   The consensus is that this expression originated with the railroad.

derail a project or idea   A train's progress stops abruptly when this happens, too.

getting on board   Possibly a nautical origin here, but we'll claim it anyway.

doubleheader   Originally, two locomotives coupled together to pull a long, heavy train.

over the hump　When freight cars are pushed over the hump, or high point, in a rail yard, they roll easily by themselves to a siding.

hell on wheels　This expression was a reference to the gamblers and prostitutes who followed railroad crews in their own rail cars (on wheels) while the transcontinental railway was being built.

CHAPTER 3

Amtrak to the Rescue

The great trains are gone. Of course it's a pity, but, with the advantage of 20/20 hindsight, most people agree it probably wasn't realistic to think that a nationwide system of privately operated passenger trains could have survived. It certainly hasn't worked out that way anywhere else in the world.

Anyway, after a decade or more of struggle, by 1970 it had become clear that the private railroads were simply not going to provide the country with anything even remotely resembling a nationwide rail passenger system. Even government oversight and regulation of the railroad industry wasn't going to save the passenger train. The railroads' claim that their financial health would be threatened if they were forced to continue providing passenger service was quite true in most cases. In fact, the Interstate Commerce Commission had all but officially acknowledged the plight of the railroads during the 1960s by granting various railroads permission to eliminate what amounted to almost 60 percent of the nation's passenger trains. Even that relief wasn't enough help for some, however, and private railroads continued to go broke at an alarming rate.

Time for Some Hard Decisions

Politicians had been watching these convulsions in the railroad industry with consternation. It had become clear to most members of Congress that sooner or later they would have to confront a very fundamental question: Did America really need some kind of rail passenger system? There were loud and vocal arguments on both sides, but the answer finally came up "yes," helped along at least in part because there was already a mandate to that effect on the books, the High Speed Ground Transportation Act passed by Congress in 1965. It had created and funded a federal office to look into the feasibility of, among other ideas, high-speed rail. Some of the funds had gone into study of far-out futuristic schemes, but a lot was put to practical use—helping the Penn Central begin high-speed Metroliner service between Washington, D.C., and New York, for example.

Things came to a head during the summer of 1969 and, after a great deal of argument and discussion, several different members in both the House and the Senate introduced a variety of bills. There was the usual dithering as the several versions slowly began working their way through the legislative process. Then, in June of 1970, the Penn Central collapsed into bankruptcy, and the resulting shock waves galvanized Congress into action. What emerged was something called the Rail Passenger Service Act, which finally allowed the private railroads to give up their passenger service. It also created a half-private, half-public company to take over the job of providing the country with a nationwide rail system. Although a bit short on specifics, the bill was nevertheless a commitment of support for passenger trains by the federal government. It was also pretty much a bi-partisan effort. (Cynics have noted—in fact, they *continue* to note—that support of rail passenger service has less to do with political philosophy than with whether or not there are trains serving the district of any given congressman.)

The method of funding devised to launch Amtrak was pretty complicated. Essentially, it allowed private railroads to make a cash payment to Amtrak in exchange for permission to get out of the passenger business. On a case-by-case basis, Amtrak could also elect to accept payment in the form of passenger equipment or operating crews. By the time it all shook out, twenty railroads had given Amtrak nearly 1,200 pieces of equipment and a total of just over $197 million in cash. Congress added to the pot with $40 million in cash and another $100 million in loan guarantees, giving Amtrak some $340 million to begin operations.

The final hurdle was a presidential signature. Richard Nixon had been keeping a low profile on the subject, but, in retrospect, that part of the process was probably never really in doubt. Nixon was already looking ahead to his reelection campaign in 1972 and worrying about how the unpopular war in Vietnam would affect his chances. Politically, he couldn't afford having the death of the passenger train laid at his doorstep, too. He signed the bill on October 30, 1970.

Any sighs of relief from pro-rail people were premature, however. Many who were there at the time now believe that the intent of the Nixon Administration, if not actually the president himself, was to give lip-service support to the creation of the new rail system and then quietly kill it behind the scenes. These suspicions were subsequently borne out by a succession of power plays and roadblocks aimed at undermining Amtrak. They were usually orchestrated by Nixon aide John Erlichman (later of Watergate fame).

A Shortage of Know-How

The formal name for this new public/private corporation was the National Railroad Passenger Corporation and, as a matter of fact, that's still its name. Given the American propensity for nicknames, it's not surprising that the company

almost immediately became known simply as Railpax—
"pax" being common shorthand in the travel industry for
"passengers." Within months, supposedly because a few
critics of rail travel had begun referring to the new company as Railpox, the name was changed to Amtrak, an
acronym for AMerican TRavel by trAK. A new logo was
also adopted—the same arrow-shaped mark still in use. It
was almost instantly dubbed "the pointless arrow," prov-
ing, I suppose, that someone will always find something
to pick on.

As President Nixon named directors to the board of the
brand new company, not one railroad person was among
them. Then, continuing this puzzling precedent, the board's
choice for Amtrak's first president was Roger Lewis, who
was available for the job by virtue of having been recently
fired from his position as head of General Dynamics. Lewis
assumed his new job just one week before Amtrak's scheduled start date. Don Phillips, a Washington-based journalist
whose credentials include stints as a transportation writer at
UPI and the *Washington Post,* came to like the man personally,
but publicly speculated on Lewis's real assignment: "I am
persuaded that [Lewis] took the job with orders from the
White House—direct or indirect—to oversee an orderly
shutdown [of Amtrak]."

Some were startled by Lewis's priorities as he under-
took what was undeniably a daunting job. One early
Amtrak employee, Kevin McKinney, recalled in a *Trains*
magazine story that the first memo Lewis distributed to his
staff complained about the appearance of the reception area
outside Amtrak's executive offices. The memo further
directed that thereafter the number of magazines permitted
on the coffee table would be limited to no more than four.

In putting together his team, Lewis surrounded himself
with other executives equally unfamiliar with the business
of railroading. Graham Claytor, himself a future Amtrak
president and head of Southern Railway at the time, grum-
bled that "Amtrak doesn't have a railroader above the level

of trainmaster" and dourly predicted that the new Amtrak brain trust, people Claytor considered near-hopeless amateurs, would "screw it up beyond . . . redemption."

It took a while—organizing a coast-to-coast system of passenger trains would be a monumental task under even the best of circumstances—but the first train to operate under the Amtrak banner rolled out of Washington, D.C.'s Union Station headed for New York City on May 1, 1971.

A Rocky Start

An old Madison Avenue axiom says, "Nothing can kill a business faster than great advertising." Translation: If you create demand for a product or service, it had darn well better meet customer expectations; if it doesn't, the negative word of mouth can destroy you. Amtrak stumbled into that trap in its early days with a catchy advertising slogan: "We're making the trains worth traveling again." Unfortunately, they weren't.

From day one, Amtrak people found themselves with a maintenance and operations nightmare on their hands. Being saddled with a variety of equipment collected from more than a dozen railroads caused some nasty surprises. Amtrak soon discovered, for example, that the electrical systems in one or two passenger cars of a train's consist were incompatible with the rest of the train. Rolling stock, most of which had been old to begin with, was deteriorating rapidly, and little money was available for repairs, let alone any kind of orderly maintenance program. Worst of all, in Amtrak's first few years, locomotive failures occurred at the rate of ten per day. *Per day!* There was no money for new ones, of course, so Amtrak had to scrape together whatever cash it could and go back on the used locomotive market, buying poor equipment to replace terrible equipment.

In many areas of the country, Amtrak had to haul all that run-down equipment over poor track, adding to the woes of beleaguered passengers. Railroads were in poor financial shape after the disastrous 1960s, and rather than spend money to maintain their track, most simply let it deteriorate, reducing the speed of their freight trains accordingly. Amtrak passenger trains running over that same track had two options: run at the highest safe speed possible and cause discomfort to your passengers from the bouncing and swaying, or reduce speeds and frustrate your passengers with slow trains and late arrivals. Some choice!

Finally, many of the on-board crews, which Amtrak had inherited from private railroads along with all that run-down equipment, brought with them casual if not downright unpleasant attitudes. After all, they had probably been working for a railroad that had been actively trying to discourage passenger business for years.

For the record, a few railroads continued to guard their reputation for quality and service. One was the Santa Fe, which had begun operating the deservedly famous *Super Chief* between Chicago and Los Angeles in 1948. Amtrak had taken over the route, but Santa Fe's chairman, John Reed, was so distressed at the level of service being provided on the train that he indignantly withdrew permission for Amtrak to use the *Super Chief* name. That decision was never reversed and today, although it has become one of the company's better trains, Amtrak continues to call it the *Southwest Chief.*

Too Many Trains, Not Enough Dollars

Despite these very serious concerns, Amtrak's biggest problem was financial. Within months, the company's deficit had begun to mount alarmingly. For one thing, start-up costs had been huge. For another, Amtrak's route system was highly political from the get-go, with influential pro-rail members of Congress demanding trains into their districts whether or not there was any serious demand for the service. As an example, early in its existence, Amtrak began service between Washington, D.C., and Parkersburg, West

Virginia, at the behest of one Harley O. Staggers, the powerful and influential congressman from guess-which-state? In its first several years of operation, and despite increasing deficits, the Amtrak system had actually increased from some 23,000 miles to more than 27,000 miles.

About the only thing holding steady during Amtrak's turbulent early years was the public's support for rail. That support was reflected in the opinion polls, which, as we all know, are avidly read by the politicians. So, while Congress remained committed to the passenger train, it nevertheless recognized that too much was being demanded of the company and that a cutback in service would be necessary. After months of hand-wringing—no one in Congress wanted *his* train eliminated—the Amtrak system was reduced by about 14 percent, which, ironically, left the company just about the size it was on its very first day.

After several years of operations to provide some kind of track record, Congress at last began to evaluate Amtrak in a more realistic light. Clearly, the notion that Amtrak could operate at a profit had *not* been realistic—not as long as every other manner of public transportation, from airplanes to sidewalks, was being subsidized by government at one or more levels. In 1978, Congress formally acknowledged Amtrak's need for government support by ordering the company to generate enough revenue on its own to cover at least half of its operating costs. Then, a few years later, Congress finally dealt with the problem created by its own members. Specific monetary guidelines were set up for judging every train in Amtrak's system. Trains that fell below certain minimums for ridership and revenue would face elimination, even over the inevitable objections of individual members of Congress.

No Friend in Reagan

Somehow Amtrak managed to muddle through the 1970s, meeting and at least trying to deal with one obstacle after another. Another obstacle would come along in 1981 when Ronald Reagan took office as the country's fortieth president. Reagan was opposed to *any* subsidy for Amtrak and, with Budget Director David Stockman at the point, the first of many attempts to reduce or eliminate the flow of federal dollars to Amtrak was not long in coming. Instead of proposing plans for the future, Amtrak found itself having to justify its very existence with an administration that was almost blindly anti-rail. (Ironically, for many years Ronald Reagan had appeared in advertising campaigns extolling the virtues of the Union Pacific's passenger service.)

Another Change at the Top

It had taken almost four years, but influential pro-rail members of Congress had finally gotten the idea that Roger Lewis was not the right man to run Amtrak. One clue came when, in spite of all its problems, Lewis would not support a request to Congress for additional funding. Responding to congressional pressure, the Amtrak board replaced Lewis with Paul Reistrup. Reistrup was a railroader, all right, but proved artless when it came to dealing with the politicians. After a 3 1/2-year hitch, he was replaced by Alan Boyd. Yes, once again Amtrak found itself with a non-railroad man as its president, but Boyd had been the country's very first Secretary of Transportation and was a consummate Washington insider. During his four-year tenure, and despite Reagan's policy of benign neglect toward Amtrak, Boyd managed to bring about some kind of political stability among the various players.

During most of Amtrak's first dozen years, however, the timing for its top leadership somehow seemed to be wrong. When circumstances cried out for someone with operational know-how, they got a politician; when they needed someone who could talk turkey with the power brokers on Capitol Hill, they got a railroader. Fortunately for

Amtrak, Graham Claytor became the company's fourth president in the summer of 1982.

The Cavalry Arrives Just in Time

W. Graham Claytor Jr. was a railroad man first and foremost. He was known to "walk the train" on every Amtrak trip he took, relentlessly looking for the smallest out-of-place detail. But Claytor also proved to be a skilled politician. Already greatly respected by his peers, he was soon viewed in the same way by members of Congress as well, many of whom felt a good deal more comfortable about continuing federal support for Amtrak with the no-nonsense former president of Southern Railway in charge. Unlike most of his predecessors, Claytor was able to speak from experience and with authority. Happily, under Claytor's leadership, Amtrak began to deliver.

Claytor began a shape-up program at Amtrak that would continue through the 1980s. Training improved for employees and gradually—because of elaborate procedures required by union contracts—those with unsatisfactory performance records were weeded out. As did the railroad barons of a century before, Claytor knew that what passengers most remember is having a meal in the dining car. Little by little—when you're habitually underfunded, there's no other way—plastic was replaced by china and stainless steel utensils in Amtrak diners, and airline-type food gave way to meals prepared on board. Claytor was a hands-on leader who took a personal interest in every aspect of the Amtrak operation. Many an Amtrak passenger who had written a letter of complaint about some lapse in service was surprised to receive a personal letter from Claytor himself in response, including an assurance that the matter would be addressed.

One day at a time, Amtrak began working through many of its problems. Engineers and conductors, who had continued to be employees of the freight railroads, became Amtrak employees. New contracts with labor unions resulted in more productivity from on-board crews. In addition to support for operating expenses, Congress provided funds for new equipment: bi-level Superliners to replace traditional rail cars on Amtrak's western runs were ordered in 1975, followed by an order for new locomotives in 1976. In the late 1980s, Amtrak placed an order for a new generation of passenger car, dubbed the Viewliner, which would enable the company to start getting rid of the old single-level coaches and sleepers still operating on eastern routes. In 1993, a new locomotive appeared—the first one in several decades specifically designed for passenger train service—and a new order for updated Superliners was placed.

A New Era Arrives

In December of 1993, Graham Claytor retired at the age of 81, and Thomas M. Downs became Amtrak's fifth president. Downs had his hands full from the start. Minimal funding during the eight-year Reagan administration had continued under George Bush and was beginning to take its toll. Replacement and maintenance for locomotives and cars was being deferred because of a lack of funding and equipment failures; the same problem that had plagued Amtrak in its start-up years was happening all over again. President Bill Clinton was vocally pro-rail, but his budget requests for Amtrak, generous compared to those of Reagan and Bush, were drastically reduced by a suddenly conservative Congress.

During his first year at Amtrak's helm, Downs moved quickly to streamline the company's operations, transferring both responsibility and authority farther down toward front-line employees. As a direct result, and with reduced costs clearly part of the picture, some 600 middle-management people were laid off. In December of 1994, Downs had the dubious distinction of announcing the most drastic reduction in service in Amtrak history—more than 20 percent.

Still, every day Amtrak trains continue to carry Americans to and from thousands of cities and towns from one end of the country to the other. In terms of cost to the taxpayer, it's all being done at bargain prices. It is a fact that revenues from the sale of rail tickets and other sources—carrying the mail for the Postal Service, for example—cover some 80 percent of Amtrak's operating cost, making Amtrak the most cost-effective public rail transportation system in the world.

Another Era Comes to an End

Graham Claytor died in May of 1994 at the age of 82, less than six months after retiring. It is universally agreed that without him Amtrak would probably never have survived.

CHAPTER 4

Planning Your Own Train Trip

If you want to fly between two large U.S. cities, there will probably be several airlines from which to choose. But if it's a long-distance train ride you're after, Amtrak is your only option. The Amtrak system covers most of the continental United States, which means you can reach or get close to most major cities by train. (See Amtrak System Map on pages 38–39). Before you begin to work out the details of any rail trip, however, you should know a few things about present day train travel and ought to consider a few others.

Beware Great Expectations

To avoid disappointment, it's important to have a clear understanding of what you can reasonably expect from your train trip—and, probably more important, what you shouldn't expect. One Amtrak car attendant I spoke to is still astonished about the couple on a cross-country honeymoon train trip who had somehow gotten the idea that there would be a fireplace in their compartment. Many of these misunderstandings, at least according to the on-board crews, are caused by advertising that gives people the idea that a train is like a cruise ship. There are indeed similarities, but the two experiences are opposite in the most fundamental way: Cruise ships focus on a wide variety of on-board activities because most of the time there's nothing to see but ocean beyond the railing. Trains, on the other hand, offer constantly changing scenery outside the window and, for the most part, leave passengers to create their own activities and diversions.

Things You Should Know Before You Start

First, and probably most important, do your planning as far in advance as possible. Your first priority should be deciding on specific dates for your train travel. Most long-distance trains, especially the sleeping car accommodations, sell out very quickly. That's particularly true during the busy summer months, but no matter when you travel, it's a very good idea to make your train reservations at least ninety days in advance—sooner if you can.

For years, trains operating east of the Mississippi River were comprised of the traditional single-level rail cars, while long-distance trains running west of the Mississippi were equipped with Amtrak's two-level Superliner cars. As new equipment has come into service, however, that's begun to change. Superliners are now being used on the *Capitol Limited,* the *City of New Orleans,* and *Auto Train;* and new Viewliners will also start showing up on trains in the eastern part of the country.

On all long-distance trains, Amtrak offers its passengers a choice between two distinct types of service: coach or first class. On those trains, the term "first class" always refers to the sleeping cars (also called "sleepers"). In fact, the two terms are interchangeable. Some all-coach trains also have two levels of coach class, referred to as "coach" and "club coach" (also called "parlor car," usually by the old-timers). With club coach, you will get wider, more comfortable seats

A Superliner coach. Passengers ride on the upper level of these cars. (Photo courtesy of Amtrak.)

and complimentary food and beverages served at your seat. There is, of course, a surcharge for these extras.

The information and suggestions in the following pages are intended to help you plan a rail trip that's best suited to your individual preferences and budget. While most of the examples refer to longer and more detailed itineraries, shorter rail trips deserve no less attention. Whether you're considering a four-day excursion through New England to admire the fall colors or a four-week rail tour of the West, the planning process should be the same: as thorough and as unhurried as possible. After all, any vacation, whether short or long, requires an investment of your leisure time and your money, neither of which should be wasted.

Consider a Package Tour

This chapter is about planning your own train trip because it's fun to do, and you can design it exactly the way you want. You should be aware, however, that Amtrak has packaged a wide variety of rail tours of varying lengths which include train fare, hotels, and some sightseeing. These trips can usually be scheduled at your convenience, and the cost will probably be somewhat lower than if you book the identical itinerary yourself. You are limited to the pre-planned itineraries, however. For information and a detailed brochure, call Amtrak's Great American Vacations at 1-800-321-8684.

A Word About Rail Fares

When traveling by train, *all* passengers pay a basic rail fare that covers the cost of a seat in coach class. That fare will vary, depending on how far you're traveling. If you opt to travel in first class—meaning in one of the several different sleeping car accommodations—you'll be upgrading your ticket by, in effect, paying a first-class surcharge. The cost of the upgrade will vary, depending upon the type of accommodations you select and how far you're traveling. Both the basic rail fare and the first-class surcharge will fluctuate, depending on the time of year you travel; that is, you'll pay more during the busy summer months, less other times.

Special Fares

With Amtrak's special "All Aboard America" fares, you can add a surprising amount of traveling to a simple itinerary without increasing the cost of your basic rail ticket. And, unlike most airline fares, these are easy to understand.

Amtrak has divided the country into three zones: **East** (between the eastern seaboard and Chicago or New Orleans), **Central** (between Chicago and Denver), and **West** (from Denver to the West Coast). How much you'll pay on an All Aboard America fare depends on whether you travel in one, two, or three zones.

Amtrak's Rail

Passenger System

You can use an All Aboard America fare as long as you aren't traveling for more than 45 days and don't stop off in more than three places. Stick to those guidelines and there will be no increase in your basic rail fare no matter how many miles you travel, including round-trip itineraries. Just remember that this is the basic rail fare for which you get a coach seat. If you want to travel in a sleeping car, you'll pay the first-class surcharge on top of this special fare.

Look for Other Discounts

Your age can also save you money . . . at either end of the spectrum. Children under 2 travel free. Those between 2 and 15 pay half fare when accompanied by an adult. And seniors 62 and over get a 15 percent discount on their rail fare when traveling Monday through Thursday. The seniors' discount does not apply to sleeping car accommodations. As noted already, fares vary according to the season, so once you have tentative dates, check with Amtrak to see when those changes in price occur. It may be that you can save some money just by changing the dates of your trip by a week or so.

Who Should Plan Your Trip?

There's no reason at all why you can't do all the preliminary planning yourself. For me, that's part of the fun. Besides, the more personal thought you put into your trip, the more successful and rewarding the whole experience is likely to be. Get as far into the details as you want, even selecting the specific trains you want to take. But once you think you're ready to make reservations, you should probably turn things over to a knowledgeable travel agent. There is usually no additional cost involved since he or she is paid a commission by Amtrak (as well as by airlines, rental car companies, cruise ships, hotels, etc.) for handling the details and doing your ticketing. I'd suggest letting the travel agent double-check what you've done then take care of the reservations and the ticketing. A good one will know a few "tricks of the trade," which could mean you'll pay a lower fare.

How to Find a Knowledgeable Travel Agent

Ah, therein lies the rub! Notice I've used the word "knowledgeable" as opposed to "experienced." The unfortunate fact is, most travel agents—even those who have been in the business for a long time—don't necessarily know much about train travel. I tell you that from bitter experience. It's easy to have the train trip you've always dreamed about turned into a nightmare by the wrong travel agent. Never fear. Here are a few suggestions to help you find the *right* one.

Every year Amtrak presents Golden Spike Awards to a very small percentage of travel agents across the United States and Canada. To be recognized with one of these awards, a travel agent must have written a *lot* of Amtrak tickets. Chances are good that any one of them will be able to handle even a complicated rail itinerary. (A list of 1994 Golden Spike travel agencies is included in the appendix.)

You might also stop by a local newsstand and look for one of the popular magazines directed at the serious rail fans—*Passenger Train Journal, International Rail Traveler, Railfan & Railroad, Trains,* etc. Any travel agent advertising in one of those publications had better know his stuff!

Finally, a real pro in the business, Carl Fowler of Rail Travel Center in St. Albans, Vermont, suggests you simply ask your travel agent to explain the difference between a roomette and a slumbercoach. If you get a lot of hemming and hawing, be careful! (You'll already know the answer, of course, because you will have read all about slumbercoaches in Chapter 9.)

Going to Do It Yourself? Start with a Timetable

To get started, just take things in a logical order, starting with the two most important decisions: How long will you be gone, and where do you want to go? Everything else is simply a matter of filling in details, and that's when you'll need an Amtrak timetable. You can get one free by calling Amtrak's nationwide toll free number: 1-800-USA-RAIL. They'll mail one to you, although it may take several weeks to arrive. If you don't want to wait, contact the closest Amtrak office or try your travel agent, who may have a few. Just be sure to ask for the "National Timetable" (sometimes referred to as the "System Timetable"), which includes schedules for all Amtrak trains from coast to coast. There is also a "Northeast Timetable," which provides a detailed schedule of trains running between New York and Boston. You may want to ask for both.

Learn How to Read It

Amtrak has done a good job with their timetables. The format is simple and well presented, making them easy to read. The timetable contains much more than just train schedules. Depending on your specific itinerary, much of the information may be of little or no concern, but some could be very important.

Below each schedule, for instance, is a paragraph describing the different services available on that particular train. That's where you can find out if your train has a dining car serving full meals or if there's only a lounge car serving snacks. Some of Amtrak's long-distance trains run daily, but others don't. The eastbound *Sunset Limited*, for example, departs from Los Angeles on Sunday, Tuesday, and Friday evenings. When you select a specific train for your itinerary, it's certainly important to know if it runs daily or just three days a week. The timetable will give you that and other important information.

Some cities not served by Amtrak may be reached by buses scheduled to connect with the trains. That information is also in the timetable, along with the locations of all Amtrak stations and whether or not you can check baggage there.

One more thing about timetables in general: Remember that minor changes in train schedules occur frequently. A train that departs at 10:00 A.M. today, and is listed accordingly in the current timetable, could leave 30 or 40 minutes *earlier* three months in the future when you're planning to travel. So once you've worked out your itinerary and are ready to book your reservation, be sure to confirm all departure and arrival times for your specific dates, either by calling Amtrak directly or through your travel agent. Then check again a few days before you leave.

Following is a sample Amtrak timetable. Study it for a few minutes, and you'll discover that there is order and logic to the format. The schedule for the westbound *California Zephyr,* Train 5, runs top to bottom in the left-hand column, while the schedule for the eastbound *Zephyr,* Train 6, is listed bottom to top in the right-hand column. (Please note that this is just an example of a typical timetable's format. The *Zephyr's* current schedule will no doubt have a number of changes.)

Deciding on Your Destinations

Study the map of Amtrak's coast-to-coast system, which is found on pages 38–39, and settle on a primary destination. Then, assuming you have the time, consider adding two more stopovers. Using those special All Aboard America fares, you can do that without any increase in your basic rail fare. How's *that* for a bargain!

California Zephyr

Chicago...Denver...
(San Francisco)

5 Daily			◄ Train Number ► ◄ Days of Operation ►			6 Daily
ReadDown	**Mile**	▼		**Symbol**	▲	**Read Up**
3 05P	0	Dp	*(Burlington Northern)* Chicago, IL–Union Sta. (CT)	Ⓢ 🅲 ♿	Ar	4 15P
⑲ 3 40P	28		Naperville, IL (METRA/BN Line)	♿		⑲ 2 54P
4 50P	104		Princeton, IL	● ♿		1 45P
5 44P	162		Galesburg, IL–S. Seminary St. ⑥ 🚌	♿		12 55P
6 37P	205		Burlington, IA	♿		12 00N
7 12P	233		Mt. Pleasant, IA	🅲 ♿		11 25A
7 47P	280		Ottumwa, IA	🅲 ♿		10 38A
9 13P	360		Osceola, IA (Des Moines)	● ♿		9 16A
9 46P	393		Creston, IA	● ♿		8 47A
🚌 Amtrak Thruway Bus Connection—Kansas City, MO/Omaha, NE—Schedule Below						
11 35P 11 59P	501	Ar Dp	Omaha, NE	🅲 ♿	Dp Ar	6 50A 6 25A
1 02A 1 12A	555	Ar Dp	Lincoln, NE	🅲 ♿	Dp Ar	5 25A 5 15A
2 45A	652		Hastings, NE (Grand Island)	🅲 ♿		3 47A
3 36A	706		Holdrege, NE	● ♿		2 55A
4 46A	784		McCook, NE (CT)	● ♿		1 47A
6 07A	960		Fort Morgan, CO (Sterling) (MT)	● ♿		10 15P
8 10A 9 10A	1037	Ar Dp	*(Southern Pacific Lines)* Denver, CO (Colorado Springs 🚌)	🅲 ♿	Dp Ar	9 00P 7 40P
11 05A	1100		Winter Park, CO–Fraser	● ♿		4 55P
11 35A	1113		Granby, CO (Rocky Mt. Nat'l Park)	● ♿		4 30P
2 50P	1222		Glenwood Springs, CO (Aspen)	🅲 ♿		1 20P
4 55P	1311		Grand Junction, CO	🅲 ♿		11 35A
✖ 6 10P	1390		Thompson, UT	● ♿		✖ 9 35A
8 00P	1488		Helper, UT (Price)	● ♿		8 00A
10 05P	1564		Provo, UT	● ♿		5 55A
🚌 Amtrak Thruway Bus Connection—Ogden/Salt Lake City—Schedule Below						
11 36P 12 35A	1608	Ar Dp	*(Union Pacific)* Salt Lake City, UT (MT)	🅲 ♿	Dp Ar	5 05A 3 45A
3 48A	1871		Elko, NV (PT)	● ♿		9 55P
5 55A	2009		*(Southern Pacific Lines)* Winnemucca, NV	● ♿		7 50P
7 30A	2082		Lovelock, NV	● ♿		6 42P
9 15A 9 30A	2180	Ar Dp	Sparks, NV	● ♿	Dp Ar	5 12P 4 57P
9 41A	2184		Reno, NV	🅲 ♿		4 37P
10 34A	2218		Truckee, CA (Lake Tahoe)	● ♿		3 40P
12 42P	2284		Colfax, CA	● ♿		1 29P
1 48P	2319		Roseville, CA	● ♿		12 39P
2 40P	2337		Sacramento, CA	🅲 ♿		12 12P
D 3 00P	2350		Davis, CA	🅲 ♿		11 38A
D 3 24P	2377		Suisun-Fairfield, CA	● ♿		11 10A
D 3 46P	2393		Martinez, CA (San Joaquin Trains)	🅲 ♿		10 48A
D 4 15P	2413		Richmond, CA–BART Sta.	♿ 🅱		10 16A
D 5 00P	2420	Ar	Emeryville, CA (PT)	🅲 ♿	Dp	10 05A

Connecting Services

			🚌 Amtrak Thruway Bus Connection–Emeryville, CA 🅢/San Francisco, CA			
5 05P	0	Dp	Emeryville, CA (PT)		Ar	9 45A
5 25P	9	Ar	San Francisco, CA ● ● 🚌 –Ferry Building	🚕	Dp	9 25A
5 35P	10	Ar	–CalTrain Sta.–4th & Townsend	● 🅱	Dp	9 10A
			🚌 Amtrak Thruway Bus Connection–Kansas City, MO/Omaha, NE			
6 30P	0	Dp	Kansas City, MO		Ar	12 00N
8 00P	54		St. Joseph, MO	●		11 00A
10 30P	198	Ar	Omaha, NE (CT)		Dp	8 00A
			🚌 Amtrak Thruway Bus Connection–Ogden, UT/Salt Lake City, UT			
9 15P	0	Dp	Ogden, UT	🚕	Ar	5 50A
10 00P	36	Ar	Salt Lake City, UT (MT)	🚕	Dp	5 05A

This is a recent timetable for the *California Zephyr.* Read down for Train 5's schedule (Chicago to Emeryville/San Francisco) and up for Train 6 (Emeryville/San Francisco to Chicago). The "Symbol" column indicates if there is checked baggage service or if the platform is handicapped accessible at that particular station. The black dot means that tickets are *not* sold at that station, but can be purchased when you board the train.

For instance, suppose you live in Washington, D.C., and want to spend some time with your favorite Aunt Tillie in Pittsburgh. Of course, the obvious thing to do is hop Train 29, the *Capitol Limited,* to Pittsburgh, have your visit, then return home on the same train. But by taking advantage of the All Aboard America fare, look at the nifty vacation you can arrange for yourself *without* increasing the cost of your rail fare:

- Washington to Pittsburgh for your visit with Aunt Tillie
- Pittsburgh to Chicago to see the Redskins play the Bears
- Chicago to New Orleans for some jazz and Creole cooking
- New Orleans back home to Washington

As long as you're traveling on a coach ticket, you pay nothing more for all those extra miles. If you want to go first class, you'll pay extra for each additional night spent in sleeping car accommodations.

One of the main reasons for taking the train is to see the country, so bear that in mind when working out the details of your rail itineraries.

The Plane/Train Option

There's still another option to consider: Amtrak has arranged special joint fares with United Airlines that permit you to fly one way and take the train the other. For instance, you could take the train from Los Angeles to Seattle to Chicago to Boston, and then fly back to L.A. from Boston.

A Little Research Will Pay Off

After you make a list of places you want to visit, find out something about those areas *before* deciding how long you'll stop there. Any good bookstore will have travel guides for most major cities and for every region of the country. Public libraries are also excellent sources for free information, as are the tourism promotion offices in each of the various states.

For example, if you want to visit historical sites associated with the opening up of the American West, you'll probably head for Nebraska and Wyoming. Both state governments fund offices whose function is to get promotional literature into the hands of people exactly like you. *Call them!* Information operators in Lincoln and Cheyenne, the two states' capitals, will almost certainly be able to find the right phone numbers for you. If not, take an easy shortcut: Ask for the number of the governor's office and call there. They will know exactly whom you should contact for your information and will be delighted to tell you.

You'll find that the research you do will pay big dividends in the form of a better trip. There's a wealth of information out there and most of it's free.

Bus Connections

Almost every Amtrak train passes near, but not through, one or more large towns or cities. In many of those cases, Amtrak provides connecting bus service. For instance, if you're traveling from Chicago to Phoenix on the *Southwest Chief,* then Flagstaff, Arizona, 140 miles north of Phoenix, is the closest station stop. No problem. Amtrak has a bus that will take you there, and it will be waiting at the station when the *Chief* pulls into Flagstaff. Book the bus when you make your train reservations so your ticket to Phoenix will be right there in your Amtrak ticket booklet when you board the bus.

Starting Your Itinerary

Okay, so you know how long you can be gone and where you want to go. Now you're ready to begin developing a detailed itinerary. Some travelers refuse to prepare itineraries in the mistaken belief that they will somehow become locked into a rigid schedule from which they can't deviate. What nonsense! A carefully prepared itinerary is nothing more than relevant information compiled in an orderly fashion. Not having one with you as you travel is foolish; not leaving one behind with friends or family in case of emergency is irresponsible.

Begin with a rough worksheet listing the days you'll be gone. At this stage, don't worry about specific dates. Remember that trip to Chicago and New Orleans via Aunt Tillie's? Here's how it would look on a worksheet, planned to fit neatly into a two-week vacation.

Day 1	Washington to Pittsburgh
Day 2–5	At Aunt Tillie's
Day 6	Dep. Pittsburgh
Day 7	Arr. Chicago
Day 8	Chicago
Day 9	Dep. Chicago
Day 10	Arr. New Orleans
Day 11,12	New Orleans
Day 13	Dep. New Orleans
Day 14	Arr. Washington

Next, plug in real dates for your trip, beginning with those you can't change. In this example, you'll have to start with Day 8 when our hypothetical Redskin-Bears football game will be played. That's your one firm date that the rest of your itinerary must revolve around. Once that's done, use your timetable and add specific trains to the rough itinerary.

Nov. 2	Dep. Washington, Train 29, 4:15 P.M.
	Arr. Pittsburgh 11:27 P.M.
Nov. 3–6	At Aunt Tillie's
Nov. 7	Dep. Pittsburgh, Train 29, 11:42 P.M.
Nov. 8	Arr. Chicago 8:45 A.M.
Nov. 9	**Chicago—'Skins vs. Bears**
Nov. 10	Dep. Chicago, Train 59, 6:30 P.M.
Nov. 11	Arr. New Orleans 1:50 P.M.
Nov. 12, 13	Tour New Orleans
Nov. 14	Dep. New Orleans, Train 20, 7:00 A.M.
Nov. 15	Arr. Washington 9:20 A.M.

Your itinerary may go through many additions and changes before you actually leave so keep things simple until seats are booked and hotel rooms are reserved. (See the example of a finished itinerary at the end of this chapter.)

A Word of Warning About Connections

If you're flying, a missed connection seldom turns out to be a big deal. Chances are there'll be another plane from either the same or a different airline before long. It's different with Amtrak. There *are* no other passenger railroads, and most of Amtrak's long-distance trains run only once a day. In fact, some, like the *Cardinal* or the *Sunset Limited,* operate just three days a week.

When you're traveling by train, a missed connection can be a real disaster, perhaps even a vacation buster. So as you prepare your rail itinerary, be careful of any close connections. If there's a later train that would allow more time to make the connection, choose that one . . . even if it means spending a few extra hours somewhere. Or consider stopping at that point, spending the night, and continuing your journey the next day. (Note: If you're traveling on an All Aboard America fare, you're permitted a total of three stopovers once your trip begins. If that extra night's stay counts as a stopover and puts you over the limit, it will affect the price of your ticket. Check that detail with Amtrak or your travel agent.)

How Safe Is a "Guaranteed Connection"?

If a connection can't be avoided, be sure to find out if it's a "guaranteed connection." If it is, Amtrak will do everything within reason to make sure you and other passengers affected make your connections. Usually that means holding the second train until yours arrives. As a practical matter, however, they can't delay the departure of a train for very long since it will undoubtedly be connecting with another train somewhere else.

If you do miss a guaranteed connection with a train that runs once a day, any of several things could occur. As a first choice, Amtrak will pay for your overnight stay in a hotel and put you on the same train the next day . . . assuming there's space, of course. Unfortunately, if you're traveling in a sleeper during one of the frequent busy periods, available space is not likely. In that case, even though you're holding a first-class ticket with a guaranteed connection, you could end up riding overnight in a coach seat. The eventual refund of your sleeping car accommodation cost will be small consolation. If the entire train is sold out the next day, you could be sent on your way by plane. Or, depending on your destination, by bus . . . hardly the way you expected your carefully planned train trip to end up.

Many factors could affect how your missed-connection problem is solved, but keep in mind that the final decision is up to Amtrak. (For more on this subject, see Chapter 8: When Things Go Wrong.)

Should You Ride in Coach or in First Class?

You'll have to choose whether to go coach or first class before you book your train reservations. There are a number of factors to consider.

With a coach ticket you'll ride in one of 50 or 60 seats in a standard passenger rail car and 70 or more in a Superliner coach. A first-class ticket puts you in small but private accommodations that include a bed to sleep in at night. We'll discuss other differences in the next few pages, but that's it in a nutshell.

For short trips, even if it's an all-day ride, the choice is easy: Coach is the way to go. For overnight journeys, the coach versus first class decision becomes much more difficult, although the differences are easily defined: It boils down to cost and comfort.

Save Big Bucks in Coach

The biggest difference between coach and first class is cost. Coach is cheaper. In fact, it's a *lot* cheaper. Depending on the time of year, it's possible to travel from coast to coast and back again for less than $250, as long as you ride in coach class. That same trip in a sleeping car could cost $1,200 or more, depending on the type of accommodations you choose.

Here's an example: Let's assume you're traveling during the first three weeks of May between Los Angeles and Chicago on Train 4, the *Southwest Chief.* Here's how the cost of riding in a first-class economy bedroom compares with that same trip on the same train in coach. Remember, this is a two-night trip.

Los Angeles–Chicago, One Way

Class of Service	Coach	Sleeper
Basic Rail Fare	$217	$217
First Class Surcharge		$232
Total Cost	$217	$449

The cost differential between coach and first class really widens if you're traveling round-trip. There's only a slight increase in the coach fare, but now you're paying for a total of four nights in the sleeper.

Los Angeles–Chicago, Round Trip

Class of Service	Coach	Sleeper
Basic Rail Fare	$224	$224
First Class Surcharge		$464
Total Cost	$224	$688

Those costs would be somewhat higher in June, July, and August, the peak travel period, and somewhat lower in the winter months, when travel is lighter. The bottom line? Coach travel wins hands down if cost is your most important consideration. There are other considerations, however, and we'll get into those just a bit further on.

One Other Coach Option

On several of its short-haul routes, Amtrak offers something called "Club Coach" service. Basically, it's a higher class of service provided in an all-coach train and, naturally, it comes at a higher fare. Club coach passengers traveling along the Northeast Corridor are located in a special section of a coach that includes a snack bar. The surroundings are somewhat more plush and a free tray meal is served to you in your seat. Go for it if you've got the money and are into traveling first class. On other routes, principally the Los Angeles to San Diego trip, the club coach surcharge is minimal, but so is the difference in service.

The Unreserved "Reserved" Seat

You already know that securing a coach seat on any of Amtrak's long-distance trains requires a reservation. You also need to know that your reservation does *not* mean you have a specific seat assignment; it means simply that there will be one empty coach seat for you somewhere on that train. This is a small, but important detail—especially if several people are traveling as a group. See Chapter 5 for suggestions on what you can do ahead of time and during the boarding process to get a good seat and to help make sure that your family will be seated together.

Can You Sleep Sitting Up?

The seats in coach class are wide and comfortable, and there is ample leg room even when they're fully reclined. Many seats are equipped with special extenders for your feet and legs so you can really stretch out. All things considered, your coach seat on the train will be comparable to a first-class seat on an airplane, but with much more leg room. Make no mistake, however—it may be comfortable and roomy, but it's still a chair and you'll still have to sleep in it! If experience tells you that sleep just won't come under those conditions, consider opting for a sleeping car.

Are You a People Person?

Is privacy a big consideration for you? Coach seats are comfortable and the car itself is spacious; but if it's full, you'll be in fairly close proximity to 50 or 60 other people. If you're traveling alone, you could be lucky and end up with an empty seat beside you, but you could also be sitting next to a stranger or find a young mother with a couple of restless toddlers directly behind you. Some people see this as a great way to meet people and make new friends; others soon find themselves longing for the chance to be alone. Before letting cost alone dictate your decision, think about how much value you put on your privacy.

Comfort and Privacy in First Class

Life in the sleeping cars is undeniably luxurious compared to coach class. While none of the first-class accommodations can be described as spacious, they are private and, come nighttime, you've got your own room and a real bed to sleep in. Most, but not all, first-class accommodations are equipped with their own toilets. Sheets, blankets, pillows, and towels are all provided. For some travelers, the privacy and comfort found in the sleeping cars is an essential luxury for which they're happy to pay.

Free Meals: A First-Class Bonus

While all passengers are welcomed in the diner, the cost of dining car meals is *included* in the price of your first-class ticket. Coach passengers pay the regular menu prices for their meals. Since the prices in Amtrak dining cars are quite reasonable, and you can always bring food aboard or purchase sandwiches and snacks in the lounge car, this may not be a major issue for you. Note that meals are *not* included when traveling in slumbercoaches.

Other First-Class Extras

Amtrak serves up additional extras for sleeping car passengers that add to the pleasure of the trip. On most trains, you'll receive a complimentary copy of a morning newspaper. The attendant in each sleeping car will provide a number of other services either automatically or on request. Some of these include wake up calls, free juice and coffee each morning, making up of your berth each evening, and serving food or beverages in your room.

Which First-Class Accommodation Should You Choose?

Coach seats are all pretty much alike, but when it comes to sleeping car accommodations, there will be several choices, depending upon the specific train you've chosen. Eastern trains offer slumbercoaches and roomettes accommodating one person and bedrooms that are designed for two people. Doors between adjoining bedrooms can be opened to provide four-bed compartments for families. Superliners operating west of the Mississippi River offer economy bedrooms for one or two people, deluxe bedrooms for two and possibly a small child, and family bedrooms that sleep two adults and two young children. Special compartments designed for handicapped passengers are also available. Superliners are now in use on a few eastern trains, too.

How to Lower the Cost of Going First Class

It may sometimes be possible to cut the total cost of your ticket by booking your sleeping car accommodations for only the evening portion of the trip. Consider, for example, a family of three traveling between Tampa and New York. Train 88, the *Silver Meteor,* leaves Tampa in the late morning and arrives in New York just before noon the next day. Instead of reserving both a bedroom and a roomette for the entire trip, why not book the roomette only between Savannah, Georgia, and Washington, D.C.? All three can sit together during daylight hours and one family member can pay for a separate room just for the night . . . a significant savings.

The cost of first-class accommodations is based on the room, not on the number of people occupying it. That means the first-class surcharge for an economy bedroom on a Superliner, which has two berths, is the same whether it's occupied by one or two people. And, as long as everyone understands they'll be sharing the rather small berths, kids can join their parents in first-class accommodations without paying the extra first-class charges.

Finding and Booking the Right Hotel

Unless you have several Aunt Tillies scattered around the country, one or more nights in a hotel could well be part of your train trip. For some people, a hotel is just a place to sleep and almost any one will do. But others want their hotel to be another interesting and enjoyable part of the experience. In other words, where you stay during your stopovers is also a matter of your own personal taste and budget.

You can always turn the matter over to a travel agent. Just give your agent some idea of the type of hotel you want and a price range, and he or she will suggest a place to stay and take care of the booking.

If you want to make the arrangements yourself, the easiest approach is to call the central reservations number for one of the national hotel chains. They'll probably have a hotel where you want to go, and at least you'll know your room will meet the minimum standards of that particular chain. If, however, you prefer smaller hotels that may offer more in the way of taste and charm, your best bet is to browse in the travel section of your local bookstore. They'll have any number of guidebooks to help you make your choice, be it deluxe accommodations or a listing of quaint bed-and-breakfast spots. Once you find a hotel that seems to meet your requirements, call or write for rates and a brochure.

If all then seems to your liking, go ahead and book your room. Do it by phone if you wish, but be sure to have the hotel send you a written confirmation. At the very least, ask for and make note of a confirmation number. It's normal practice for the hotel to ask you to guarantee your reservation with a credit card. If you would prefer not to, make sure they will still honor your reservation. And be aware that without the credit card to guarantee it, your reservation will cancel automatically, probably at 6:00 P.M. on the day you're supposed to arrive.

What's All This Going to Cost?

After you've done it a few times, you'll be able to estimate the cost of your train tickets fairly accurately. But why guess at it? Once you've decided when and where you're going, just call Amtrak (1-800-USA-RAIL) for a fare quote.

Now start on estimates for the other costs connected with your trip. Do *not* try to anticipate *every* individual expense. Instead, think in terms of daily averages, either per person or for the whole party, whichever is appropriate. The following guidelines are the ones I use and should provide you with a rough starting point. Adjust you own guidelines according to personal tastes and preferences.

Using your rough itinerary, figure out how many nights you'll be in hotels. For big city hotels, allow no less than $80–$100 per night; for hotels in smaller cities and rural areas, figure room rates at half to two-thirds of those amounts.

For food costs, figure $35 per day per person for adults and kids over 12. That's $7 for breakfast, $10 for lunch, and $18 for dinner. Yes, it could be less and, obviously, it might well run much more, depending on where and what you eat. For younger children, reduce your estimate appropriately. (Note: Remember that a first-class rail ticket includes the price of your dining car meals. If you're riding in a sleeper, figure out how many meals you'll be having on board the train and don't budget for those.)

Will you be renting a car somewhere along the way? Allow $40 per day. (Remember that there will likely be a "drop charge" if you return the car to a different location. Check that out ahead of time.)

How much sightseeing will you be doing? Better figure at least $10 to $20 per person per day. (Don't count the days you'll be on the train. All of *that* sightseeing is free!)

Going to be shopping and buying souvenirs? Don't guess at an average daily amount. Instead, decide what you can afford and budget that lump sum for the entire trip. If you're traveling with children, I'd suggest deciding on an appropriate shopping allowance for each of them, then giving each child the money up front—and when it's gone, it's gone.

You'll also have small but frequent miscellaneous expenses such as tips, snacks, fees for checked baggage, film, etc. Allow a total of $15–$20 per day for such costs.

Be realistic, work with daily averages, and you'll be amazed at how accurate your estimate will be. A good estimate of your travel expenses done now is an important double-check that your trip will be affordable. It will also be a valuable guide to keep you on budget during your vacation.

Book Your Space Early!

Make your rail reservations as soon as your dates of departure and return are definite, when you've decided on your destination and other stopovers, and when you know whether you want coach or first-class seats. The other details—hotel rooms, rental cars, sightseeing tours, and the rest—can be filled in later. Early booking is especially important if you want sleeping car accommodations. They're very popular and fill up rapidly, particularly in the summer months. Better to make tentative reservations then cancel or switch dates than wait too long and find nothing available.

You can either have a travel agent handle the booking or deal direct with Amtrak by calling 1-800-USA-RAIL. If you elect to call an Amtrak reservations agent, you'll find them very capable and usually extremely helpful. Do *not* call Amtrak direct if you're still uncertain about significant details of your itinerary. The reservations agents are usually very busy and will not be able to give you the help you might need to make up your mind. They may try, but that's when some small but important detail is sure to fall through the cracks. Besides, filling in those details is how a travel agent earns his commission.

Whether you use a travel agent or call Amtrak direct, be sure to cover these important things with them before you hang up:

- Ask if they're sure you've been quoted the lowest possible fare.
- Ask if there are any changes you could make in your itinerary that might further reduce the cost.
- Ask if there are any connections in the itinerary that could be a problem.
- To avoid some of the less desirable accommodations, be sure to request specific room numbers if you're booking sleeping car accommodations (see Chapter 9: Passenger Train Equipment).
- Be sure to ask for the cancellation date for your reservation. You must purchase your tickets by a specific date once you've booked space. Usually it's about thirty days after the actual booking, but that can vary. If you don't pay for your tickets by that date, your reservation will cancel automatically and your seats will go back into inventory for sale to someone else.
- Get a reservation number when you book. *This is important!* If you need to make any changes in your itinerary, or if a problem should occur during your trip, that number will help Amtrak locate your complete record quickly.
- Finally, be sure to look at your tickets carefully when they arrive and check each date and train number against your itinerary.

Do You Need Special Services?

If you or someone traveling with you should require any kind of special assistance or service—a wheelchair or a special diet, for instance—call Amtrak at 1-800-USA-RAIL at least 72 hours before you leave. It would also be a good idea to call the Amtrak representative at the station ahead of time. And then plan to arrive at the station early.

How to Get Last-Minute Sleeping Car Space

If you have to make a train trip on short notice, you may find that no sleeping car space is available. Don't despair. It might not be a convenient hour, but about 4:05 A.M. eastern time, call the Amtrak reservation number; 1-800-USA-RAIL. Every morning at 4:00 A.M. the Amtrak computer is purged of passengers who have canceled space and, at that hour, you'll probably be first in line if a vacancy has occurred for the train you want. If worse comes to worst, board the train with your coach ticket and ask the conductor right away if there's a vacancy in one of the sleepers. There are no-shows more often than most of us would imagine.

Paying for Your Tickets

If you book with Amtrak direct, you can pay for your tickets by phone with a major credit card and they will be mailed to you. If you live near an Amtrak station or office, you can pick up and pay for your tickets there. If you wish, you can pay for tickets through a travel agency, whether they handled the details or not. All they will need is your reservation number. By the way, it's a good idea to pay for your tickets with a credit card. It automatically provides you with a record of the purchase and a measure of protection should there be any solvency problems with the travel agency.

Make Copies of Your Tickets

Before you leave on your trip, make two photocopies of your tickets. Give one copy to a friend or relative and take the other set with you. Just be sure to keep that second copy in a different place than your original tickets. This is a basic precaution that should be taken routinely by all travelers. As a matter of fact, you should photocopy all important travel documents, especially passports and plane or train tickets.

If You Need a Refund

Should your plans change or circumstances force you to cancel your trip, there's a right way to go about getting a refund. Go back to the travel agency if that's how you bought the tickets, although in some cases Amtrak can handle the refund. Contact Amtrak if you booked direct. Either way, you will need the original tickets for a prompt refund. Amtrak has a liberal refund policy, even handling many refunds by mail. There are some restrictions, though, so be sure to ask which might apply when you make the reservation.

What About Travel Insurance?

Travel agents sell this insurance. The policy will compensate you if you have to cancel your trip, either before you start out or while you're traveling. Almost any reason will constitute a valid claim. Think carefully before buying because it's a better deal for some people than it is for others. Realistically, what are the chances that you'll have to cancel your trip at the last minute or interrupt it in progress? How old are you? How's your health? Are there other family or business circumstances that could cause you to abort your plans? There are several kinds of travel insurance, so talk it over with a travel agent. Before you decide, however, remember that he or she receives as much as a 30 percent commission for each sale. The bottom line is that it's a crapshoot and only you can make the call.

Putting Your Itinerary into Final Form

The last step in the planning process is to produce a final version of your itinerary. Remember that an itinerary is much more than just a day-by-day schedule; it should be your one written source of information, including everything you need to know about your trip—train arrival and departure times, addresses and phone numbers of all hotels, confirmation numbers for all reservations (train, hotel, and rental car), and other pertinent information and relevant notes.

The format may vary, but every itinerary should record information in appropriate chronological order. As an example, here's a section from one of my itineraries as it existed about a month before departure. I note relevant details such as reservation and confirmation numbers in a second column to the right.

Monday, May 10

Dep. Ft. Myers, Amtrak bus,   Amtrak Res. #406020
  6:50 A.M.

Arr. Tampa, 9:50 A.M.

Dep. Tampa, Train #88,   Car 8800, roomette #2
  10:22 A.M.

Tuesday, May 11

Arr. Washington, 5:06 A.M.

Hotel Bellvue   Conf. #100BG6
15 E Street NW
Washington, D.C. 20001
Tel. 202-638-0900

Thursday, May 13

Dep. Washington, Train #60,   Car 6000, roomette #2
  4:10 P.M.

Friday, May 14

Arr. Montreal, 10:45 A.M.

Queen Elizabeth Hotel   Conf. #456885
900 René Levesque Blvd.
Montreal, Quebec H3B 4A5
Tel. 514-861-3511

Saturday, May 15

Dep. Montreal, Train #61,   VIA Booking #XB2894
7:15 A.M.

Arr. Toronto, 11:52 A.M.

Dep. Toronto, VIA Train #1,   Car 1200, roomette #6
12:45 P.M.

Tuesday, May 18
Arr. Vancouver, 8:00 A.M.

Westin Bayshore Hotel   Conf. #RB1135J
1601 West Georgia St.
Vancouver, BC V6G 2V4
Tel. 604-682-3377

When finishing up your itinerary, avoid unnecessary verbiage, but include everything you will need to know once you've left home. While you're away, this will be your bible, and you'll refer to it many times each day. *Make three copies of your itinerary*—one for your shoulder bag, one for your suitcase (in case the shoulder bag is lost or stolen), and one to leave at home with a neighbor or relative.

That's it. You're just about ready to leave.

CHAPTER 5

Packing and Last-Minute Details

Someone who no doubt learned the hard way once said, "There are only two kinds of travelers—those who are traveling light and those who wish they were." Certainly, when you travel by train, you're permitted to bring more baggage than the airlines allow. But why would you *want* to?

When in Doubt, Leave It Out!

If you pack intelligently, you can be away from home almost indefinitely and get along very well with only one medium-sized suitcase. All you need is the resolve to do it.

Before you start packing, go over your itinerary. What's the longest stretch you'll be without access to a washing machine? Four days? Okay, then give yourself a margin for error and pack in fives.

- For a man, that means five shirts, five changes of underwear, five pairs of socks, etc. Pack two pairs of pants, making sure they'll both work with all of the shirts.
- For a woman, take two or three slacks and skirts, plus five tops that will go with all of them.

- For men and women, two pairs of shoes, one casual, one a little dressy (both comfortable). Wear one pair and pack the other.

When it comes to toiletries, don't bring large sizes of *anything* with you, be it toothpaste, mouthwash, Kleenex, or whatever. Instead, buy the smallest available tubes or packages, then replace them along the way if necessary. Some items you use every day at home can be left out altogether to save space and lighten your load—that big bottle of after-shave lotion, for instance. Ladies should be sure to bring an adequate supply of sanitary supplies; they are not sold aboard the train.

A Catchall Carry-on Bag

In addition to your one suitcase, take a nice, roomy shoulder bag. There will be exceptions, but it's best to assume that while you're on the train, getting to your suitcase won't always be convenient. The shoulder bag, on the other hand, will stay with you in your room or at your seat. Knowing that, pack each bag accordingly, with your short list of essentials in the shoulder bag and everything else in the suitcase. You'll quickly develop your own list of shoulder-bag items. To get you started, here's mine:

- Toothbrush
- Toothpaste (small tube)
- Razor (an electric razor is much easier while you're on board.)
- Shave cream (small tube)
- Clean shirts (one for each day on board)
- Clean underwear and socks (ditto)
- T-shirt (to sleep in)
- Nail clippers
- A plastic zip-lock bag (for wet face cloths, etc.)

- Reading material
- Spare glasses
- Two pens and a notebook
- Postage stamps
- Small calculator (I'll explain this later)

You might also consider bringing along a pair of binoculars. Just make sure they're small enough to slip into your camera case (if you carry one) or your shoulder bag. You'll particularly enjoy them if you're traveling on one of the western trains through wide open spaces.

The bottom line when it comes to packing: Less is better. As travel writer Rick Steves notes, how many people do you know who brag that they take a little more baggage with them on each trip? You get the idea—the lighter and smarter you travel, the happier you'll be every step of the way.

What About Electric Appliances?

If you can't do without your electric hair dryer or razor, you won't have to. Standard AC outlets of 120 volts are provided in all first-class rooms and in all lavatories, both coach and first class. But before you stick either of those items into your bag, stop for a reality check: Do you want to deal with the bulk and the weight?

Packing for Kids

In addition to the usual items your kids will need during the time you'll be away, be sure to pack an assortment of books and games to occupy them while they're on the train. Adults may be able to enjoy the passing scenery for hours at a time, but not youngsters who need plenty of distractions. In particular, be sure to bring each child's favorite thing. When he or she gets tired or bored or cranky or sick, that one item—blanket, teddy bear, doll, pacifier, or whatever—will help make things all right.

Riding Coach? Bring a Blanket!

Amtrak coaches are air-conditioned and sometimes the system is hard to regulate. Even during the summer it can get quite chilly at night in those large cars. Amtrak does not provide complimentary blankets for coach passengers, so if you're riding coach, *bring your own blanket!* There ought to be a limited supply of small, lightweight blankets for sale in the lounge car, but often none are available and they don't help much anyway. Heed this advice and you will thank me for it! I know, I know . . . a minute ago I told you to pack light and now I am advising you to bring a blanket. It doesn't have to be a big one. A small thermal blanket or one for a twin-size bed that can be folded in half for extra warmth will be fine. Don't pack it; roll it up and tie it to your carry-on bag. Bottom line: *You'll need it!*

And Perhaps a Pillow

Amtrak does provide all coach passengers with a pillow and, while it's considerably larger than the puny ones handed out by the airlines, it's still less than what you're probably used to. I found a small down-filled travel pillow in a mail-order catalog some years ago and bring it along on every trip. During the days, I compress it into a tight roll that fits neatly in my suitcase. Come nighttime, I'm thankful for it whenever I find a hard foam-rubber pillow waiting for me on a train or in a hotel room. The contoured inflatable kind are okay, too.

Coping with Baggage

All Amtrak coaches, whether on short- or long-distance runs, have overhead racks running the length of the car to accommodate luggage. While the rules are not strictly followed, each passenger is allowed two pieces of baggage of "reasonable" size and weight. Additional items are no problem as long as common sense is applied.

If your baggage includes larger suitcases or boxes, they can sometimes be stacked at the end of the car or, in the case of the Superliners, in baggage racks on the lower level. My first recommendation, of course, is that each person travel with just one medium suitcase and a shoulder bag to avoid this very problem. However, if you must have large, heavy baggage, I'd recommend using Amtrak's Checked Baggage Service. Be at the station at least 30 minutes prior to departure to arrange that. Each extra piece of baggage will be tagged and placed in the baggage car. If the total weight of your baggage is more than 150 pounds, expect a small additional charge. Just remember that these pieces will be unavailable to you during your trip.

Be advised, however, that it's not always possible to check baggage. Either the station where you board or at your destination may not offer the service, or your train may not include a baggage car in the consist. This information is included in the Amtrak timetable or, of course, you can always call Amtrak at 1-800-USA-RAIL to make sure.

If you have an unusual amount of baggage, or if you're not able to handle it yourself for any reason, call Amtrak's 800 number at least 72 hours before your departure.

Will the Train Be on Time?

If you're boarding at the train's point of origin, it will almost certainly leave on time. There could be a delay in departure if your train is held for passengers making connections from an incoming train, but under no circumstances will your train depart ahead of schedule from any station . . . *ever!*

If you're boarding somewhere along its route, there's a real possibility that the train will be late. That means you should find out exactly when it will arrive *before* you leave for the station. (After all, if the station is a 90-minute drive from your home, and the train is due at 5:45 in the morning, you'd probably like to know if it's going to be two hours late on that particular day!) Here's what to do:

First try calling the Amtrak office at the station where you'll be boarding. If no one is there (you may need to leave home before Amtrak personnel arrive at the station), call Amtrak's toll-free number, 1-800-USA-RAIL. If they say the train is running on time, head for the station as originally planned. However, if they say the train is significantly late, beware! Their information could be old and, since Amtrak pads their schedules, your train could have made up a lot of that lost time since they got that information. The fail-safe method is to call the Amtrak station one or two stops up the line from your departure point a few minutes before the train is due there. By then they'll know exactly when the train will arrive, and the timetable will tell you the running time from there to your station.

Whatever You Do, Don't Miss Your Train!

Someone once said that the only way to be sure of catching a train is to miss the one before it. Maybe in the good old days, but miss one of Amtrak's long-distance trains and you've got a real problem. Most operate just once a day so at best you'll have to wait 24 hours for the next train. During peak travel times, however, you may find the train sold out for the next day . . . and the next, and the next. That's especially likely if you're riding on a first-class ticket.

For heaven's sake, allow plenty of time for the drive to the station. Any number of things could delay you, so allow for the unexpected. You may end up sitting in the station for a while, but at least you'll be waiting calmly. Don't begin your train trip with anxiety and stress.

It's commonly assumed that times listed on railroad schedules are arrival times. Not so. When only one time is listed for a specific station stop, that's when the train *departs*. If the train is running on time, it will actually arrive several minutes before that time, so plan accordingly. Be aware, too, that in most stations the train won't be there very long—sometimes just sixty seconds or so.

The point is, don't be casual about the business of getting to the station and boarding your train. It's easy to miss a train and, when you do, getting things straightened out is at best a minor inconvenience. At worst, it can be a nightmare.

Things to Know About Boarding

Some Amtrak trains do not offer reserved seating, which means that your seat is not guaranteed. Usually, however, that system is used on short-haul trains that run fairly frequently and are not often sold out.

In coach class, that "reserved seat" status guarantees you a seat on the train, but no *specific* seat has your name on it. This is particularly important to remember if you're traveling with one or more friends or as a family, because you will undoubtedly want to sit together. While there are no guarantees, you can do a few things to make sure you board quickly and, hopefully, end up in the seat or seats you want.

If you're boarding the train at its point of origin, you should have no problem. Just make sure you all get to the station *early* and check in right away with the Amtrak official at the gate. He or she will know how full the train is. Even if it's sold out, the gate official can arrange for your family to board first, if not ahead of the other passengers.

If you're boarding the train en route, however, the train could be nearly full by the time it gets to your station. Here's what to do:

- Call Amtrak at 1-800-USA-RAIL several days before departure and ask them to inform the on-board chief of your needs.

- When you arrive at the station, ask an Amtrak employee where to stand on the platform so you won't find yourself several hundred feet from the coaches when the train comes to a stop. The object is to be among the first to board.
- Better yet, designate someone in your party, unencumbered with kids or baggage, to hop aboard and look for seats as soon as the train stops.
- Once on board, if you cannot find enough seats together, ask the car attendant for help. If he or she is unable to help, ask the conductor who takes your tickets or the chief of on-board services. One of them should be able to accommodate your family.

One of the perks of riding first class, of course, is that specific accommodations have been reserved for you. All you need to do is find the right car and the attendant will direct you right to your room.

Finally, this may seem obvious, but make sure to board your train at the station stop showing on your ticket. A friend of mine once held tickets for sleeping car accommodations between Miami and Washington on the *Silver Star*. At the last minute he had to change his plans and boarded his train in Orlando instead, some 250 miles north of Miami. However, thinking that his bedroom would be waiting for him no matter where he boarded that train, he did not change his tickets or bother to notify Amtrak. Wrong! He was considered a no-show in Miami, and the conductor had sold his bedroom to a coach passenger who had asked for an upgrade.

Metropolitan Lounges

If you're boarding your train in Washington, D.C., New York, or Chicago, be sure to take advantage of the comfortable accommodations Amtrak has for sleeping car passengers in those stations. These waiting rooms, called Metro-politan Lounges, are nicely furnished with easy chairs, cur-rent magazines and newspapers, and complimentary coffee, juice, soft drinks, and snacks. Telephone and fax facilities are also available. (The lounge in Chicago actually has a work-ing fireplace.)

An attendant will ask to see your ticket when you enter, and you will be welcomed into the lounge only if you have just arrived or are about to depart on a first-class ticket. Amtrak sticks to this rule quite literally. I was once refused entry to the Metropolitan Lounge in Chicago because the first 3-hour leg of my trip—Chicago to Galesburg—was in coach class, notwithstanding the fact that I was traveling first class from there to Oakland.

Welcome Aboard!

Okay, you planned your trip, packed carefully (and light), arrived at the station early, boarded without problem, and have just settled into your seat. The train starts rolling before you realize it and you're on your way. Now you're ready to experience everything that's relaxing and fun about a rail journey.

CHAPTER 6

Life on Board

Today's long-distance trains provide passengers with most of the comforts of home. Despite all the improvements and refinements, however, don't expect things to be perfect. A train is *not* a cruise ship on wheels. With several hundred people living together in close quarters for as long as three days, there are bound to be inconveniences. Bear that in mind, and before making an issue out of something, ask yourself if you're being unreasonable under the circumstances. I once listened to a woman in an adjoining room berate the car attendant unmercifully because he had been unable to silence a minor rattle somewhere in her room. The poor man had tried several times to find it without success and clearly it was time she thanked him for his effort and made the best of things. So, before boarding, resolve to lighten up. There's too much to enjoy on the train to let minor things spoil your trip.

Where to Stow Your Baggage

If you're traveling on one of Amtrak's coaches, whether an older type or a newer bi-level car, you'll find room for one or two medium-sized suitcases in the rack above your seat.

There will be plenty of space for a small carry-on bag in the same rack or on the floor under your feet. Superliner coaches also have a large storage rack for luggage on the lower level just as you enter near the middle of the car.

Single-level sleepers have space for some baggage in the rooms. Roomettes have a small rack that can handle one medium-sized bag; bedrooms can handle two bags. The sleeping car accommodations in Superliners really have no place to store baggage conveniently. Like the coaches, however, each bi-level sleeper has a large, easily accessible luggage rack on the lower level. In my experience, the best method is to stow your baggage there, taking the bare essentials with you in a small shoulder bag to your room.

Your On-Board Crew

You'll come in contact with a number of crew members during your trip, including your car attendant, the conductor, possibly a chief of on-board services, dining-car staff, and a lounge-car attendant. (For a complete explanation of the duties and responsibilities of each crew member, including the engineer and his assistant in the locomotive, please see chapter 7: Who's in Charge Here?)

Traveling in Coach

As a coach passenger, you have not been pre-assigned a specific seat. That means you should just climb aboard and sit where you want. On short-haul trains, you'll be pretty much on your own. The only members of the train crew you'll encounter will be the conductor or his assistant. On overnight trains you'll probably be directed to a specific car, but usually you can choose any seat you wish in that car. Sometimes, to help keep track of where people are getting off, coach passengers on overnight trains will be assigned to specific seats by car attendants. Most are quite reasonable about shifting people around, so if you have a problem with your seat assignment, ask if you can be reassigned.

Where to Sit?

For a smoother, quieter ride, try to locate near the middle of the car and, if riding a Superliner, on the upper level. Some Superliner coaches do have a few lower-level seats, but these are usually reserved for handicapped or elderly passengers. Unless you require such accommodations, avoid these seats when you board.

Be Careful About Changing Seats

When your ticket is taken by the conductor, he slips a cardboard seat check into a slot in the baggage rack over your head. That tells both him and the car attendant where you're getting off. Don't change seats without notifying either the conductor or the car attendant, or without taking the seat check with you. This is especially important if you're on an overnight trip and have to leave the train in the wee hours. Many a passenger has changed seats during the night and slept through his stop, because the car attendant couldn't locate him. When that happens, the car attendants invariably get the blame—which explains why they may be uptight if you change seats without telling them.

Changing cars can also cause problems. For instance, when the westbound *California Zephyr* pulls into Salt Lake City, it's split into two trains. Most of the train continues on to Oakland, but a sleeper and several coaches are detached, hooked to a new locomotive, and, as the *Desert Wind,* heads off across Nevada bound for Los Angeles. This all happens around midnight, so if you're sound asleep in one of those big coach seats, it had better be in the right car!

Traveling First Class

"First class" on Amtrak means private accommodations in a sleeping car. It also means that the cost of your meals in the dining car is included in the first-class surcharge you paid when you bought your ticket. (Actually, most Amtrak crews don't commonly use the term "first class." Instead they'll say that you are "in the sleepers.")

As a sleeping-car passenger, you've been assigned a specific room in a specific car. The room and car numbers will appear on your ticket. Each car's number will be visible from the platform, usually in the window nearest the door where you'll enter. In any event, the first member of the train crew you see on the platform will be able to direct you to your car.

Your car attendant will be at the car entrance. He or she will have a manifest listing all passengers assigned to that car and will be expecting you. The car attendant will also carry your bags from the platform into your room if you need help doing so.

Once you're shown to your room, take your time and settle in. The car attendant will offer to show you where everything is and how it all works. You'll find everything very compact. In fact, first-time riders are sometimes startled at how small the accommodations appear. But the rooms are well designed, very efficient, and generally quite adequate.

What to Wear

In another day and time, people dressed up to travel. Cramped spaces on planes changed all that, and today casual dress is acceptable, if not always appropriate. Anyway, feel free to dress comfortably for your train trip. That's especially good advice if you're traveling in coach where you'll be sleeping in your clothes. Jeans or slacks and a sport shirt are fine for men; a skirt or slacks and a blouse are equally appropriate for ladies. My suggestions are based on personal taste, of course. You will see shorts, tank tops, T-shirts emblazoned with messages of questionable taste, and the like, but for the most part, passengers comply reasonably well with today's minimum standards.

Washroom Facilities

Superliners, both coaches and sleepers, have four lavatories located on the lower level of each car. All include washbasins with hot and cold water and a toilet. Some include changing tables for infants, and one is usually oversized. (Find and make note of that one early in your trip.) Superliner sleepers have a shower on the lower level and an additional lavatory on the upper level. All six deluxe bedrooms have toilets and showers in the room.

Short-haul coaches and coaches used on eastern long-distance trains have lavatory facilities at each end of the car, including a washbasin and a toilet. There are no shower facilities. As has been the system since long-distance trains first began carrying passengers, waste water from both the washbasins and the toilets is dumped from many of these cars directly onto the tracks below. Obviously there is still good reason for the old phrase: "Passengers will please refrain from flushing toilets while the train is in the station," and you may hear announcements to that effect on the train's public address system. Also, while the train passes through stretches where the track is being repaired, you may be asked not to use the facilities out of consideration for those doing the work.

As the result of a fairly recent federal mandate, Amtrak has begun a program to systematically convert all toilet facilities to the self-contained type found in Superliners and on airplanes. There are obvious aesthetics involved, of course, but no evidence suggests the existing practice should cause any valid health concerns.

Smoking

Smoking is permitted only in certain specific locations in the train, usually in one area of the lounge car or, occasionally, in one entire coach. Smoking has been eliminated completely on a number of long-distance trains, but, in those cases, passengers are permitted to leave the train at certain stops for a smoke on the platform. "Smoking stops" are announced over the trains P.A. system, but you can usually figure out in advance which stops allow smoking by checking the timetable for stations with both arrival and departure times listed. Amtrak periodically revises its smoking policy and, in fact, more and more trains are being designated as completely non-smoking.

Pets

Pets are a no-no. Not at your seat, either in or out of a container, and not even in the baggage car. At first I thought this policy was too severe, but after hearing a number of horror stories from crew members about pets running loose on trains, I've come to agree that it's the only approach. An exception is made is for certified guide and service dogs, and documentation is required.

Things That Go Bump in the Night

Many a passenger has bedded down for the night in a cozy sleeping-car room, only to become aware of a persistent rattle or squeak coming from somewhere inside the compartment. It's not unusual and may happen to you. If you're bothered by such things, just get up and track it down. Most of the time it's something easily located—a coat hanger swinging with the motion of the train against the sides of the skinny little closet or a ladder not stowed quite right in the upper berth. It's amazing how effectively a washcloth wedged into a crack can silence a rattle. If you can't locate that elusive noise, call the car attendant. He or she has found and fixed many a rattle and will probably have better luck.

Security for Your Belongings

It is an absolute fact that incidents of thievery are rare aboard Amtrak trains, but that doesn't mean you can ignore everyday common sense. The best rule is to leave real valuables at home. If you must bring them aboard, take them with you whenever you leave your seat. That's true for sleeping-car passengers, too, by the way. You can lock the door to your private room once you're inside, but the doors *don't* lock from the outside. My advice to both coach and sleeper passengers is to always carry your identification, your money, your credit cards, and your tickets with you. *Always!* Sleeping-car passengers can feel comfortable about leaving other items—cameras, tote bags, even handbags—in their rooms, but put them someplace out of sight and close the drapes and door to your room securely when you leave. If the car attendant is around, tell him or her that you're going to be out of your room for a while. Notify the attendant if someone opens the door to your room, apparently by mistake. (Don't be overly concerned, however. It's almost always a case of right room, wrong car.)

Personal Food and Drink

Passengers are permitted to bring food and drink aboard the train. My advice, however, is to eat in the dining car or get snacks from the lounge car. The food is quite good, moderately priced, and it's an opportunity to get up, move around, and meet some of your fellow passengers. Besides, especially in the coaches, foods with strong aromas can be annoying to people seated around you.

If you're riding in coach, don't bring any alcoholic beverages aboard since you are not permitted to consume them in your seat. Beer, wine, and a variety of mixed drinks are available in the lounge car and must be consumed there. If you're in a sleeping car, you may bring your own alcohol aboard, but it must be consumed in your room. (Amtrak train crews generally have a low tolerance for passengers who overindulge and cause problems. Conductors can and do put offenders off the train. Literally a sobering experience, I'm sure.)

Dining on Board

Part of the enjoyment of train travel is the unique experience of eating in a rolling restaurant, and a pretty good one, too. Amtrak is into food service big time. The systemwide total is impressive: An average of nearly 11,000 meals are served every day year-round, and that will increase to as many as 14,000 meals a day in peak season. Since the early 1980s, when budget problems brought the Amtrak dining experience to its lowest ebb, there has been steady improvement. Today, considering long hours and the busy, crowded conditions under which they work, Amtrak's food-service crews do an incredible job. As an example, the dining-car crew on the *California Zephyr* serves between 500 and 600 meals a day depending on the time of year.

There are fewer choices on the menu than you would find in a restaurant because storage space in a dining-car kitchen is quite limited. Nevertheless, the portions are generous, the food is good and reasonably priced, and the service is usually cheerful and efficient. Happily, despite the added costs, Amtrak is steadily phasing out the Styrofoam plates and plastic utensils that became necessary during the budget-slashing years. On most long-distance routes, plastic has been replaced with real china and stainless-steel tableware on linen tablecloths. Hooray!

In a full-service dining car, the kitchen crew consists of a chef and at least one food specialist. In the Superliner kitchens, there are always two and sometimes three food specialists to assist the chef, depending on the passenger load. In fact, as real china replaced the disposable plates, an additional worker has been added to help with the dishwashing. In the dining area itself, there will be either a steward or what Amtrak calls a lead service attendant, plus as many as four service attendants, again depending on the type of equipment and the number of passengers on board for that trip.

The dining car is usually located near the middle of the train so no one has to walk the length of the train to reach it. When you enter the diner, wait for the dining car steward or the attendant in charge to seat you. Meals are family style in Amtrak dining cars, meaning that you'll be seated with one or more fellow passengers. In my experience, it's best to take the initiative and break the ice immediately. Introduce yourself and get the conversation started: Where are you from? How far are you traveling? Are you enjoying your trip? I've met some very interesting people in Amtrak dining cars. Besides, the alternative is to sit in uncomfortable silence for the better part of an hour.

Kids are welcomed in the dining car. Booster seats are not always available, although they're supposed to be. In the Superliner dining cars, the top portion of the seat lifts off and can be used for youngsters to sit on. For whatever reason, most dining car crews either don't know about this feature or don't volunteer it, so you'll have to ask.

Menus will vary from train to train and individual chefs are given a fair amount of latitude in what they serve and how it's prepared so it's hard to generalize about dining-car food. Nevertheless, here's an idea of what you can expect in terms of selection and cost when you enter an Amtrak dining car. Remember, coach and slumbercoach passengers pay for their meals while sleeping-car passengers pay out-of-pocket only for soft drinks, beer, or wine.

Breakfast. The dining car is usually open for breakfast from 6:30 A.M. (double-check the exact time with your car attendant) until about 9:30 A.M. You'll hear announcements over the train public address system when the diner opens. The busiest hours are usually between 7:00 and 8:30. Since you'll be seated on a first-come, first-served basis, to avoid a wait, try to get to the diner just as it opens or wait until 9:00. Usual breakfast fare is served: fruit juice, cereal, eggs (fried or scrambled), pancakes, French toast (a tradition of train travel), bacon or sausage, toast, and tea or coffee. Grits are served on most trains traveling to or through the South. Cost: $4.00–$5.00.

Lunch. Dining-car service begins around 11:30 A.M. and continues until everyone is served, closing usually about 1:30 P.M. As with breakfast, there are no reservations. The lunch menu will probably include soup, a choice of hamburger or cheeseburger, chicken sandwich, individual pizza, or a salad plate. For dessert there's pie, cake, or ice cream; drinks include coffee, tea, milk, soft drinks, beer, and wine. Cost: $5.00–$8.00.

Dinner. On most long-distance trains, dinner in the dining car will be by reservation. Normal procedure is for the dining-car steward to move through the train assigning passengers to the various seatings, starting at 5:00 or 5:30 P.M. Usually, he or she will be able to seat you when you would prefer to eat, especially if you're in first class. Again, P.A. announcements through the train will tell you when to head for the diner. The evening menu is quite a bit more extensive than lunch. There will be several entrees, probably a choice from among a chicken, fish, or pasta dish, a steak, roast beef, or a chef's special; dessert includes pie, cake, or ice cream; coffee, tea, milk, soft drinks, beer, and wine are the beverages. Cost: $8.00–$15.00.

You may pay for your meals in the dining car with cash, personal check, or credit card. As already noted, when you travel first class on Amtrak, all your meals are included at no additional charge. If you're traveling first class, either the chief of on-board services or your car attendant will provide you with a meal voucher shortly after you board. Just present it each time you have a meal in the dining car. You'll have full choice of the menu and will not be charged except for beverages other than coffee, tea, milk, or juice.

Coach passengers are also welcomed in the dining car, of course, and can choose from the same menu as folks from the sleeping cars. The only difference is that meals are not included in the cost of the coach ticket.

Amtrak has some interesting ideas under consideration to improve the food service on board their trains. One is to serve only the appetizer and main course in the dining car, having passengers move into the adjacent lounge car for dessert and coffee. This system would permit the dining car to serve more people in a shorter period of time and eliminate the problem of requiring some passengers to choose between very early or very late seatings. There are also plans to prepare special menus for each long-distance train, meaning that trains such as the *Empire Builder* and the *Coast Starlight* would have their own personalized menus.

As noted elsewhere, your car attendant will bring meals from the dining car to sleeping-car accommodations if you request it. But unless you're unable to move throughout the train without difficulty, why do that? Part of the train experience is going to the dining car and meeting fellow passengers over a meal. If you do elect to eat in your room, be advised that it could take a while to arrive and will probably not be piping hot.

The Lounge Car

The other dining option available to all passengers is the lounge car where a variety of hot and cold sandwiches, snacks, and drinks are almost always available. The attendant does stop serving several times a day for meals and an occasional break, but generally the lounge car will be open from 6:00 A.M. until midnight. On shorter runs, the lounge car will remain open for the entire trip. Sleeping car passengers do have to pay for their purchases in the lounge car, by the way.

Beware the "Denver Cocktail"

If you're on one of the western trains and would like a mixed drink or two in the lounge car, or perhaps wine or beer with your meal in the diner, don't forget that altitude increases the effect of the alcohol on the human body. For example, the *California Zephyr* climbs to more than 9,200 feet as it crosses the Continental Divide west of Denver. At that altitude, one glass of wine will have the effect of two. This physiological phenomenon is usually the reason that otherwise sedate passengers are sometimes seen tottering back to their seats from the dining car as the eastbound *Zephyr* begins its descent into the Denver area.

What About Bathing?

Taking a bath, in the literal sense, can't be done. But you can manage to approximate one with a little effort and some ingenuity. As with almost everything else, a lot depends on what kind of accommodations you have.

Superliner sleeping cars have a shower on the lower level. It's cramped (especially if you're tall) and a little tricky, but it works. The prescribed method is navy style: water on, get wet, water off . . . soap up . . . water on, rinse off, water off.

There is a shower in each deluxe bedroom in the Superliners. Well, actually it's a compartment the size of a phone booth that contains both a toilet *and* a shower. The shower works like the one on the lower level, except that you have even less room to maneuver because of the toilet. Be careful not to press the "shower" button when you meant to flush the toilet. You'll need a good sense of humor if you do.

If you're much over six feet, showering on the train can be an awkward task. Even when riding in a sleeper, I usually opt for an all-over sponge bath instead. It's just easier and faster. Towels and washcloths are supplied in the sleeping cars, but if this is your choice, ask the car attendant for an extra towel to stand on.

Superliner coaches don't have showers. There are simply too many passengers to convert a much-needed washroom into a shower. In coach, the only solution is the sponge bath.

Likewise, there are no showers on the older trains operating throughout the eastern part of the country. The answer for all passengers alike is a sponge bath, which is performed by coach passengers in washrooms at the end of the car and by sleeping-car passengers in their roomette or bedroom. Here again, ask the car attendant for an extra towel to stand on.

Sleeping in Coach

Any way you cut it, you'll still be sleeping in a chair. That's not nearly as bad as it sounds, though, because Amtrak's coach seats are large and comfortable, they recline, and most have leg rests. In fact, they're pretty much like that nice recliner in your living room, the one you fall asleep in while watching Jay Leno. The major difference, of course, is the noise and motion of the train and the other people around you. Some passengers don't manage this part of the train experience very well, but some tips can make it easier:

- Bring a blanket and your own pillow.
- Don't eat a huge dinner . . . and skip the coffee or coke.
- Change into loose clothing—an extra-large sweatshirt and sweatpants are ideal.
- Stay up as late as you can reading or chatting quietly with your seatmate; don't even *try* to sleep until you're really ready for it.
- Earplugs and a sleep mask will help.
- So will a sleeping pill. Perhaps your family doctor will prescribe something before you leave.

Sleeping in First Class

Most people—and I'm one of them—don't truly appreciate their sleeping car accommodations until bedtime. But when I'm under those clean sheets and into a good book, glancing up occasionally as we pass through a town, I have a feeling of contentment that makes that extra fare worth every dime. I get the same feeling all over again when I wake up the next morning after spending a restful night in reasonable comfort.

Remember that the car attendant has a lot of beds to prepare—as many as 44 if you're traveling in a Superliner and the car is full. Try to give him or her as much advance notice as possible when you want to have your beds prepared. Ideally, get one of the later seatings in the diner and let the attendant know when you're heading off to dinner. He'll have your beds made up when you return.

Here are a few suggestions to help ensure a good night's rest in your first-class bedroom:

- You won't need to bring a blanket, but you might want to bring a pillow—one of those small, down-filled kind you can roll up and pack in your suitcase.

- Don't overdo it at dinner, even though your meals are free, and avoid the caffeine.
- Stay up as late as you can reading; turn out the light only when you're really sleepy.
- You can easily darken your room, so a sleep mask won't be necessary; but consider the earplugs.

Incidentally, the car attendant would rather you didn't try to prepare the bed yourself. And don't try to close it up in the morning, especially if you're going to be occupying the room for another night. There's a right way to do it, and the attendants would rather you left that job to them.

Tipping

For some reason, the issue of whether to tip members of the train's on-board crew confuses many travelers. Fear not, here are the ground rules:

- Do *not* tip the conductor, the chief of on-board services, or the dining car steward.
- *Do* tip the car attendant. In the sleepers, a good rule of thumb is $5 per night per passenger. Increase that appropriately if you ask to have meals brought to your room. I'd suggest at least an additional $2 per person per meal. In coach class, assuming you've been helped with baggage and have received cheerful and friendly attention, my suggestion is $1 or $2 for a one-night trip; $3 or $4 for two nights. Most passengers tip the car attendant as they leave the train at their final destination, although others prefer tipping after each special service is provided.

  (By the way, I've interviewed numerous car attendants during my many travels on Amtrak and, although it's deplorable, all agree that female car attendants tend to receive lower tips than their male counterparts. Please be sensitive to that inequity.)

- *Do* tip the lounge-car attendant. Extra change left behind on the counter after each purchase is appropriate.
- *Do* tip the service people in the dining car. Follow the same rules you would in any other restaurant: Start with the standard 15 percent, moving up for really good service and down for casual or unfriendly service.

Some first-class passengers have the misconception that they're under no obligation to tip dining-car staff because their meals are complimentary. Not so! If you have the means to ride first class, you can afford to tip generously where warranted. Please do so! The IRS *assumes* you will be tipping these people, by the way, and requires them to pay income tax on an amount equal to 8 percent of each meal check they serve.

If done right, no jobs on a long-distance train are easy. Car attendants routinely put in 18–20 hour days; the dining-car staff often prepares or serves 700–800 meals a day; the lounge-car attendant is on duty almost non-stop for 16–17 hours, often, I'm sorry to say, in a smoke-filled environment. Crews working the cross-country trains are on duty for 45 or 50 hours straight, spend one night in a hotel, then work the same train back home. I would encourage you to recognize and reward people who perform efficiently and cheerfully under those conditions.

Finally, you should be aware that official Amtrak policy says no employee shall solicit tips. I've never once run into it, but should it happen to you, especially if it's flagrant, I would encourage you to report the individual to the on-board chief. It's not that the sin is so great; it's just a pretty good indication of a bad employee.

Taking Pictures

If you enjoy taking photographs on your vacation trips, traveling across the country by train will provide you with a limitless number of photo opportunities, both inside and outside of the train. I carry two cameras when I travel—a good quality "idiot proof" camera with a built-in flash for interior and nighttime shots, and a more sophisticated model that allows me to set the shutter speed and to focus manually. Between them, I'm able to cover almost any photo opportunity.

Taking interior shots on a train is no more difficult than taking photos in your own home. For shots of a party in the lounge car or of that nice couple from England you met over dinner, the little automatic camera is perfect.

Unfortunately, it's not as easy to get really first-rate shots of the scenery passing by outside. Shooting through the tinted train windows is the biggest obstacle to really good pictures. Unlike European railroads, the windows in American coaches and sleeping cars cannot be opened (although they can be pushed out in an emergency). Final results may not be perfect, but there are things you can do to improve the quality of those important souvenir photos.

Photos taken through tinted windows tend to come out looking a little "flat." To compensate a bit, use a color print film. If you prefer to shoot slides as I do, use Kodachrome, which provides more contrast than Ectachrome. Other manufacturers have equivalent film types, which your dealer can help you select. If you have a more sophisticated camera, a compensating filter will probably help. Which filter you need will depend on choice of film. Again, consult someone knowledgeable where you buy your film.

A film speed of 100 or 200 is appropriate. Anything less will require faster shutter speeds; anything more will yield grainy results.

Get the camera's lens as close to the window as you can *without touching it*. A lens pressed against the window or a camera body braced against any other part of the train can transmit the train's vibration to the camera. Result: blurry photos.

If you can control the adjustment, switch your camera from automatic to "selective focus." Some cameras with the automatic focus feature will focus on the transparent window pane instead of that gorgeous passing scene outside. Controlling the focus yourself will avoid that problem. Usually you won't have time for much adjustment, so often the best advice is to set your focus on "infinity" and forget about it.

Again, if your camera is so equipped, switch from automatic to "selective shutter speed," then set the shutter speed to 250 or 500. Because the train is moving, slower shutter speeds can result in blurry photographs.

If you take the ultra-simple approach and use one of the so-called "idiot-proof" cameras exclusively, you probably won't be able to make most of those adjustments. My advice? Don't worry about it! Your photos won't be up to *National Geographic* standards, but they'll still make dandy souvenirs.

If you have time, check for any reflections in the window and block them with your body before shooting.

Don't use the automatic flash for photos taken through the train window. It will probably cause a photo-wrecking reflection and, besides, it's of no use for objects more than 15 or 20 feet away. *Do* use the flash for interior shots, even during daytime hours.

Please don't try for clearer photos by opening the windows in the train's exit doors, either in the vestibules or on the lower level of the Superliners. You run the risk of injury from flying debris kicked up by the train, from passing trains, or from stationary objects at trackside. And, of course, there's always the cheery prospect that you and your camera could suddenly be enveloped in a fine mist— the contents of a toilet in the car ahead that has been emulsified, chemically treated, and blown out onto the tracks.

One more thing: Don't feel badly when you get home and find that quite a few of your photos have been ruined by what I call "the green blur" . . . bushes or trees that suddenly zoom in front of the camera just as you press the shutter. I'm an expert on the green blur and have hundreds of shots to prove it.

On-Board Activities

Most of the organized activities occur in the Superliner lounge cars, simply because they're so much bigger than their single-level counterparts. You'll hear about them over the train's public address system. Movies are shown and, toward sundown, there's usually a Happy Hour. Depending on how "with it" the on-board chief is, games involving the entire train are often played, with prizes offered for answering trivia questions or for producing the greatest number of objects in a scavenger hunt.

Passing the Time

Finding something to do on the train is more of a problem for some passengers than for others. Many people—and I'm one—can just turn down their metabolism and dreamily let the hours roll by along with the miles. Others need to change their activities rather frequently. Having something available to do is important, especially at night or when there's nothing much passing by outside to hold your attention.

Enjoy the Scenery

The view, of course, is the main reason for traveling by train, so take full advantage of it. On most long-distance trains, Amtrak provides passengers with printed route guides identifying the major points of interest along the way. These include a written description and a schematic map that tells you on which side of the train each feature will appear and about when to start looking for it.

Frequently a member of the crew—usually one of the conductors since they know the route best—will provide commentary about the passing scenery over the P.A. system. Unfortunately, there really isn't any standard when it comes to this kind of live narrative. Some passengers enjoy it; others would prefer not to have to listen to it. Some conductors have a real feel for this kind of thing and do a wonderful job; others don't or won't do it at all.

Several of Amtrak's trains feature special lecturers who offer commentary over the P.A. system about the countryside through which the train is passing. For instance, during much of the year a Native American volunteer boards the eastbound *Southwest Chief* in Gallup, New Mexico, and provides a fascinating narrative about the area and the people who have lived there for thousands of years. He or she leaves the train three hours later in Albuquerque and, later the same day, catches the westbound *Chief* back to Gallup, once again lecturing all the way. A few other trains—the *California Zephyr* and the *Cardinal,* for example—often have volunteers from local historical societies who come aboard to perform similar services. Without exception, I've found these people interesting, articulate, and well-informed. All deserve thanks and appreciation for their dedication and effort. Please make it a point to acknowledge them should you be on one of those trains.

Now here are some train-related diversions for passengers, either to undertake alone or with traveling companions.

Compute the Train's Speed

The train's speed varies greatly, of course, depending upon track conditions, grade, the amount of rail traffic, weather, and other factors. The maximum speed allowed for Amtrak trains is 125 miles per hour along the Northeast corridor from Washington, D.C., to Boston, and 79 miles per hour almost everywhere else in the country. "How fast are we going?" is almost certainly the question asked most often.

There *is* an easy way to figure it out, quickly and accurately. You'll need a sweep second hand on your watch and a calculator, unless you don't mind working out the math yourself. You'll also need to be able to see the mile posts passing by outside your train. (Information about mile posts can be found in chapter 10: How It All Works.)

The formula is simple: Divide 3,600 (the number of seconds in an hour) by the number of seconds it take you to travel one mile (the distance between two mileposts). Thus, if it takes the train 53 seconds to travel one mile, you're going 67.92 mph. The engineer in the locomotive cab carries a stopwatch for the same purpose, by the way. He's required to operate right at the speed limit and regularly checks the accuracy of the speedometer in the cab using this same method.

If you're not interested in doing the math, here's a chart that will shortcut the process for you.

Time Between Mile Posts	Speed (mph)
2:00.0	30
1:43.0	35
1:30.0	40
1:20.0	45
1:12.0	50
1:00.0	60
:55.4	65
:51.4	70
:48.0	75
:45.0	80
:42.4	85
:40.0	90
:37.9	95
:36.0	105
:32.7	110
:31.3	115
:30.0	120
:28.8	125

There is another, much less accurate, way to compute the train's speed. Count the number of "telephone" poles passing by in a 15-second period and multiply that number by six. Most of the time, that will give you a rough idea of the speed. (Incidentally, those are not really telephone poles. They were originally installed by the railroad to bring electricity to its signals and switches.)

Track the Train's Progress

Bring along a soft-cover road atlas of the United States and, as you travel from town to town, mark the train's progress on the maps with a colored highlighter pen. If you don't want to bring the entire atlas, just xerox the appropriate pages before you leave home. Personally, I'd bring the whole atlas because it does provide a nice record of your train trip—even more so if you're a frequent train traveler.

Estimate Your Arrival Time

I enjoy figuring out whether we're gaining or losing time along our route. It's quite easy since departure times for each station stop are listed in the Amtrak timetable. You can probably get one from the car attendant or conductor, and you may find one at your seat or in your room when you board, but I always bring one with me. Just for fun, I use this means to log our progress and to predict the exact time we'll arrive at our final destination.

Because there's plenty of time, and as the mood strikes me, I sometimes keep a running account of how we're doing in some detail. For example, here's a portion of the log I kept aboard Train 87, the *Silver Meteor,* between Jacksonville and Tampa some time ago. One little thing you discover through this exercise is where the schedule has been padded. Note that the timetable shows 25 minutes between DeLand and Sanford; in actuality, at least on this particular day, it only took 18 minutes.

Station Stop	Schd Dprt	Actl Dprt	Schd Min	Actl Min	No. Miles	Avrg Speed	Time Gained (lost)	Total Time Gnd	Est. Arvl (lost)
Jcksnvle	1:18	1:18	—	—	—	—	6:07	—	
Palatka	2:24	2:29	:66	:71	59	49.9	(:05)	(:05)	6:12
DeLand	3:09	3:17	:45	:48	52	63.7	(:04)	(:09)	6:16
Sanford	3:34	5:51	:25	:18	16	67.5	:07	(:02)	6:09

By the way, to compute the train's average speed over longer distances, use the following formula:

60 × no. of miles ÷ no. of minutes = mph

As an example, in the log shown above, it took Train 87 a total of 48 minutes to travel the 52 miles between Palatka and DeLand, Florida. Here's the math to figure out the train's average speed over that leg.

a. $60 \times 52 = 3,120$
b. $3,120 \div 48 = 65$ mph

Many people won't want to bother with these kinds of calculations, but others enjoy keeping tabs on how their train is doing.

Listen In on Train Talk

It's done with a device called a scanner, a radio receiver about the size of cellular phone that picks up conversations between members of the operating crew—usually the engineer and the conductor. These little devices rapidly scan across radio frequencies used by police, fire departments, civil defense, railroads, taxi companies, and others and automatically stop whenever they come across a channel in use. For years I thought only the real hard-core train nuts carried one of these little electronic toys, but I must confess that I bought one a couple of years ago and have enjoyed using it when I travel by train. You can not only pick up conversations between members of your train crew, but also those from yard workers, passing trains, and the recorded voices of the hot box detectors you pass. Scanners provide a fascinating look at railroad operations and are perfectly legal, but there are a couple of things to remember:

- Use an earphone—they come with the scanner—so the periodic squawking won't disturb other passengers.
- Some high-end scanners also include the ability to transmit, permitting two-way conversations. You certainly don't need that feature, but, in any event, the inflexible, carved-in-stone rule is: Listen, but *do not talk!* People who do have no sense and, if discovered, are likely to find themselves standing on a platform watching their train disappear in the distance without them.

You can buy a serviceable scanner in most electronics stores for around $150. They're powered by a rechargeable battery, which typically will operate the scanner for five or six hours. If you're traveling in a sleeping car, you can save your battery and operate the device by plugging the adapter into the electric receptacle in your room. The battery can be recharged in the same manner. Just be sure the model you buy will pick up the frequencies commonly used by the railroads (160.215 to 161.565 megahertz). There's also a nifty little publication called *Trak Tables* which lists Amtrak frequencies by train numbers. To order a copy, contact Three Rivers Press, Box 70285, Bellevue, Washington 98007.

There are a plethora of other ways to put some variety into your day aboard.

Take a Walk

Once or twice between each meal and usually after each stop, the conductor "walks the train," literally passing through from one end to the other. He does it to collect tickets from passengers who have just boarded or just to satisfy himself that there are no problems. You should do it to get the juices going a bit and just for the exercise. After all, before you know it, you'll be back in the dining car for another meal! You'll find it's more exercise than you might think since you'll be working more than normal to keep your balance in the moving train.

Read a Book

Most of us have any number of books we haven't been able to get to because of our busy daily schedules. Here's the perfect opportunity to start on that tome you've been holding onto. I try to save most of my reading for the evening when there's little or nothing to see outside.

Or a Newspaper

Sleeping-car passengers usually get a morning paper delivered to their room by the car attendant and sometimes there will be other copies in the lounge car for coach passengers. These newspapers are put aboard the train at major stops early every morning. For example, Train 48, the westbound *Lake Shore Limited,* stops in Buffalo, New York, at about 6:00 A.M., so first-class passengers will usually find the Buffalo newspaper under their door upon waking. I enjoy looking through these unfamiliar newspapers since I'll probably pass through some of the towns and cities they're writing about. Sometimes, instead of the local paper, *USA Today* will be put aboard, but either way you'll feel in touch with what's going on in the world.

Listen to Audio Tapes

A number of mail-order catalogs feature audiotapes and most good bookstores stock a large selection, too—everything from children's stories to classic literature to old radio shows from the 1940s and 1950s. This can be the best of both worlds. I once sat gazing out the window of Train 7, the *Empire Builder,* as it rolled through the farm country of Minnesota while listening to an audiotape of Garrison Keillor spinning some of his wonderful yarns about Lake Wobegon. It was rather a strange feeling.

Do Puzzles and Games

Bring along a book of crossword puzzles. Most also include other games: anacrostics, cryptograms, and other word games. Bring a deck of cards (or buy a souvenir deck in the lounge car) for solitaire or other card games with your traveling companion or new friends in the lounge car. If you're traveling with children, by all means pick up a book of games for kids in your hometown bookstore before you leave. Several are available, and each can give you lots of new ideas for games and other diversions you'll all enjoy.

Write Letters

Finally you have the time to write to friends and family—and something to tell them about, too. You can buy Amtrak post-cards in the Superliner lounge car, but bring some along or buy a few in the station before you leave just in case. And be sure to bring your own postage stamps or, better yet, put stamps on them before you leave home. Otherwise you're likely to carry those cards and letters with you the entire way.

See a Movie in the Lounge Car

There are TV monitors in Superliner lounge cars, usually one at each end of the upper level and another downstairs. Recent feature films are shown in the evening, usually twice, and often video entertainment geared toward youngsters is presented in the afternoons. In any case, as on the airlines, all movies shown will have been sanitized for family viewing. As new equipment is added and older cars refurbished on the eastern trains, video monitors will appear in those coaches, with headsets available for rental.

There's Romance on the Rails—Literally

Some passengers take the idea of a romantic train trip quite literally. For them, an overnight train trip seems to have a direct affect on the libido. Train crews grin and shake their heads when asked about some of the more inventive means passengers have taken to enjoy the pleasures of sex on board a long-distance train. Amorous couples have been discovered in the baggage car, in vestibules, in the lounge car, in the washrooms (quite a trick, given their size), and wherever else opportunity, desire, and, I suspect, a sense of mischief or daring collide.

Because of the lack of privacy at their assigned seats, coach passengers are most often the ones who seek somewhat more secluded locations for these activities. But not always. Sleeping-car passengers are occasionally discovered having sex in parts of the train other than their rooms. And it's not unknown for couples safely ensconced in private accommodations to deliberately leave their window shades up during their lovemaking as the train flashes—sorry, no pun intended—through small towns.

For the most part, Amtrak crews try to look the other way when encountering these situations. The unofficial common-sense response seems to have a lot to do with whether or not other passengers are being disturbed or offended.

By the way, those who successfully engage in these amorous on-board activities are said to have joined the 80-Mile-an-Hour Club, the rail equivalent to the Mile-High Club of the airline industry.

A Few Do's and Don'ts

Most of these suggestions probably apply more to coach passengers because of the communal seating arrangement. But whether you're sitting in coach or a sleeper, you're still living with a lot of other people in fairly confined circumstances. Being a good neighbor is really just a matter of common sense and basic courtesy, so . . .

- Use earphones with radios, tape and CD players, and scanners. (Amtrak will enforce this.)
- Loud conversations, even in private sleeping-car accommodations, can be very disturbing to people located nearby, many of whom will be relaxing, reading, or dozing.
- Tidy up after yourself in the washroom. One car attendant cannot possibly keep all of them clean all of the time.
- Let your car attendant know right away if you find something wrong—a malfunctioning toilet, for example. Early attention to these problems will minimize inconvenience to fellow passengers and can frequently prevent things from getting worse.
- Don't hog a seat in the Superliner lounge or the dome car if other passengers are obviously waiting for their turn.
- As pleasant as it may be, don't linger in conversation for more than a few minutes over coffee in the dining car. There's either another seating scheduled or the dining-car crew is ready for a well-earned break.
- Unless it's truly important, don't bother a member of the crew who's on a meal break in the dining car. It's a tough job, and they deserve that short time to themselves.
- If you're traveling with children, don't let them run around the train without supervision. It's dangerous, especially in the vestibules between the cars, and it can be very annoying to other passengers.

One last word on the subject of behavior: Some passengers are under the impression that there are *no* laws on board a train and actually think they can indulge in drugs, liquor to excess, and any number of other illegal activities with immunity. Wrong! Wherever the train happens to be, the laws of that particular state apply to everyone on board. Passengers can be removed from the train and arrested in exactly the same way they can be kicked out of a hotel or a restaurant and into the waiting arms of the law. It can and does happen.

Train travel is meant to be an enjoyable experience. Agitation and impatience are simply incompatible with a leisurely cross-country train ride, so once on board and set-tled into your surroundings, relax. Gear down. Start notic-ing the new and the different in the passing scenery. Meet some of your fellow passengers. In fact, try to adopt the philosophy of an English gentlemen I met over lunch in the *Empire Builder*'s diner a few years back. The conductor had stopped by our table and informed us that we would be at least two hours late into Seattle because of work being done on the tracks. My English friend fairly beamed at the news. "Jolly good!" he exclaimed. "We're getting our money's worth and then some, aren't we!"

CHAPTER 7

Who's in Charge Here?

The success of any company, whether a manufacturing firm or a railroad, depends on its employees and, ultimately, how well they perform their jobs. When it came into existence in 1971, Amtrak inherited thousands of employees from private railroads. Along with all those new people came a kind of compendium of pecking orders, systems, and procedures which somehow had to be forged into one way of doing things. In many respects the resulting operation didn't work out well and, in some instances, change for the better has taken years.

When Thomas M. Downs took over as Amtrak's president in 1994, more than two decades after the company was created, he was startled to discover that *he* was the first common supervisor for both a train conductor and a chief of on-board services. Largely due to Downs' urging, Amtrak reorganized its systems and introduced newer and better management techniques. Happily, that included the granting of more authority to front-line employees and today, at least in theory, key members of the on-board crew can take action on the spot to rectify most problems.

A Word About Race and Gender

Although there are still some inequities in a number of areas, Amtrak has consistently demonstrated a progressive approach to the problem of discrimination by race or gender. The most obvious example is the position of car attendant. In the days of the Pullman porter, these jobs were limited to black males. Today, however, passengers are just as likely to find that their car attendant is a white female.

This enlightened attitude also extends to giving women an opportunity to work in other railroad jobs that were traditionally the exclusive province of men. Women are now serving in every capacity on both freight and passenger trains, including the head end. For traditionalists, not to mention sexists, that will take some getting used to. My brother Pete was on a short-haul trip in the Midwest recently when a railfan, seated across the aisle from him, turned on his scanner to listen in on chatter among the crew. The man suddenly sat bolt upright in his seat and exclaimed to everyone within a 20-foot radius, "Holy ----! The engineer's a woman!"

Who Does What and Why?

First, you should know that a distinction is made between "operating crew" (the engineers and the conductors) and "service crew" (everyone else working on board). As the terms imply, the operating crew is responsible for actually running the train, while the service crew looks after the needs of passengers. There is another significant difference: The service crew stays with the train for the entire trip, while the engineers and conductors are restricted by federal law to working no more than twelve hours in a row.

Most Amtrak crews tend to become quite close and treat each other like family. For instance, car attendants will switch off during the night, with one person covering two cars through a couple of stops so the other one can get a bit more sleep. If one of the dining-car crew becomes ill, it's not unusual for the chief of on-board services to pitch in and help out. Often one train crew will help out another. Once, while I was traveling eastbound on the *Southwest Chief,* our train slowed to a stop when we met our westbound counterpart so that several cases of soft drinks and a bag of ice could be handed from our lounge car to theirs.

The ability to get along with people is certainly a prerequisite for anyone considering a job with Amtrak. By the time someone becomes a veteran employee, he or she has seen it all and can deal with most of it pretty darn well.

There are, of course, many other key jobs in the operational structure of a railroad, but this section focuses on those employees who are directly responsible for getting you to your destination in safety and comfort.

In addition to learning more about what these people do, I thought you would find it interesting to know what they're paid for their efforts, so I've included some rough compensation figures for members of the on-board and operating crews—starting pay and the maximum possible under the current contracts. Most employees receive increases of 5 percent a year until they reach the ceiling. I've rounded off the numbers and made an effort to standardize the information by computing the annual pay from current hourly rates, assuming everyone works a full year of 40-hour weeks. Obviously, many of these people put in additional hours, adding to their base salary with overtime pay. And, of course, some of the on-board crew also earn tips.

Dispatcher

Wherever the train may be, whether it's running over Amtrak or contract railroad tracks, its progress is controlled every inch of the way by a dispatcher. The airline equivalent is the air traffic controller, but there is an important difference: Railroad dispatchers are employees of the individual railroads, while air traffic controllers are employed by the Federal Aviation Administration, an agency of the U.S. Department of Transportation. (One more hidden government subsidy of the airline industry not enjoyed by the railroads, by the way.) Dispatchers who control trains traveling in the Northeast Corridor between Washington, D.C., and Boston are Amtrak employees because those tracks are owned by Amtrak. Elsewhere throughout the country, the movement of Amtrak trains is controlled by dispatchers employed by the host railroads—that is, the railroads over whose tracks the Amtrak train is traveling.

Like their aviation counterparts, dispatchers are critical to the safe operation of the nation's railroads. Typically, they work in darkened rooms, keeping track of trains on an illuminated display of the tracks for which they are responsible. The job requires complete concentration and their fellow employees take pains not to interrupt or distract them.

Dispatchers communicate directly with the train's engineer by radio. They also control the signals seen by the engineer along the route. The dispatcher's main and constant concern is knowing exactly where each train is at all times. To assist the dispatcher, the engineer checks in by radio regularly—when the train passes specific checkpoints, when it leaves each station stop, and at other times along the way. Many engineers even "answer" the recorded voices of automated hot box detectors they pass—just one more way of letting the dispatcher know where they are.

There is other, more specific communication between the train crew and dispatcher, of course. The dispatcher frequently directs the train to slow down, stop, or resume normal speed. He may remind the engineer that men are working on the track at a certain location, or instruct him to reduce speed between two specific mileposts where the track has just been laid. When receiving such instructions, the engineer will acknowledge the call and carefully repeat the message so the dispatcher will be sure it was heard correctly. The engineer will often conclude his part of the transmission by verbally noting the time and the train number, and then identifying himself by name. For important matters, the dispatcher is also the train's link to the rest of the world. If a passenger becomes seriously ill, for instance, the engineer can call the dispatcher and ask him to arrange for paramedics to meet the train at the next station stop.

Engineer

This is the job many of us wanted when we were kids and, if you've ever been one of the privileged few to ride in the cab of a locomotive, you'll know why. It's a thrill to sit up there with all that horsepower, grandly acknowledging the waves from kids of all ages as you thunder past. But make no mistake: It's a tough job and, while it's generally agreed that being a freight engineer is more demanding, the men and women who haul Amtrak trains around the country are acutely aware that they're responsible for the lives of as many as 500 passengers.

Becoming a locomotive engineer isn't easy. It's particularly difficult if your goal is the head end of a passenger train, not quite so hard if you're after a job as a freight engineer. Basically, it boils down to supply and demand. Most engineers, or at least the older, married ones, seem to prefer working for Amtrak because of convenience. An Amtrak engineer works a set schedule and thus has the luxury of knowing in advance when he'll be at home and when he'll be away. A freight engineer, however, is usually on call and goes whenever and wherever he's needed.

Then there's the matter of training. Before someone can even be *considered* for an engineer's job, he or she has to spend six weeks in a classroom. One section covers instruction in the mechanical aspects of the equipment, another deals exclusively with air brakes (reflecting the obvious importance of knowing the hows and whys of stopping a train weighing many thousands of tons), and the third is a detailed review of the operational rules of railroading. From the classroom, an engineer/trainee moves into the cab of a locomotive as an assistant to the engineer for a minimum of 480 hours of on-the-job training. Even after the classroom and on-the-job experience, there's still no guarantee that the trainee will be selected. Some would-bes are rejected because, according to one veteran engineer, they "just don't seem to have a *feel* for it." And, no matter how long they've been on the job, every engineer goes through refresher training periodically and must take regular exams to qualify and re-qualify for the specific territory he works.

Of course the engineer is the person who controls the locomotive that pulls the train. He alternately operates the throttle to start the train in motion and keep it moving, and the brakes to slow or stop the train. He also controls the whistle and constantly uses the radio to communicate with the conductor and the dispatcher.

To start the train, the engineer opens the throttle, which causes the diesel motors to run faster, generating more electricity and increasing the flow of power to the traction motors on each of the locomotive's axles. As he or she does that, the engineer leans out the window and looks straight down at the ground. In that way, he or she can tell the instant the train starts to move and can adjust the throttle accordingly to keep the wheels from slipping. A slipping wheel is a real no-no, because it can cause a jerk that can be felt throughout the train. Passenger train engineers pride themselves on their smooth starts, so starting with even a small jerk is embarrassing. But there are more serious potential consequences to a rough start. If the jolt is strong enough, it can cause passengers or crew to lose their balance momentarily and even fall.

Because freight trains are longer than passenger trains, there is a lot more slack or "play" built into the coupling mechanism hooking each car together. As a freight starts moving, the slack is taken up in one car after another down the length of the train. Brakemen in the cabooses can hear the jolt coming toward them and hang on. As the slack is taken up in car after car, it builds in intensity. By the time it gets to the last car of a long train, it can literally knock you off your feet.

As strange as it may seem, freight engineers must handle their trains very gently. Taking up slack abruptly while a freight train is rolling can actually break the train in two. In fact, to prevent massive derailments, the knuckle in the coupling device is deliberately designed as the weakest link in the chain so it will break under severe stress. How many times an engineer breaks a train is one way of measuring his or her performance and abilities. Sometimes it happens because the engineer caused it, but other times a knuckle gives way from metal fatigue or because it's old and rusted. When that happens, the engineer will replace the defective knuckle (spares are carried in freight locomotive cabs) and keep it to show his superiors as proof that the break was not his fault.

Once under way, the engineer's attention is almost always directed toward the track ahead, looking out for obstructions, but also watching for signals, speed-limit signs, whistle posts (warning him to blow the whistle for an approaching grade crossing), and other trackside markings. The locomotive cab is equipped with two large side mirrors, which the engineer uses to inspect the rest of his train on every curve for problems such as smoke from an overheated bearing or shifting loads in the case of freights. The assistant engineer does the same on his side of the cab. Traditionally, the engineer sits on the right side of the locomotive cab because, in the days of steam locomotives, that's the side of the tracks where all the signs and signals were placed.

The visual inspection was also an important function performed by railroad personnel riding in cabooses at the end of freight trains, but both the cabooses and the people who rode them have been replaced by an electronic device mounted at the end of the rear car. Called FRED by railroad people (an acronym for "Flashing Rear End Device"), it picks up reports from the automatic detectors alongside the track and relays them by radio to the engineer in the head end.

Unlike the smooth ride passengers are treated to, it's pretty bouncy in the cab of a locomotive, and the rough ride can affect the accuracy of the speedometer. Because trains must run at or close to the prescribed speed for any given stretch of track, most engineers carry a stopwatch, which they use regularly to determine precisely how fast the train is moving. This is done by recording the exact time it takes the train to pass between two mileposts then computing the speed from that. (See table on page 92.)

Most Amtrak engineers came to the job with freight experience, and most agree that being a freight engineer is the more difficult of the two jobs. Because freight trains are so long—a 150-car train can be over a mile and a half from end to end—the engineer of a freight train often finds himself with one part of the train coming up a hill and the other part heading down the other side at the same time. Just to complicate things, the number of cars on either side is constantly changing as the train passes over the crest of the hill. That's very tricky because the engineer must make sure he's pulling all the cars all the time. Now suppose there's a curve in that stretch of track. That means he also has to think about centrifugal force affecting the part of the train that's going around the curve. Veteran engineers will tell you that in many ways their job is tougher and more demanding than that of an airline pilot. The cockpit of a modern jet certainly looks complicated, but, as one engineer friend of mine says, "Those are all fancy gizmos to help the pilot do his job. We don't have any of that stuff to help us." And he's quite right. In that sense, there is indeed a greater burden placed on a locomotive crew. If the train is running in fog or snow, there is no radar to help the head-end crew. The engineer must be so familiar with his route that he can "see" the track ahead in his mind's eye.

Another apt comparison between the locomotive engineer and an airline pilot is that both are expected to operate their machines in a manner that will minimize the use of fuel. The pilot does it by adjusting the attitude of the aircraft in flight so it passes through the air with the least possible resistance. The locomotive engineer conserves fuel in much the same way the driver of a car does—with a delicate touch, both on the throttle and the brakes.

Federal law permits an engineer to be on duty for no more than twelve hours. For that reason, one pair of engineers does not stay with a long-distance train for the entire route. For instance, along the westbound route of the *California Zephyr,* operating crews change in Galesburg, Illinois; in Lincoln, Nebraska; in both Denver and Grand Junction, Colorado; in Salt Lake City, Utah; and so on all the way to Oakland, California. Usually, a crew coming off duty will sleep overnight at one of those points, then, the next day, take the eastbound train back to where they started. Under no circumstances is an engineer permitted to continue operating a train after he reaches his twelve-hour limit. If it appears that an operating crew will "go dead" before reaching its scheduled crew-change stop, Amtrak must anticipate the problem and arrange for a fresh crew to meet the train somewhere along the route before that happens.

Engineers are intimately familiar with the track in their territories—that is, with the stretch of track over which they operate their trains. They know that track the same way a commuter knows the roads between home and work. They *have* to—and must take regular tests to prove it. In many cases—probably most—they also get to know some of the people who live along their regular routes. These folks sit in their windows or step out into their backyards to wave as the trains go by. The crews get to know their "regulars" and wave back when they appear, usually with a friendly toot from the whistle, too.

One more tidbit I found interesting: Unlike the airlines, where meals are provided for the cockpit crews, head-end crews on Amtrak trains bring their own food in lunch pails. The only thing they're permitted to get from the dining car is coffee. On occasion, however, a chef will bend the rules and send up food that would otherwise spoil and be thrown out. But the steak or half chicken that can be used another day stays in the diner's freezer.

As with almost any job, there is a downside to being a railroad engineer. The first thing a visitor to the head end discovers is that it's *noisy* up there. That shouldn't be surprising because you're sitting just a few feet in front of as many as 4,000 horses. All that power makes quite a racket, and it's magnified several times whenever the train enters a tunnel. The real culprit, however, is the whistle, which is blown constantly. While the volume can be controlled to a degree, it still ranges from loud to damn-near unbearable. Earplugs are provided, but aren't practical since there's a lot of necessary conversation going on. One obvious solution would be to retrofit the whistles farther back on the roof of the locomotive. It wouldn't eliminate the problem, but it would certainly help a lot. So far, presumably for budgetary reasons, that hasn't been done. Amtrak's newer locomotives are air-conditioned, permitting the crew to keep the windows closed. That will help, too. But for most engineers, operating older locomotives, which still comprise 90 percent of the fleet, no immediate answer to the noise problem is in sight.

There is only one real negative to the engineer's job, but it's a big one. Almost every engineer, freight or passenger, has struck and killed someone while at the controls of the locomotive. Perhaps it's someone who thought he had plenty of time to drive across the tracks before the train reached the crossing. Maybe it's a teenager playing chicken with the train on a dare. And maybe it's just some poor soul who has decided it would be a quick way to end it all. Whatever the circumstances, they're all equally tough on the person who happens to be at the controls of the locomotive. Spend a few hours riding in the head end and you somehow sense a touch of uneasiness as every grade crossing is approached. Most engineers manage to keep it in perspective. One told me, "As long as I've done everything possible—if I wasn't speeding, used the whistle, and applied the brakes—I can't take it personally." There is, of course, no way in the world to stop in time, although they always try.

Amtrak engineers are assigned to specific runs which range from ninety minutes to ten hours in length. They are paid for no less than eight hours for every day they work, so it's Amtrak's responsibility to schedule their hours efficiently. Base pay for an Amtrak engineer ranges from $36,000 to $48,000 a year.

Assistant Engineer

Once upon a time, even after steam locomotives had been taken out of service, these people were called firemen. Today, the assistant engineer provides a second set of eyes and ears in the locomotive cab, calling out the signals as they're passed, noting any change in the speed limit, sending and receiving messages on the radio, and generally assisting with the many details, which allows the engineer to focus on the primary task of driving the train. Assistant engineers are fully qualified to operate the locomotive and regularly do so, spelling the engineer along the route. As a rule, the only difference between the two is years of experience. (Assistant engineers are used on all long-distance trains, but on short-distance runs, only one engineer is in the cab.) The annual salary range is $34,000 to $45,000.

Conductor

There is a conductor on every train—passenger or freight, long or short, and whether it's traveling 1,000 miles or 1,000 feet. This is the person who is actually in charge of the train, roughly equivalent to the captain of a ship at sea. That means the conductor has to be thoroughly familiar with both railroad operations and the train itself. (The conductor is the one who can tell you why the train is running late and when you'll arrive at your destination; he's *not* the one to ask for a wake up call.)

Anyone who's an Amtrak conductor has worked his or her way up the ladder and knows a lot about railroad operations. Every new conductor goes through an initial training program of 244 hours, which includes train operations, emergency procedures, passenger relations, and all procedures necessary for handling tickets. There are periodic refresher courses after that.

As do engineers, each conductor works a specific territory, usually a section of the route just a few hundred miles long. He knows it intimately—every switch and every crossover. Conductors are required to take an annual test on the operating rules, which is based on the specific territory they work. If a conductor moves his residence, a new test must be taken and passed before he can begin working a new territory. By the way, it takes a grade of 85 percent or better to pass those tests. Conductors are also required to pass a physical exam every two years.

The conductor is in regular contact with the engineer by radio throughout the trip and, in this manner, stays up to date on the train's progress, track conditions, other rail traffic, and any number of other details. If there's some kind of mechanical problem with the locomotive, the conductor (in consultation with the engineer) decides when or if the train can continue on its way. While the train is en route, it's the conductor who must deal with all the little idiosyncrasies that are found in every car—a bedroom door that comes off its track, a circuit breaker that trips for no obvious reason, and who knows what else? Finally, the most obvious duty: He or she is responsible for collecting tickets and supervising the loading and unloading of passengers and baggage. Even when nothing apparent is going on, most conductors "walk the train" once or twice every hour just to keep an eye on things.

The conductor also has the authority to deal with any other problem if it involves the safety or well-being of the passengers. If a passenger becomes ill, the conductor can arrange for an ambulance to meet the train at an upcoming stop. If a passenger becomes disorderly, the conductor has the authority to stop the train and put him off.

Because he's so thoroughly familiar with the train's route, the conductor is usually the one to make periodic announcements over the public address system about points of interest along the way. It's also the conductor's responsibility to inform passengers of the reasons for any delays that may occur. (Some conductors don't do this, however, which is a real sore point with many frequent passengers. In my opinion, there is simply no excuse for not informing passengers about delays that are longer than a few minutes.)

Finally, there is also paperwork to do. The conductor officially notes all arrival and departure times (which he confirms with the engineer by radio). Should the train be late, the conductor is responsible for filling out a Delay Report, which includes both the length of the delay and the reason it occurred.

Base pay for conductors runs from $30,000 to $40,000 a year.

Assistant Conductor

Originally, this person was called "trainman," "flagman," or "brakeman." Today he has the same duties and responsibilities as the conductor, but in a subordinate role. One vestige of the old job remains, however, since the assistant conductor is often assigned to look after the rear portion of the train.

Finally, and this brings us back to the issue of gender once again, if the assistant conductor happens to be female, many passengers assume that she has little or no responsibility other than taking tickets. Not so. She takes the same tests, meets the same requirements, and must have the same knowledge of railroad operations. Usually the only real difference between the conductor and assistant conductor position is their length of service.

Annual pay for an assistant conductor ranges from $26,000 to $35,000.

Yard Workers

As your train passes through major stations around the country, you'll see railroad employees in hard hats working around the trains—both freight and passenger. This is tough, dangerous work. They'll be hanging onto ladders on the sides of rolling cars and working between rail cars for the coupling and uncoupling process. They talk with the engineer by radio and help direct him when he's backing up to add more cars to the train. They'll do this by calling out car lengths (". . . two cars . . . one car . . ."), then switching to feet (". . . 20 feet . . . ten . . . five . . ."). Finally—and this is a curious railroad tradition—they will all call out, "That'll do!" just before the cars bump together.

Station Agent

While not part of the on-board crew, station agents deserve at least some mention since they're often the first Amtrak employees that passengers encounter. Depending on the size of the station, the station agent's job may or may not be full time. Basic responsibilities include keeping the station clean, selling tickets, and handling baggage. They'll also direct you to the spot on the platform to wait so you'll be near your car when the train stops. Frequently, however, an agent is called on for other things. For instance, if the lounge car on an incoming train is running low on ice, the on-board chief may have a radio message sent, asking the station agent to have several bags of crushed ice waiting when the train pulls in.

Train Manager

The on-board operation of every long-distance train run by Amtrak is the responsibility of someone called a train manager. For example, one train manager supervises all of the Amtrak trains operating as the *California Zephyr*. It's a big job because the *Zephyr* operates daily in each direction between Chicago and Oakland, California, and the train manager is ultimately responsible for *all* of those trains. He is primarily concerned with staying in contact with the crews—maintaining good lines of communication between the crew and the company on one hand and between passengers and front-line Amtrak employees on the other. Train managers can and do board their trains unannounced anywhere along the route to check on the crews and interview passengers. What do the crews need to do a better job? What do passengers want that they aren't getting? The train manager is the management person responsible for making sure that Amtrak's standards of quality are met on all trains.

Chief of On-Board Services

The chief of on-board services is immediately responsible for the quality of service on your train. Earlier in the company's history, quality control for on-board service was the responsibility of train inspectors who would board unannounced to conduct random inspections. This changed in the mid-1980s when chiefs were put aboard all long-distance trains. By the time the 1990s came around, and cost-cutting was clearly a factor, the chiefs were eliminated on some trains. It's easy to justify having an onboard supervisor for trains such as the *California Zephyr* or the *Silver Meteor,* which have service crews of more than twenty people. But having an extra person on a train where the entire service crew is just five or six people makes much less sense.

Whether you're riding in coach or first class, you should be able to spot the chief within the first thirty minutes of your trip. He or she sports a navy blue blazer with gray slacks or skirt and is quite clearly someone in authority. While the conductor is primarily concerned with the operation of the train, the chief of on-board services is responsible for just about everything else that goes on inside the train. She double-checks all supplies, greets passengers, distributes meal vouchers to first-class passengers, makes regular public address announcements, and keeps tabs on every aspect of service during the trip. On long-distance trains, it's usually the chief who organizes activities in the lounge car or offers prizes for trivia contests or scavenger hunts conducted over the P.A. system.

About the only way to become a chief is to work your way up through the ranks. And a good thing, too, because the chief must be prepared to pinch-hit for another crew member in the event of illness, accident or, as sometimes happens, if a regular crew member is a no-show.

After the car attendant, the chief is your best recourse for any problem you might encounter. In fact, a good chief will anticipate and deal with problems before they occur—like finding a more appropriate seat for the mother with two youngsters who was seated right behind a retired couple, or taking a teenager aside and quietly asking that he change that T-shirt with the obscenity on it. A chief's constant focus should be the safety and comfort of the passengers, and on keeping the rest of the crew on its toes. When you get a good chief, you'll know it right away.

Unfortunately, Amtrak still has a few "invisible chiefs," who are seldom seen or heard throughout the trip.

Average salary for an Amtrak chief is a bit over $38,000 a year.

Dining-Car Steward

There are fewer and fewer stewards these days and, personally, I think that's a pity. Being greeted by a polished *maître-d'* as you enter the dining car certainly adds to the overall experience. In most cases now, that function is performed by the lead service attendant (LSA), who also waits on tables.

The steward is responsible for the quality of the service in the dining car. He or she seats people, distributes the meal checks on which your order is noted, records the complimentary meals of sleeping-car passengers, and collects payment from the coach passengers. He's also responsible for all cash collected in the dining car. Over the duration of a two-day trip, that can amount to many thousands of dollars. His accounts had better balance at the end of the trip, too, because any difference must be made up from his personal funds.

Theoretically, the LSA has the same responsibilities as the steward. Because he must also work tables, however, there just isn't much time to spend on the niceties of dining. Lacking a steward, the emphasis is necessarily on getting people seated and served in a reasonable amount of time.

Whether a steward or an LSA, this person is responsible for making sure everyone gets fed—whatever that entails. If a power failure knocks out all the ovens in the diner's kitchen, for example, the steward will dash to a telephone at the next stop and arrange for hot meals to be delivered to the train at a station up ahead. (I've often tried to imagine the scene in a KFC restaurant when the phone rings and an Amtrak steward wants 250 chicken dinners delivered to the local station when the train pulls in ninety minutes later.)

Stewards are paid between $25,000 and $34,000 a year; LSA's a bit less—$24,000 to $33,000.

Service Attendants

This is Amtrak's gender-neutral term for waiter or waitress. Call it what you will, on a long-distance train it's a tough job. Each day they'll start serving breakfast in the dining car as early as 6:30 in the morning and the final seating for dinner often lasts until 9:00 P.M. In between, the service attendants may have served as many as 700 meals. It's quite true that the chef and his assistants in the kitchen had to prepare all those meals, but the service people had the added responsibility of maintaining a cheerful disposition throughout that 16-hour day. It's especially grueling on one of the western trains, which take two nights to reach the west coast. After a scheduled 50-hour trip from Chicago to Oakland, crews working the *California Zephyr* spend one night in a hotel, then depart the next morning for the trip back home—two more tough 16-hour days. A compensating factor, usually the most important one for Amtrak crews, is that they'll get six or seven days off before the next trip.

In addition to waiting on tables, each member of the service crew has other specific duties: setting the tables, filling the salt shakers, sorting and stocking the packaged condiments, and performing a host of other tasks—pretty much the same things you would do to prepare for a dinner party in your home.

In Amtrak's early days, most crew members were veterans of the railroad, many being third or even fourth generation. Some of these folks remain, but through normal attrition and as more women have been hired, their numbers have diminished.

Annual pay for a service attendant starts at $21,000 and goes up to $29,000.

Chef

Once you enter the kitchen in an Amtrak dining car, you're on the chef's turf, and a good chef keeps a sharp eye on everything that happens within his domain. He boards the diner several hours before the train departs to make sure the kitchen has been left in proper order by the previous crew. Occasionally things are not shipshape. In such cases, a long trip begins by cleaning up after someone else.

Amtrak's computer determines in advance the amount of food and supplies that should be put aboard the diner before each trip. The first order of business for the chef is to check supplies against that list to be sure he's received everything the computer ordered. That's important because every steak and piece of chicken must be accounted for at the end of the trip, and anything missing must be paid for out of the chef's own pocket. Some food is prepared or cooked ahead of time. Bacon, for example, is precooked, then heated prior to serving.

Amtrak chefs are permitted a fair amount of latitude within the framework of the current menu. The chicken dish can take many savory forms depending on how the chef chooses to prepare it, and the "chef's special" offers another outlet for culinary creativity. Although there isn't a lot of variety on the menu because of limited storage space, many chefs bring their own personal collection of spices on board to give several items on the bill of fare an additional bit of individuality.

A few years ago, in a determined effort to improve the quality of on-board meals, Amtrak began sending its chefs to "Chefs College," otherwise known as the Culinary Institute of America in Hyde Park, New York. Everyone agrees it worked and, in a domino effect, morale among the entire dining-car crew has gone up, too. It's pretty simple: Better food means happier passengers who leave more generous tips.

Once under way, and as mealtime approaches, activity in the diner's kitchen increases to a pace that's somehow frenzied and orderly at the same time. The chef is still clearly the one in charge and handles most of the actual cooking. Orders come in, are filled, and sent out (or *up* via dumbwaiter, in the case of Superliners) with amazing dispatch. And they'd better be! On some of the more popular trains, as many as 250 meals have to be prepared and served over a four-hour period. A Superliner dining car can seat 72 passengers at a time, and even under optimum conditions that translates into four one-hour seatings. Meals have to be prepared and served efficiently or the dinner hour will stretch into bedtime—annoying to passengers, exhausting for the dining-car crew.

One veteran Amtrak supervisor, who worked his way up through the ranks, says that a chef has the toughest job on a passenger train—for which he's paid anywhere from $23,000 to $32,000 a year.

Food Specialist

Food specialists are the people who work in the kitchen under the supervision of the chef. Responsibilities are divided, but include all of the tasks we all perform at home in our own kitchens, from putting the groceries away to cleaning up the pots and pans after the last meal is served. The days are long and the work is hard. As with many other on-board employees, what makes it all worthwhile is good pay for the hours you work and lots of time off for leisure or, in many cases, another job for additional income. Newly hired food specialists go through an initial training program of 105 hours, but must take a number of trips and perform satisfactorily under the watchful and usually very critical eye of a veteran chef. Pay ranges from $23,000 to $31,000 a year.

Car Attendant

Car attendants are the folks who look after the comfort of passengers on all of Amtrak's long-distance trains. There are no car attendants on short-haul trains or on trains that may cover a lot of distance but don't operate overnight.

Note that the correct term is *car attendant* and not *porter*. It's not a major issue with most, but, in the minds of some, porter is a term that carries a reminder of another time. Its origins date back to the days when virtually all sleeping cars were manufactured, owned, and operated by the Pullman Company. Only black males were hired to staff those cars. The jobs were highly prized, especially during the Great Depression, and those who got them took justifiable pride in the quality of their work. Not surprisingly, however, a good deal of latent racism came with the territory. It became the unfortunate custom for many passengers to call every porter "George," after the company's founder, George M. Pullman. Hearing that every day from passengers who neither knew nor cared what their given names were was certainly a humiliating and dehumanizing experience for many Pullman porters and, it seems to me, accounts at least in part for the passing of the term. Incidentally, that bit of history is one reason Amtrak has made a point of providing all employees with name badges.

New hires go through a minimum training program of 105 hours and, if they're going to be working on eastern trains or on the *Auto Train* where they'll run into a greater variety of equipment, an additional 15 hours is required. There are periodic refresher programs and, as with all new hires, car attendants have to take a number of "student trips" and perform up to standards.

I had always assumed that brand-new attendants start out working in coaches and gradually work their way up to sleeping cars, but that's not necessarily true. Amtrak people bid for their assignments, and whether or not they get their request is determined partly by seniority and partly by how popular the particular trip is. Whether or not an attendant works in coaches or sleepers seems pretty much a matter of choice and, in fact, many attendants prefer the coaches. Sleeping-car attendants make more money because of tips, but even under normal circumstances they work harder and their passengers can be much more demanding.

Amtrak assigns one car attendant to every sleeping car whether it's one of the older single-level sleepers or a bi-level Superliner. Not so with coaches. You'll find one car attendant for every three coaches on single-level eastern trains while one attendant looks after two coaches out west in the Superliners. (By the way, in Amtrak slang these folks are known as "tacos," an acronym for "Train Attendant, COach.")

Whether she's working in coach or sleeper, many of the attendant's duties are the same: boarding passengers, helping to stow their baggage, maintaining a seating chart, keeping the car orderly and the bathrooms clean, making sure each passenger gets off at the right stop, and generally doing whatever is necessary to make sure the trip goes pleasantly for everyone. Coach attendants distribute pillows throughout the car and retrieve them after each passenger leaves the train.

Sleeping-car attendants have fewer people to look after, but much more to do. I once had a wonderful conversation with a long-time car attendant who provided the best description of the job I've ever heard. "This here sleeper," he said, "is just like a small hotel . . . and I'm the only employee!" That's just about right, too. The attendant is doorman, receptionist, bellhop, maid, room-service waiter, and concierge all rolled into one. Spend forty-eight hours watching a good one in action and you'll have a real appreciation of what a demanding job it is.

A sleeping car attendant reports for duty about three hours prior to the train's departure. He makes sure every room is in order and has towels, face cloths, soap, the current issue of *Express* (Amtrak's on-board magazine), and anything else that's supposed to be in the rooms. He cleans mirrors, removes any dirty linen, stocks and cleans the rest rooms, and looks for anything that may not be in working order. (If a toilet doesn't function properly, *now* is the time to find out and get it fixed!) He also checks to be sure all the beds have already been made up. Most of the time they have, but not always. In those cases, he'll have to do it himself. Even if he finds everything in order, there's a great deal of bed-making in the life of a car attendant. When a passenger is ready to retire for the evening, his berth has to be lowered into position and arranged for sleeping and, on two-night trips, it must be made up again the next morning. Often there is as much as a 50 percent turnover on a 48-hour trip, meaning half of the bedrooms could be occupied by different individuals on successive nights. The first passenger may ride overnight from Chicago to Denver with the second traveler boarding in Salt Lake City for the trip from there to Oakland. The attendant must pull off the old sheets and remake the bed before the new arrival boards, ready for a good night's sleep. There's even more bed-making to do on turnaround trips. The *California Zephyr,* for instance, originates in Chicago and is turned around in Oakland. The car attendant makes up all the beds in the car for the train's return trip to Chicago the next day. In a Superliner sleeper, that could be a total of 44 beds.

You'll first meet your attendant on the platform where he will check your name off against his passenger manifest and direct you to your room. Once the train is underway, he should also take the time to make sure you understand where everything is in your room and how it all works.

Some sleeping-car passengers enjoy the idea of room service and ask the attendant for beverages or meals served in their rooms. Strange as it may seem since the dining-car experience is one of the unique things about train travel, it's not unusual for a sleeping-car passenger to have *all* meals brought to the room for the entire trip. Of course, that's the norm for handicapped passengers and for those who have difficulty moving about the train.

The sleeping-car attendant will also give you a wake-up call if you would like one or if you're going to be leaving the train at an early-morning station stop. He'll offer to bring juice or hot coffee to your room at whatever time you might wish in the morning. Also, the same attendant will usually slide a morning paper, put aboard at a major city the train passed through in the wee hours, under the bedroom door. In theory, attendants are still supposed to shine passengers' shoes during the night, but in actual practice it doesn't happen. The shoe shine is one of the last vestiges of the days of the Pullman porter and is highly symbolic for many Amtrak car attendants. There is almost universal agreement that it's no longer appropriate for them to perform that service.

The car attendant is the person you should first contact with any problem or need. Whatever it may be, you can be sure that the attendant has heard it before and will take it in stride. (I always make it a point to ask the attendant in my car to tell me about some of the unusual experiences he or she has had. They all have dozens of stories, some so bizarre they couldn't possibly be invented.) Coach attendants usually occupy one of the rear seats in their car. Sleeping-car attendants are usually assigned one of the rooms in the car. Some will make a point of telling you which room they're in, should you need something during the night. If your attendant doesn't volunteer that information, ask. But, please, be considerate. Don't roust the poor soul in the middle of the night for a trivial request. By the same token, don't hesitate to call if you have a legitimate need—illness, for example.

Car attendants work a base of 180 hours a month. It figures out to just over 40 hours per week, but that's deceiving. The typical work day for a car attendant is 16–18 hours long. It would be worse than that, but they help each other out—one attendant will handle the boarding of passengers for several cars in the middle of the night so a colleague can get a bit more sleep. The up side is the time off. Every attendant I've talked to lists this as a major benefit to the job. Although it varies according to the schedule of the employee, car attendants average four days off for every three they work. Base pay—$21,000 to $28,000 a year.

Lounge-Car Attendant

The specifics of this job vary somewhat according to the kind of equipment involved. On eastern trains, especially the short-haul trains without a dining car, it's a particularly busy job. The attendant operates behind a counter in a galley located in the middle of the lounge car and provides hot and cold sandwiches and a variety of beverages for passengers. On western trains, the attendant is located in a similar facility on the lower level of the Superliner lounge car.

The lounge-car attendant's schedule is a killer: On the long-distance trains, he or she will be up at 5:00 A.M. making coffee and preparing the little galley to open at 6:00. The attendant takes three 45-minute meal breaks during the day and finally closes down around midnight. For most of that 18-hour day, the lounge car attendant is on her feet serving a constant stream of passengers—heating packaged meals in the galley's microwave oven, serving potato chips and other snacks, pouring cold drinks, selling decks of cards or souvenir blankets, and making change—all the while maintaining a cheerful disposition.

(As an interim measure in its smoking policy, Amtrak did away with smoking anywhere on the train *but* in the lounge car. Most passengers applauded, but it made life miserable for the lounge-car attendants who found themselves working that grueling schedule in a constant haze of tobacco smoke. When new policies eliminated smoking entirely from some trains, no one was happier than the lounge-car attendant.)

Base pay for these people ranges from $22,000 to $29,000 a year.

CHAPTER 8

When Things Go Wrong

Every year, Amtrak carries more than 20 million passengers over 25,000 miles of track on trips ranging from short commuter runs to cross-country odysseys. To the company's credit, most train trips are an enjoyable experience from start to finish. Our national rail passenger system, however, is an immensely complex operation and, not surprisingly, things can and do go wrong. Knowing what *could* happen can help head off problems in the first place or help you deal with situations if they do occur. *Not* knowing and being unprepared, mentally or otherwise, can turn a minor inconvenience into a major problem.

Whom Do You Turn to for Help?

When a problem occurs, the best advice is to ask for help calmly, politely, and early. Since areas of responsibility are divided, knowing which on-board crew member to talk to is also helpful.

- The car attendant has primary responsibility for your comfort and safety. See him or her about problems within your car.

- The chief of on-board services is responsible for the service you get anywhere on the train. (If there's no chief on your train, start with the car attendant. If he or she can't help, take your problem to the conductor.)
- The conductor is responsible for problems of an operational nature. Like the captain of a ship at sea, the conductor is the ultimate authority aboard a train.

There is a welcome trend at Amtrak to give more authority to on-board employees. Conductors can now waive penalties for passengers who purchase their tickets after they board the train, and both conductors and on-board chiefs can upgrade passengers into first-class accommodations if, in their judgment, the circumstances warrant it. Conductors and chiefs can also issue Amtrak travel vouchers on the spot in order to handle problems. The amounts given are rather small, but just about everyone concerned applauds the management principle involved.

That being said, let's look at some typical problems that can crop up during your trip.

What if You Get Sick?

If you experience some kind of a health problem while on board, inform your car attendant right away. An unexpected illness can happen to anyone so don't be embarrassed. And don't wait until you're in a real emergency situation before asking for assistance. For one thing, the sooner you notify the crew, the more time they'll have to consider the options and make the appropriate arrangements.

As with any problem, go to the car attendant first. Give him your best assessment of what's happening and, if it's something you've experienced before, what you think you'll need. He'll probably alert the chief of on-board services or, if there is no chief on your train, the conductor.

Sometimes they'll use the train's public address system to ask if there is a physician on board who can take a look at you. The conductor may also decide to radio ahead and arrange for paramedics to meet the train at the next station stop. They'll evaluate your condition and take the appropriate action. Sometimes that means providing medication; sometimes it means leaving the train and taking a trip to the local hospital. Whatever the circumstance, you can take some comfort in the knowledge that a sick passenger is not an unusual occurrence on Amtrak trains. You'll find crew members concerned, sympathetic, and capable.

Missed Connections: The Number One Problem

Trains running behind schedule are the single biggest headache Amtrak has to deal with—at least in terms of their day-to-day operations. When trains are late, passengers miss connections and, when those are "guaranteed connections," it's Amtrak's responsibility to make things right. Unfortunately, it's almost a certain lose-lose situation for Amtrak. Missed connections, or "misconnects" as they're called, cost the railroad a lot of money and, no matter what kind of a solution is worked out, the affected passengers will not be happy.

Regular riders, and people who understand the unique complexities of running a long-distance railroad operation, are usually more tolerant of delays than the infrequent or first-time traveler. Veteran rail travelers also take the likelihood of delays into consideration when they make their travel plans, allowing plenty of time between connecting trains. When working out a rail itinerary, I figure the train could be as much as two hours late for each night I'm aboard and schedule my connections accordingly. For example, if I'm traveling between New York and Chicago (one night on board), I make sure the second train departs at least two hours after my scheduled arrival. If I'm traveling from Los Angeles to Chicago (two nights on board), I'll allow no less than four hours in Chicago before connecting with a train going on to the east coast. I usually follow this rule of thumb even if it means spending the night in a hotel and continuing my trip the following day. Far better to play it safe than to find yourself finishing your journey by bus.

You'll probably be aware that your in-bound train is running late, so get ahold of the chief of on-board services even before you arrive to get his advice on your options. Once you pull into the station—it will most likely be in New York, Washington, D.C., or Chicago since most scheduled connections take place in one of those three locations—go *immediately* to Amtrak's Passenger Service Desk in the station. Other passengers from your train will be in the same situation, so the object is to be one of the first instead of one of the last problems solved. The Amtrak employee at the desk will already be aware that a connection was missed and will probably have some tentative answers for you by the time you show up. If you don't get immediate help or if you're not satisfied with the alternative arrangements offered, ask to see the supervisor for station services.

The important thing is to let them know what *you* want. Be reasonable, however. Amtrak may be willing to meet your request, but unable to because of the time of year, the weather, the time of day, the number of people involved, the availability of nearby hotel accommodations, and many other factors. Through it all, try to keep your cool. The person you're dealing with isn't the cause of the problem and is no doubt doing her best to help you.

Problems with Accommodations

Occasionally, passengers with first-class tickets find themselves in the wrong type of room or, more typically, *think* they are in the wrong room. Some first-time travelers—especially if traveling as a couple—take one look at an economy bedroom on a Superliner and are convinced they can't possibly spend two days in a room that small. These problems almost always occur because whoever booked the trip—either the passenger himself or a travel agent—wasn't familiar with Amtrak accommodations. Sometimes, of course, real mix-ups do indeed occur. Whatever the problem, if you want to change your sleeping car accommodations, start with the car attendant and, if he or she can't help, ask to speak with the chief of on-board services or the conductor. Bedroom space is very tight, especially in the summer months, but sometimes a last-minute cancellation or no-show will enable the chief to take care of your problem.

Plan for a Late Arrival

If your train runs late, that can cause a real inconvenience for those who plan to meet you at your destination. When you make pick-up arrangements, by all means instruct them to call Amtrak at 1-800-USA-RAIL to get the latest arrival time before they leave for the station. It's a basic precaution that could keep them from having to sit in a station parking lot—perhaps in the middle of the night—waiting for a train that's two or more hours late.

Poor Service

In any organization of 25,000 employees, there will be some bad apples. That certainly doesn't excuse poor service, but it should serve to remind us all that maintaining a high level of competent service is an ongoing effort. For instance, if you're traveling in a sleeper and ask for a meal to be served in your room, remember that your car attendant can be looking after as many as 44 people. He has to take your order to the dining car, wait until your meal is prepared, then bring it to you. In the meantime, other passengers are asking to have their beds made up, and there may be a station stop coming up. Cut him some slack if you can.

Car attendants and serving personnel in the dining cars have a very tough job. Sometimes even the best of them will get cranky and let slip a brusque remark. Be understanding, try to keep things in perspective, and don't let one person who is having a bad day spoil your trip. In the unlikely event that you run into a real problem employee, seek out the chief of on-board services or the conductor. If you're not satisfied with the action taken, note the employee's name and, after you get home, write to Amtrak about the problem. How can they deal with problem employees if you don't? (See details of how and where to write at the end of this chapter.)

Rattles and Squeaks

As mentioned in an earlier chapter, the rail car in which you're riding may have been around a long time. The constant motion of the train can cause strange noises to develop and, if you're like me, they can drive you crazy when you're trying to sleep. Usually it's something easy to find and simple to fix—slamming a washcloth in a loose cabinet door, for instance—so at least make the effort. The next step is to call your car attendant, who will probably be able to locate the problem and take care of it quickly. On rare occasions, mysterious squeaks and rattles just can't be silenced. When that happens, it may be possible to change rooms. Otherwise you'll just have to tough it out. Heck, if a rattle will bother you that much, you won't be sleeping much anyway.

Problem Passengers

Occasionally the stranger sitting next to you turns out to be something of a problem—a constant talker, for instance. When it happens on a plane, most of us just suffer through it for three or four hours. On a long-distance train, however, a chatterbox can become a 48-hour ordeal. At the very least, you can get up and sit for a while in the lounge car.

But if your seatmate or someone nearby turns out to be significantly more than just an annoyance—makes sexual advances, becomes drunk or quarrelsome, for instance—you can and should ask for help from your car attendant or the on-board chief. Amtrak personnel are more than willing to take firm action against the occasional serious troublemaker . . . to the point of putting them off the train, baggage and all.

The conductor is the ultimate authority in these matters. One told me with a smile, "Occasionally there'll be a group in the lounge car that gets rowdy from drinking too much. That keeps families from enjoying the lounge car, so I tell 'em pretty firmly to settle down. If they don't, I'll just put the ringleader off the train. When that happens, his pals are like little lambs the rest of the way."

In extreme cases, the local highway patrol is contacted by radio and a police car meets the train where the tracks cross a major highway. I was once aboard the *Desert Wind* when it stopped at a grade crossing somewhere near the Nevada-Utah state line. An obnoxious character who had staggered aboard the train in Las Vegas and had been drinking steadily ever since was suddenly confronted at his seat by two state troopers and hustled off the train—to the enthusiastic applause of several dozen fellow passengers. When last seen, he was twisted around and looking back at us through the rear window of the police car, on his way to at least one night in the jail at Caliente, Nevada. Incidentally, in order to avoid a loud argument or worse, a disorderly passenger who refuses to cooperate with train crew members is given no warning before being put off the train.

Equipment Failures

Mechanical breakdowns occur and can be very disruptive, depending on how and when they happen. Unfortunately, the problem has not been getting better. Severe budget restraints have forced Amtrak to keep a limited amount of equipment in more or less constant use and to stretch out the time between equipment maintenance and overhauls.

The most significant problem, as you might expect, occurs when a locomotive breaks down. Even a partial loss of power at the head end can disrupt an entire schedule. For instance, if you're on the *California Zephyr* heading west out of Denver and one of the three engines fails, it could be enough to delay the entire train until a replacement unit arrives. Two units might not be enough to haul that entire train over the Rockies as well as provide electricity to the rest of the train.

The most common problem is the breakdown of toilets in a Superliner or other new equipment. Sometimes it's mechanical, sometimes they're clogged, and in the winter they occasionally freeze. Whatever the reason, it's unpleasant, annoying, and inconvenient for all concerned, passengers and crew alike. (The original toilets in the older cars simply emptied onto the tracks and, because they were so simple, almost never failed. This is yet another reason why the federal mandate to retrofit all the older Amtrak cars with self-contained toilets is an expensive and unnecessary idea.)

Electrical problems in the dining car can be bad news for the entire train. When the ovens or the grills go down, the kitchen crew has to improvise. Sometimes the only answer is a frantic phone call to a fast-food restaurant near the station at the next scheduled stop. One way or another, however, they make sure folks get fed.

Follow Up on Your Complaint

There may be a certain amount of nostalgia attached to the image of the grizzled old railroad veteran brought up on steam and with railroading in his blood. Because the odds were against Amtrak in its early days, hard-nosed railroad people were necessary to make it all work and keep things running. The trouble is, many of those old-timers thought of passengers as a necessary evil . . . just a particularly bothersome type of freight. And that attitude was felt by passengers.

With the passing years, the old-time railroad men are leaving Amtrak and a new crop of younger executives is taking their place. As a result, there is a much broader understanding that, first and foremost, Amtrak is in the service business. Should you follow up on complaints? You bet! How else can someone in a position of authority improve or correct things? Amtrak takes all complaints seriously. They're categorized, the source of the problem is tracked down, and—in my experience anyway—a reasonable effort is made to take corrective action.

Here's how to pursue your complaint most effectively: Avoid the temptation to gripe about relatively trivial problems. Put your complaint in writing. Be specific, but as brief as possible. Stick to the facts, and try to express the issue unemotionally. Send your letter to Amtrak Customer Relations, 60 Massachusetts Ave. NE, Washington, D.C. 20002.

Their phone number is 202-906-2121, but you should telephone only if you need *immediate* assistance and are not able to work through normal channels for some reason.

Try to remember that Amtrak is a very large organization performing a complex service for millions of people. Things are bound to go wrong from time to time. Give them a reasonable amount of time to investigate and make things right. Above all, don't just take your grievance home and bad-mouth the entire Amtrak system to all your friends. Outraged letters to the editor won't solve anything either, and complaining to your representatives in Washington could have a negative effect on what is already inadequate funding by the federal government. In other words, by all means go ahead and complain, but try to keep your complaint constructive.

CHAPTER 9

Passenger Train Equipment

As you will notice, both Amtrak across the United States and VIA Rail in Canada use quite a variety of equipment. We'll get into a few details in this chapter, but will focus on some basic standards that are common to all or most rail cars.

Most passenger cars are about 80 feet long, give or take a foot or two, and no more than 10½ feet wide. The traditional single-level rail car is about 13½ feet high, but newer cars are taller. The bi-level Superliners, which Amtrak began adding to its fleet in the 1970s, measure 16'2" from the rails to the top of the car itself. The new Viewliners, which are single-level cars, are 14 feet high. Dome cars, still in use on a few of Amtrak's eastern routes and on Canada's premier trains, have a glass viewing dome mounted on top of the standard rail car, which increases their height to nearly 16 feet. Height is an important consideration when determining which type of rail car will be assigned to certain trains. For example, on a number of eastern routes, Superliners can't be used because they're just too tall for some of the bridges and tunnels along the way.

Each car has a total of eight wheels, four at each end of the car. Those four wheels are part of a unit called a *truck,* and there's one truck at each end of the car. The number of wheels on the locomotives vary, depending on what it's used for. Some have eight wheels, others twelve, and some of the really heavy-duty freight locomotives can have as many as sixteen wheels.

Locomotives

All told, Amtrak has over 400 passenger locomotives in its fleet. Most Amtrak trains are pulled by one of four basic types, but others are used for specialized service.

- The most common Amtrak locomotive is referred to as an F40 or, more completely, as an F40PH. The "P" stands for "passenger" and the "H" indicates that it's equipped to provide head end power (electrical power) to the rest of the train. More of these diesel-electric locomotives, which are made by the Electro-Motive Division of General Motors, are in service than any other type. In fact, they're the backbone of the Amtrak fleet—tough, reliable workhorses, each capable of producing 3,000 horsepower.
- A new generation of diesel/electric locomotive has appeared fairly recently and deserves special mention. Originally, they were called AMD-103s. Then, because it was the first locomotive in probably 40 years to be specifically designed for passenger service, Amtrak began referring to them as the Genesis Series. That was a bit too exotic for railroad folks so today this locomotive is known simply as the P40. Over the past few years, Amtrak has taken delivery on a number of these new machines and, depending on whom you ask, they're either the best-looking or the worst-looking locomotive ever to come along. One thing is for sure: You certainly can't miss P40s. They look very big and very powerful—as indeed they are. Each P40 produces 4,000 horsepower, meaning that two of these new units can haul a train that

Brawny F40PH locomotives, used by both Amtrak and VIA Rail, are the backbones of their long-distance fleets. Chances are a pair of them will be pulling your train. These two, at the head of VIA's Train Number One, the *Canadian*, were photographed in the heart of the Canadian Rockies during a servicing stop at Jasper, Alberta, on a cross-country trek from Toronto to Vancouver. (Photo by the author.)

previously required three engines. To provide an example in another context, one P40 can produce enough electrical power for 700 homes. The P40 offers better acceleration and greater reliability. It's also modular in design, so a faulty component can be pulled out and replaced immediately, keeping the locomotive in operation.

- Along the Northeast Corridor and between Philadelphia and Harrisburg in Pennsylvania, Amtrak trains are pulled by pure electric locomotives called AEM-7s. They draw their electric power directly from an overhead wire (a catenary) the way old-fashioned trolley cars did. Built from a European design, they can pull trains at much

Amtrak's newest locomotive, the state-of-the-art P40, has more horsepower than the venerable F40 and can operate at speeds up to 105 miles per hour. It also has an air-conditioned cab, an unaccustomed luxury for head-end crews. (Photo courtesy of Amtrak.)

higher speeds than the F40s and, at 7,000 horsepower, are a lot more powerful.

You may encounter one or two other types of locomotives.

- A number of gas turbine locomotives are used on the Hudson River route in New York State. These trains are always kept intact in what's called a *trainset,* and have a power unit at each end, which means they're capable of operating in either direction.
- Twenty diesel/electric locomotives, built by General Electric and called P32s, were put into service in 1992. They look a lot like the locomotives you see hauling freight trains and are primarily used on trains running out of Los Angeles.

Currently the fastest and most powerful locomotive in Amtrak's fleet, the all-electric AEM-7 operates along the Northeast Corridor at speeds up to 125 miles per hour. (Photo courtesy of Amtrak.)

Information on how locomotives operate can be found in Chapter 10: How It All Works. For a description of the engineers job, see Chapter 7: Who's in Charge Here?

Mail Cars

Hauling the mail is big business for Amtrak. Most of what the company carries for the Postal Service is 2nd class mail—newspapers, magazines, and other dated material. Amtrak does carry first-class mail to some areas with spotty air service. Amtrak also offers an express service, carrying packages between cities throughout its system. All told, almost $60 million a year is generated for Amtrak from these services. Everything—express packages and mail—is carried in what Amtrak people refer to as MHCs or Materials

Handling Cars. In lay terms, they're simply boxcars built to run at high speed. Amtrak's fleet includes almost 200 of these cars, and you'll usually see at least one and perhaps even two or three in every Amtrak consist, up front right behind the locomotives.

Baggage Cars

There's always at least one baggage car on every long-distance train, located right in front of the first coach. This is where Amtrak carries baggage checked by passengers as well as other parcels shipped from one point to another along the route. And, occasionally, these cars will carry mail, too.

Amfleet Equipment

You'll be able to spot these cars right away because the exterior shape is more rounded than the classic passenger rail car. You may also notice that the windows are rather small compared to either newer or older Amtrak equipment. When these cars were designed and built, air travel had become *the* way to go and, apparently, the idea behind the small windows was to evoke the feeling that you were in an airliner. There may be something to that, since Amtrak uses these cars along the Northeast Corridor where trains travel at speeds up to 125 mph. Amfleet cars are primarily used on shorter routes around the country: Los Angeles–San Diego, Boston–New York–Washington, Springfield–Hartford–New York City.

Standard Coach

These cars have two comfortable seats on each side of a center aisle. The seats recline and an airline-type tray will fold down from the seat-back in front of you. There's an overhead reading light and a luggage rack above all seats. Each car has two lavatories, one of which is designed to accommodate a wheelchair. Coaches used on longer routes have more leg room and each seat has a fold-out leg rest.

Club Coach

This is where Amtrak provides first-class service on all-coach trains. It's sometimes referred to as a "parlor car," although that's really a term from another era of railroading. Club coach seats are wider than those in the standard coach and, therefore, are placed in a 1-2 configuration—that is, two seats on one side of the center aisle and only one on the other side. These seats are really plush and recline wonderfully. There's a footrest, a service tray that folds down from the seat-back in front of you, and an overhead reading light. The club coach section occupies about a third of the rail car. In the middle of the car is a cafe service area from which complimentary meals and drinks are provided to club coach passengers. A lounge area serving all passengers is at the opposite end of the car. As you would expect, there is a surcharge for these accommodations. Frankly, if you make a strictly objective decision, the wider seat and free meal isn't worth the extra cost. If you can afford it, however, it's fun to take a what-the-hell attitude and treat yourself.

Lounge Car

These cars are found on medium- and long-distance trains. A very efficient service area is located in the middle of the car from which you can buy hot or cold sandwiches, a variety of snacks, and beverages, including soft drinks, beer, and some mixed drinks. An arrangement of tables and chairs is available where you can sit and relax, or you can take your food back to your seat.

Dinette Car

These cars—also found on medium- and long-distance trains in the east—are basically a step up from the lounge car. A compact food-service area turns out complete hot meals in addition to the fare provided in lounge cars. The seating area is set up in the more traditional dining car configuration—booths for four people on each side of the center aisle—and usually someone is there to provide table service. Don't mistake this for full dining-car service, however. The meals are prepackaged and heated in a microwave oven. Basically, it's big airline food.

Metroliners

This is Amtrak's designation for the high-speed trains that operate along the Northeast Corridor between Washington, D.C., and New York. The cars are really standard Amfleet coaches, but have fewer seats. That translates to more leg room and, because of the extra space between seats, they also recline a bit more. Metroliner locomotives are the all-electric AEM-7s, the only type able to run at 125 mph. Metroliner consists are limited to either five or six cars, which is one way to identify those high-speed trains.

Heritage Equipment

If you're on one of the overnight trains operating east of the Mississippi River, chances are that all or some of the cars will be part of what Amtrak euphemistically calls its Heritage fleet. They once belonged to one of the many former passenger railroads, but were acquired and refurbished by Amtrak when it began operation. In other words, most of these cars were built in the 1950s and 1960s and, in contrast to the rounded shape of the Amfleet and Metroliner cars, have the classic, boxier look of the traditional rail passenger car. Amtrak has begun phasing them out in favor of Superliners and a new generation of Viewliners. Trains with Heritage cars as part of the consist have a maximum speed limit of 110 mph.

Coach

Coaches have rows of two seats on each side of a center aisle running the length of the car. The seats are wide, comfortable, and will recline as much 35 degrees. Each is equipped with a fold-out leg rest, so you can stretch out pretty well at night. There is a reading light over each seat and a call button for the car attendant. If you're traveling overnight, the attendant will provide you with a pillow, but—I'll say it again!—bring a blanket. Each car includes an overhead luggage rack, which runs the length of the car on both sides, and two lavatories.

Slumbercoach

There aren't many of these cars left, but Amtrak will continue to run them on several of the overnight eastern trains. Slumbercoaches are by far the least expensive of all rail accommodations that provide passengers with a bed. You'll find them a reasonable compromise if you don't want to sit up all night in a coach seat, but are unwilling to pay the significantly higher fares for a roomette or bedroom. There are twenty-four single and eight double rooms in each slumbercoach car. In addition to the one or two berths, each room has a toilet and a sink. These accommodations are quite a bit smaller than a roomette, however, and the berths are just 24 inches wide and marginal in comfort. One more thing you need to know is that your meals are *not* included in the fare when you ride in a slumbercoach. On the other hand, meals are complimentary when you travel in any other type of Amtrak sleeping car and, assuming you plan to eat in the diner, that narrows the price differential somewhat.

Sleeping Cars

Don't be put off because the sleeping cars in Amtrak's Heritage fleet are old. They come from the golden age of rail travel and were built for comfort, which you will appreciate at bedtime when you settle down on that nice, thick mattress. Each car has ten roomettes and six bedrooms, capable of accommodating a total of twenty-six people. Railroaders refer to these cars as "10-6 sleepers," a reference to the two kinds of accommodations. Most of these sleepers have a storage area at one end of each car where the attendant can keep oversized baggage for you. In others, one roomette has been converted to be handicapped accessible and Amtrak will give booking priority to disabled passengers.

The **roomette** is compact but efficiently designed and will accommodate one person very neatly. The facilities include a fold-down berth, washbasin and toilet, call button for the car attendant, a small fan, and temperature controls. There's a rack for one suitcase and a shoulder bag, and a skinny little closet where you can hang a jacket or overcoat. The berth folds down from the wall, but be advised that when it's locked into position for sleeping, it covers the toilet. Have the car attendant show you how to unlatch and raise it in case you need the facilities during the night.

The **bedroom** will accommodate two adults quite comfortably. The seat converts to a bed and there's a fold-down upper berth. These rooms include a separate phone-booth-sized lavatory with toilet, washbasin, and mirror. A luggage rack will handle one or two suitcases. As with the roomette, bedrooms include a call button for the attendant, a small fan, temperature control, and a tiny closet. The six bedrooms in a Heritage fleet sleeping car come in one of two configurations. Bedrooms A, C, and E are more square in shape. One of the two seats is fixed in place while the other can be moved around in the room. Bedrooms B, D,

Sleeping car in Amtrak's Heritage fleet.

and F feature one bench-type seat running the width of the room. To accommodate families, a door between two bedrooms may be opened to form one large compartment.

An Insider's Tip

Flushing toilets in these older cars is a simple process: Just step on a pedal that starts a flow of water and opens a little trapdoor in the bottom of the toilet. However, more often than not, the seal between the trapdoor and the toilet isn't tight. When water in the toilet leaks out, track noise leaks in. Passengers in Heritage roomettes are particularly affected by this noise because the toilet is not enclosed in a little washroom. Although perhaps not for the faint of heart, there is a solution that I was taught by a veteran Amtrak car attendant: Wind toilet paper around the fingers of one hand eight or ten times. Keep your fingers spread so that the resulting ring of paper is about the same size as the hole in the bottom of the toilet. Then drop this improvised seal into the toilet and, working the pedal carefully, position it where the little trapdoor closes against the hole in the bottom of the toilet. The whole process will have produced a slight flow of water which, with your new seal in place, will now stay in the toilet. *Voila!* No more—well, okay, much less—track noise. Of course, you won't have much more time to put this little trick into practice; these cars are gradually being retrofitted with new toilets or are being phased out in favor of Viewliners, or, in some cases, Superliners.

Two more items: Both the roomettes and the bedrooms have a shoe locker. In the old days, passengers could place their shoes in these lockers before going to bed, and the Pullman porter would polish and shine them during the night. No more. I mention this because some passengers use the shoe locker as a place to store their valuables—a bad idea, since anyone can access the locker from the corridor outside. Finally, if you want to play cards or write, the car attendant will bring a portable table to your room.

Lounge Car

These cars are open throughout the day and into the night to serve hot and cold sandwiches, snacks, and a variety of beverages (including beer, wine, and a few mixed drinks). There are two or three layouts, but they all feature a service area either in the middle or at one end of the car. Most include an arrangement of tables and chairs, too. There will often be a dining car on the same train.

Dining Car

Heritage diners, which can serve as many as 56 people at a time, are available on most overnight eastern trains. While some of the food is necessarily precooked, most is prepared on board and the quality is usually quite good. Dining is family style in all Amtrak diners, which means you'll have fellow passengers at your table unless you happen to be traveling as a party of four. This is where you'll meet some very nice and interesting people—and some real characters, too.

Buffet Car

Amtrak's long-range plans call for the phasing out of these cars, which are still being used on *Auto Train*. Frankly, that's a good thing. A buffet car is actually two cars permanently attached. In one car the food is prepared then served from steam tables on a buffet line. Waiters carry your tray to a table in the adjoining car. This configuration is necessary because *Auto Train* is Amtrak's biggest—often with more than 20 cars—and large numbers of passengers must be served as efficiently as possible. Needless to say, however, the dining experience leaves a lot to be desired. The obvious solution is to have two dining cars on each train, allowing for a more leisurely and more pleasant dining experience for all passengers. This is indeed the plan, but since Amtrak is chronically short of equipment, not to mention the necessary capital, it will probably be a while before we've seen the last of the buffet cars.

Viewliners

Viewliners are some of the newest single-level cars in Amtrak's fleet. In fact, they are really the first passenger cars that Amtrak has been able to create from square one. After three prototypes were tested in service, fifty Viewliners were ordered and are being phased into the fleet as they're delivered. Amtrak also has an option on another fifty of these cars. The Viewliners, which have been ordered as both diners and sleeping cars, were designed for long-distance overnight service in the eastern part of the country. The single-level Viewliners are not as tall as the Superliners, but are nevertheless significantly larger than the traditional Heritage-type cars.

Sleeping Cars

The most obvious innovation in the Viewliner sleeper is the double row of windows, which provide additional viewing for passengers in the upper berths. The berths are larger than those in Superliners, too, and that combination of features should pretty well eliminate the claustrophobic feeling some passengers get when tucked away in an upper berth. Each sleeping car can accommodate a maximum of thirty people in fifteen different rooms.

Every Viewliner sleeping car includes three **deluxe bedrooms.** Each is designed for two people, and includes a washbasin, a toilet, and a shower. There's a temperature control in each room and, of course, a call button if and when you need the car attendant. There is also a small clothes closet and space for storing two suitcases. One of these large bedrooms has been designed to accommodate a handicapped passenger and a companion. The other two can connect to form a large suite with plenty of room for four people.

The twelve other **compartments** are quite a bit smaller, but will adequately accommodate two people. Because the room is much narrower than the deluxe bedroom, whoever draws the upper berth will especially appreciate that second window. Each compartment includes a washbasin and a toilet. There's a small closet where three or four garments can be hung on hangers and room for a couple of suitcases. Passengers in these compartments will have access to a shower located at the end of the car.

Dining Cars

Like the sleeping cars, these new diners also feature a second row of windows and, while not as dramatic as the Superliner lounge cars, the effect does allow more light into the car as well as provides a greater feeling of spaciousness. Each diner can accommodate forty-eight passengers at twelve tables. The kitchen is also state of the art and includes—what an obvious, but great idea!—a trash compactor. For shorter hauls, the Viewliner diners can also be converted to provide the more informal lounge-car service.

Superliners

These bi-level cars operate on all of Amtrak's western routes, including the *Sunset Limited,* which now extends to Florida. As new Superliners are added to Amtrak's fleet, they're beginning to show up on a few other eastern trains: *City of New Orleans, Capitol Limited,* and *Auto Train.* Superliners are newer, bigger, and heavier than the cars of the Heritage fleet, which means the ride is more comfortable. Passengers move between cars on the upper level only.

Coaches

Coaches have minor variations based on the way the cars are laid out, but a typical Superliner coach can accommodate seventy or more passengers. Most of the seating is on the upper level, although many coaches include some seats on the lower level primarily for the use of handicapped and elderly passengers who might have trouble climbing the

Passengers from a Superliner sleeping car stretch their legs while the *Southwest Chief* is serviced in Albuquerque, New Mexico. (Photo by the author.)

narrow stairway. They have plenty of room for baggage. You should stash your suitcases in the large storage racks located near the lower-level entrance to the car. Don't worry about leaving your luggage in these racks. Just be sure that each of your bags is clearly and prominently identified so someone with a similar-looking suitcase doesn't take yours by mistake. There's also a luggage rack above the seats running the full length of each car, which is the best place for your shoulder bag and any other carry-on items you'll need while in your seat.

The coach seats themselves are wide and comfortable. Most will recline as much as 35 degrees, and each is equipped with a fold-out leg rest. If you have to sleep sitting up, this is definitely the way to do it. Don't pick a seat in the last row, however, because those seats are in front of a wall and won't recline as far as the others. And, because they face a wall, avoid the first row of seats, too. No big deal—but they have slightly less leg room there.

Sleeping Cars

When fully occupied, a standard Superliner sleeper will accommodate as many as forty-four people in four distinct types of accommodations. As do the coaches, sleeping cars have a large luggage rack located on the lower level of the car just as you enter. This is where you should keep all your luggage—everything except the few personal items you'll need in your compartment. These should be in a shoulder bag. You will have access to your luggage during the trip; it's just a lot easier to take the few necessities with you to your room. As already mentioned, don't worry about your bags, which will be perfectly safe in the rack. Just make sure they're clearly tagged with your name.

A total of fourteen **economy bedrooms** are available on both levels. They're very adequate for one person, but are intended to accommodate two. Facing seats slide together to form the lower berth. The upper berth folds down from the wall over the window. Since it's just 24 inches wide (by comparison, a standard twin bed is 38 inches) and rather close to the ceiling, I don't recommended it for large passengers. There are no toilets or washing facilities in the room, so you'll have to use one of four unisex lavatories in the car—one on the upper level and three on the lower level. There

SUPERLINER SLEEPER (UPPER LEVEL)

Lavatory   Economy Bedrooms
Deluxe Bedrooms   Stairway

SUPERLINER SLEEPER (LOWER LEVEL)

Lavatory   Shower   Economy Bedrooms
Special Bedroom   Lavatories   Stairway   Family Bedroom

Amtrak Superliner sleeping car.

is also a shower on the lower level. There is no room for luggage, which is why I suggest putting some essentials in a shoulder bag. You'll be able to accommodate one under each seat. There is room to hang two or three garments in a little closet. No doubt about it, these rooms are small. But because you pay for your sleeping-car accommodations by the room and not per person, this is by far the most economical way for two people to enjoy the advantages that sleeping cars provide.

Be sure to ask for an economy bedroom on the upper level in the Superliners. Lower level rooms have a bit less of the side-to-side sway, but you'll get better viewing and a quieter ride up top. Economy bedrooms 1–10 are located on the upper level; numbers 11–14 are below. Although it's located on the upper level, avoid economy bedroom number 1, which is right next to a lavatory. Every time it's flushed during the night—*Whoosh!*—you will wake up with a start. Number 1 is usually occupied by the car attendant, but not always.

The five **deluxe bedrooms** are all located on the upper level and are very adequate for two adults. There's a long bench-type seat facing a comfortable chair. The seat flattens out to form the lower berth. It's three-quarters the width of a standard double bed and can accommodate an adult and a small child. Two adults will find it either crowded or cozy, depending, I suppose, on the couple's priorities at the time. The upper bunk folds down and is 32 inches wide—a good deal roomier than the upper bunk in economy bedrooms. The room includes a washbasin with lighted vanity mirror and a combination toilet/shower. (I'll say this again, too: When using the toilet, be sure to hit the flush button and not the button for the shower. It seems obvious, but someone does it on almost every trip.) A small closet allows space for two or three hanging garments. Theoretically, there is room for one or two suitcases, but you'll have to keep them on the seat or on the floor. They'll be in your way so, as with the economy bedrooms, it's better to have some essentials in a couple of shoulder bags and keep the luggage in racks on the lower level.

As with bedrooms in Heritage cars, two pairs of these rooms have a folding partition between them that can be opened to form a rather large suite. All deluxe bedrooms are on the upper level so track noise is minimized and viewing is best. Given a choice, however, avoid deluxe bedroom "A." It's at the very end of the car and has a more cramped configuration than the others.

Each Superliner sleeping car has one **family bedroom.** These were designed for two adults and two small children and do the job quite well. Two of the berths are good-sized and will handle the adults very nicely. The other two—one upper and one lower—are definitely for kids since each is just 4'9" long. Family rooms include a washbasin, mirror, and a changing table for infants. There is no toilet in the room, but three lavatories and a shower are just a few feet

Deluxe bedrooms on the upper level in Amtrak Superliners offer spaciousness and privacy. (Photo by the author.)

from the door. If you need to have luggage in the room for the kids, it's less of a problem here simply because there's more floor and seating area on which to put the bags. As a practical matter, however, I'd keep all bags in the luggage racks, which are right outside in the corridor.

These family bedrooms offer two big advantages. One is that they extend the entire width of the car, providing a look at scenery on both sides of the train. I once rode for the better part of an hour with a rocky cliff passing by just a few feet outside the window of my economy bedroom, unaware that a beautiful vista was on the other side of the train. The other advantage is cost. Family bedrooms will sleep two adults and two kids, but Amtrak has priced them well below the deluxe bedrooms, which really accommodate only two adults. And all four people will get complimentary meals when traveling in a family bedroom. Just remember that there is only one such room in each car—another reason to make your reservations well ahead of time.

There is also one **special bedroom** in each sleeping car. This is really just a politically correct term meaning that these accommodations are for a handicapped person and a companion. The room itself is well-designed and handles a wheelchair very neatly. There are two beds, a toilet, a washbasin and mirror, a little closet, and—ta-da!—a storage rack for two suitcases. Like the family bedroom, the special bedroom runs the entire width of the car and there is only one in each Superliner. These rooms will be sold to non-handicapped passengers *if* the rest of the car is sold out or within 72 hours of a specific train's departure time.

Only the deluxe bedrooms have a shower, but Amtrak has been systematically modifying all Superliners to add a shower for the use of passengers in the other accommodations. No matter which room you're in, all upper berths have straps to prevent the occupant from rolling out at night. (Use them! It's a long way down.) All Superliner rooms include a small built-in fold-down table for playing cards or games. Likewise, all rooms have a temperature control and you can also adjust the flow of air through a vent in the ceiling.

You should know one other little quirky thing about Superliner sleepers. To summon the car attendant, pull, don't push, the call button. When the button is pulled, a bell rings and a small light goes on outside your door. *Don't push the button back in until the attendant arrives.* If you do, the light will go out and he or she won't know which passenger rang.

Lounge Car

This is the place to be for the best look at passing scenery. The upper level features comfortable chairs and huge windows that wrap halfway up the roof of the car. Below is a snack bar where you can buy sandwiches and a variety of beverages, non-alcoholic and otherwise. The lounge car opens early in the morning and, except for several well-deserved breaks for the attendant, stays open until about midnight.

Dining Car

These cars will accommodate seventy-two people at one sitting, although one table for four is usually reserved for members of the crew. The food is prepared in a kitchen on the lower level and sent up in a dumbwaiter.

Transition Sleeper

This is always the first bi-level car in the Superliner consist, located right behind the baggage car. Amtrak people call it simply "the dorm car" and, as that name implies, it's for most of the on-board crew members. Sleeping-car attendants usually occupy economy bedroom number 1 in their cars, but other crew sleep on the upper level of the dorm car, which is configured with economy bedrooms only. The lower level includes combination bedroom/offices for the conductors and the chief of on-board services, toilets, showers, and a crew lounge. Most of these cars originally came

from the Santa Fe when Amtrak was created in 1971, but a
few of them are newly built.

Other Factors in Choosing Accommodations

Most veteran rail travelers feel they sleep better if they're
facing forward; that is, they prefer lying in the same direction the train is moving. In Heritage fleet sleepers, you'll
sleep facing forward in all roomettes and in bedrooms A, C,
and E; you'll be sleeping across the width of the car in bedrooms B, D, and F. In the Superliners, you'll sleep facing forward in all economy bedrooms, but across the width of the
car in all the deluxe bedrooms. In the family bedrooms,
adults sleep across the width of the car, kids in the two
small berths sleep facing forward.

Remember, too, that you'll get a smoother, quieter ride
if your room is toward the middle of the car, so make that
part of your request when you book. In Heritage sleeping
cars, you should ask for roomettes 1–6 and bedrooms A–D;
all economy and deluxe bedrooms in Superliner sleepers are
either not over the wheels or on the upper level where it
really doesn't matter very much. Both the family bedroom
and the special bedroom in a Superliner sleeper are at the
end of the car on the lower level and almost over the wheels.
Since each car has only one family and one special bedroom,
there's not much you can do about it. Don't let it worry you,
however; on a scale of 1–10, this is about a two.

CHAPTER 10

How It All Works

Hauling more than 20 million passengers all over the country is a complicated business. The Amtrak system includes a total of some 25,000 miles stretching from coast to coast. Amtrak itself owns only about 750 miles of that track, most of it along what is called the Northeast Corridor, the route running between Boston and Washington, D.C., by way of New York City. Almost everywhere else, Amtrak trains are operating over track owned and maintained by private freight railroads, referred to as "contract" or "host" railroads by Amtrak.

Passenger and freight operations have some distinct differences, but the basic technology and operating procedures are pretty much the same—whether it's Amtrak throughout the United States, VIA Rail across Canada, or a freight railroad hauling a variety of commodities back and forth through just one section of the county.

The Track

When you stop and think about it, the *track* is what makes rail travel different from every other form of transportation. Railroads spend a lot of time and money on the construction and maintenance of their track. It's important, too, because poor track means trains must run at slower speeds, and that means reduced revenues for the railroad. Sometimes trains run slowly because the track has been rebuilt. New track will settle a bit and, until it has stabilized, trains must travel over it at slow speed, usually about 10 miles per hour.

The first step in laying track is to carve the path (called the "subgrade") out of the terrain and, as much as possible, level it off. This is done by removing earth from the high spots and using it to fill in the low areas. Look for this as you travel. You'll immediately be aware of the terrain rising and falling as it passes your window, while the actual roadbed remains more or less level.

Once this subgrade has been prepared, two layers of ballast are added. The first is a coarse gravel; the second is crushed rock or crushed slag. These two layers of ballast can be as much as two-and-a-half feet deep, depending on the condition of the subgrade.

Next come the cross ties—traditionally wood, but more and more are made from concrete—which are embedded in the top ballast. Wooden ties are placed a foot apart, 3,000 to every mile of track; concrete ties are larger and heavier and are placed two feet apart. Concrete ties are used more in areas where there is heavy or high-speed train traffic. They'll also last up to 25 years before needing to be replaced. Under the same conditions, a wooden tie, even when it has been chemically treated to resist rotting, will last for about seven years.

When wooden ties are used, heavy metal plates, called *tie plates,* are placed on the ties. The rails are laid over the tie plates, then both are fastened to the ties with track spikes— really just huge nails. Tie plates are embedded in the concrete ties when they're made, and the rails are fastened to the ties with heavy metal clips. There are minor variations, but generally that's the way all track is laid.

The two rails are laid exactly four feet, 8½ inches apart, which is known as *standard gauge.* The importance of estab-

This is how railroad track is laid—rails and wooden cross ties on top of two layers of gravel or crushed rock.

lishing a standard width for track is obvious: It means an individual freight car can be hauled virtually anywhere in all of North and Central America. Parallel tracks are laid 14 feet apart—that's the distance from the center of one track to the center of the adjacent track.

There are a number of *narrow gauge* railroads in this country. The track is just three feet between the rails to accommodate smaller locomotives and cars designed to operate on steep grades and around tight curves in mountainous terrain. Most of these narrow gauge railroads have become tourist attractions and provide excellent opportunities to experience railroad operations typical of another era . . . not to mention a chance to view spectacular scenery up close. (You'll find a list of scenic excursion trains in the back of this book.)

For years, individual rails have been 39 feet long—not really an odd number, since they were originally hauled on standard 40-foot flatcars. They're laid end to end and bolted together at the joints. It's this joint that makes the clickety-clack when the car's wheels pass over it. Today, when track has to be replaced, quarter-mile lengths of welded rail are often used. It goes down much faster and, because the joints are some 1,300 feet apart and are welded together, the clickety-clack is gone. That, of course, is how you can tell when your train passes onto a stretch of welded rail.

The rails themselves vary in size, weighing anywhere from 112 to 145 pounds per yard. The size of the rail used depends on the amount, weight, and speed of traffic it's going to get. Heavy-duty rails are found on main lines, with lighter-weight track used for spurs and sidings.

You'll probably notice track work going on in several locations during your train trips. The equipment they use is fascinating to watch. One machine (actually, it's several machines mounted on a number of articulated cars) will remove the old wooden ties, level the ballast rock, put new concrete ties into position, and install welded rail—all in one operation. For years railroad workers laid track using only hand tools. Incidentally, back in the late 1800s, most of those tools were made by the Gandy Manufacturing Company. The word "Gandy" was stamped on the handle of every pick, shovel, and hammer. That's why, even today, track workers are still called gandy dancers.

Every so often you may see one or more cross ties smeared with white paint. That means those ties have either been marked for replacement or for treatment with a chemical preservative. Occasionally you'll also see *one* cross tie painted yellow. That tells the engineer where to stop his train so he won't activate crossing lights and barricades at a grade crossing up ahead. No sense stopping all that automobile traffic if the train isn't ready to proceed across the intersection.

The Wheel

More precisely, perhaps, the *flange* is the important element that makes a train's wheel different from all other wheels. The flange is that one-inch ridge projecting from the inside edge of the wheel that, with the flange on the wheel at the other end of the axle, keeps the wheel on the rail and the train on the track. (See illustration.)

Two things make a railroad different from other forms of wheeled transportation: the flange on the inner edge of the wheel and the welding of the wheels to the axle. Both are designed to make sure the train stays on the track. You can also see from this illustration how the rail fits into the tie plate and is fastened to the wooden cross tie with spikes.

Here's something else unique about the way a train works: The wheels of a rail car are welded to the axles and the entire unit turns. You'll notice it immediately if you look carefully at the wheels of a train rolling by at a slow speed. It's done that way to insure that the wheels stay on the rails and it provides better distribution of the immense weight of the rail car.

It All Starts with the Locomotive

The proper term for this monster is indeed *locomotive,* but railroad people also use the terms *engine* and *moto,* depending on the company. And, like ships, a locomotive is always spoken of as though it were female.

When it rolls off the production line, every locomotive is assigned a number that is unique all across the country; no two have same number, regardless of which railroad may own them.

When speaking about a modern railroad locomotive, most people refer to it as a "diesel." They're half right. Technically, it's a diesel/electric locomotive. Its diesel motors (there can be several) are not actually used to move the train, but they power electric alternators that generate DC current which is sent to traction motors on each of the locomotive's axles. And *that's* what makes the train go. In addition to powering the traction motors, a locomotive's generators run fans for removing heat and the air compressor for the braking system, and they provide electricity for the rest of the train.

There are also pure electric locomotives. Instead of producing their own electricity, they draw it directly from an overhead wire, called a catenary. These locomotives are much more powerful than the diesel/electrics. Faster, too.

In any discussion of railroad locomotives, *traction* is the key word. That's why locomotives are weighted—to provide as much traction as possible. Traditionally, traction motors have used DC (direct current), but that's changing. Some newer locomotives now have AC (alternating current) traction motors. The Burlington Northern was the first railroad in the world to use AC traction motors in freight service. AC uses less electricity and is therefore more fuel efficient. AC locomotives also have more pulling power— three AC locomotives can replace five DCs—and they require less maintenance.

Unlike automobiles or airplanes, the engineer of a locomotive sits on the right side of the cab with the assistant engineer occupying the left-hand seat. The assistant engineer is fully capable of operating the locomotive and, in fact, frequently relieves the engineer at the controls. Short-haul trains often have only one engineer.

The locomotive has a single set of controls on the right side of the cab in front of the engineer. There's a throttle to increase or reduce power to the traction motors, a control for the air brakes, and a little handle or button that blows the whistle. Of course, a number of gauges allow the engineer to monitor all the machinery, plus fuel reserves and the train's speed.

The whistle is blown as the train approaches grade crossings where automobile traffic crosses the tracks. On many locomotives, the loudness of the whistle can be adjusted to some degree, according to how hard the handle is pulled. Engineers will often ease up a bit at night when passing through a residential area, when they can clearly see no traffic near the grade crossing, or when the train is moving at slow speeds. Pull that handle all the way, however, and the whistle will make your ears ring!

A built-in device called an *alerter* is found in all locomotives. If the engineer doesn't adjust the throttle, apply the brakes, or blow the whistle for 20–25 seconds, a horn sounds and a bright light starts flashing in the cab. It pretty well guarantees that the engineer won't become distracted from his duties or fall asleep. If the engineer fails to respond after the horn and light have been activated for several seconds, the brakes will be applied automatically and the train will come to a safe stop. These devices are in place should the engineer become unable to operate the locomotive for any reason.

Head-End Power

Most of us take electricity for granted around the house and at work. Flip a switch and the light goes on just about every time. That's true on a train, too, but making sure it happens every time is a bit more complicated. A fully loaded passenger train requires a lot of electric power. In the coaches and sleepers it powers the air-conditioning, the lights, the outlets for electric razors and hair dryers, and provides hot water for washing up and showering. In the lounge car TV sets, VCR's, a microwave oven, and refrigerators are all run by electricity. The biggest user of electricity in the consist is, as you would expect, the dining car with its ovens, ranges, grills, freezers, refrigerators, dishwashers, and water heater. There's even a dumbwaiter in the Superliner diners, and it, too, is run by electricity.

We've already talked about how diesel motors in the locomotive run generators to produce the electricity that moves the train. The electric power to run all those lights and appliances comes from the same source . . . from a special generator just for that purpose in the locomotive. It's referred to as *head end power* by the crew, and you'll frequently see it abbreviated as HEP.

Long before passengers arrive, the service crew is on board preparing the train for departure. They all need to see what they're doing, of course. In particular, the dining-car crew needs to have all of their appliances working to store perishable food and to prepare meals. Before the locomotive is attached to the train, that electricity comes from a cable provided at the station. It's called *hotel power.*

Coupling

The coupling device that joins one car to another has two principal features: a drawbar with a knuckle on the end. The drawbar is attached to the car's frame and is constructed so it will slide forward or backward to provide slack. The knuckle looks like a cupped hand which grips and locks with the knuckle on the other car. The cars are also connected by hoses to provide air pressure for the braking system and cables to carry electricity from the locomotive throughout the train. The knuckles hook together automatically when two cars are pushed firmly together, but the complete coupling process requires a railroad worker to manually connect the air hoses and electric cables. When *uncoupling* cars, the yard worker simply releases a lever on the knuckles, and the cars are pulled apart, the hoses and cables parting by themselves.

Train Orders

Immediately before departing at the train's point of origin, or wherever he boards the train en route, the engineer is given a set of train orders. This is a sheaf of papers which authorizes that specific trip and notifies the operating crew of any changes from normal track conditions along the way. These could include specific locations where crews are working on the track and *slow orders* for other sections of track. Trains operate at slow speeds over new track until it has had a chance to stabilize. Train orders can also be called *track warrants*.

Starting

Smooth starts are a lot easier with a passenger train because there are a lot fewer cars and little or no slack between them. Engineers pride themselves on smooth starts, which, with practice, can be done consistently.

Starting a freight train of 100+ cars is quite another matter. In fact, theoretically it's just not possible for a locomotive to move all that weight. It does, though, and the secret is in the freight car's coupling mechanism. There's roughly a foot of slack between each car in the train. When he wants to start his train, the freight engineer first gets rid of all the slack by backing up enough to compress the entire train. Then, when he starts the locomotive moving forward, the

slack is taken up and the train starts moving *one car at a time.*
Once all the cars are moving, the locomotive can keep them
rolling, even speeding up and slowing down. But it was the
slack that got them all started.

Stopping

Being able to stop a train is critically important but not an
easy thing to do. It is, after all, a massive amount of weight
moving at high speed. For example, an eight-car passenger
train traveling at 80 miles per hour requires a minimum of
3/4 mile to stop, even under emergency braking conditions.
Much greater weights are involved with freights and, as
would be expected, they are that much more difficult to
stop. A 100-car freight train can weigh more then 10,000
tons and, at 30 mph, will simply not be able to stop in less
than one mile.

There's really only one way to stop any rolling vehicle—
by applying pressure against the wheels. That's the way we
stop cars, and it's the way trains are stopped, too. There is a
brake on every wheel of every car on every train.

Braking was done manually on the earliest trains, but it
wasn't until about 1900 that air brakes became standard
equipment on all railroad cars, whether freight or passenger.
Although the air brakes on every car in the train are controlled by the engineer from the locomotive cab, in an emergency the conductor can activate the brakes from anywhere
on the train.

The brakes are operated by using compressed air, which
is carried throughout the train by hoses that are connected
when any two cars are coupled. The first air brakes used the
compressed air to force the brake shoes against the wheels.
That method worked well as long as nothing went wrong.
But if the air compressor failed or if a hose broke anywhere
along the train, the resulting loss of air pressure meant the
entire braking system failed—leading rather quickly to very

unpleasant consequences. Then in 1887 in Burlington, Iowa, George Westinghouse had a simple but very bright idea: Instead of using the air pressure to force the brake shoes against the wheels, use it to hold them *away* from the wheels. In that manner, the brakes would automatically be applied if the system failed for any reason—and the train would stop. There have been frequent changes and improvements ever since, but the basic principle behind the air brake still applies . . . and it's still the way trains are stopped.

Another braking system is worth mentioning. *Dynamic braking* is used to gradually slow the train without applying the air brakes. In the simplest terms, instead of sending electricity to the traction motors to move the train, the whole process is reversed. The turning wheels are used to power the traction motors and *generate* electricity. The resulting "drag" causes the train to slow gradually. That electricity has to be used in some way, so it's put to work operating blowers which cool the traction motors. Any excess is dissipated through giant grids on the roof of the locomotive, like the coils on top of your electric stove. A rough—very rough—equivalent is slowing your family car by putting it into second gear.

As a passenger, you can frequently tell whether the engineer is using the dynamic brakes or the air brakes. For one thing, air brakes slow the train much more rapidly and you can hear them quite clearly—not the escaping air pressure, but the sound of the brake shoes being applied to the wheels under your car. There's no noticeable sound when the dynamic brakes are applied, but you can usually feel a slight bump just before the train begins losing speed—the slack between the engine and the baggage cars being compressed.

Spotting the Train

The tricky part to stopping a passenger train is more the *where* than the *how*. The object is to stop the train at just the right spot so passengers on the platform can step right into their cars, and boxes, crates, and heavy suitcases can be handed right out of the baggage car onto the waiting carts. The engineer often gets some help in *spotting* the train by radio—from the conductor, the baggage man, or the station agent. If the train is longer than the platform—often the case in small-town stations—the engineer will have to double-spot the train, meaning the train will stop to unload and board passengers, then pull ahead to repeat the process for passengers in the rear cars.

Hills and Curves

When it comes to railroading, flatter is better. (That is, in fact, why railroad tracks were often built along the banks of rivers.) Hills, referred to as *grades,* can be a problem. Because of the train's immense weight, the steeper the grade, the more difficult it is to negotiate. The engineer's main concern is to keep the locomotive's wheels from slipping, causing a sudden loss of traction. To keep that from happening, he must apply just enough power to do the job, reducing speed gradually if necessary. Driving your family car up a slope in icy conditions is a pretty good comparison. And speaking of ice, poor weather conditions just make the job that much tougher. Most locomotives are equipped with sanders that are operated by the engineer and sprinkle sand on the rails just ahead of the locomotive's driving wheels to give them better traction.

Railroad people measure the steepness of a grade in terms of percentage. For example, a one-percent grade means that the track rises (or falls) one foot in altitude for every 100 feet of rail. For a typical Amtrak passenger train, grades of 2 percent can be handled without any particular problem. Operating a freight train up such a grade is more complicated because they're a lot heavier and a lot longer. The steepest grade on any mainline track in the United States is

4.7 percent. That's crossing the Blue Ridge Mountains near Melrose, North Carolina. How steep is that? Well, railroaders consider anything more than 1.8 percent to be *mountain grade.*

With a train, *down* can often be a much bigger problem than *up*. The whole principle of a steel wheel on a steel rail is to reduce friction to a minimum in order to move those massive weights. Well and good, but the result is what's called a *lack of rolling resistance,* and it simply means that once a train gets rolling, it can be hard to stop. If it's coming downhill, even a hill that would be unnoticed by the driver of an automobile, a train can react like a roller coaster and accelerate. As mentioned elsewhere, an engineer can find himself at the head of a long train that's actually going downhill and uphill—part pushing and part pulling—all at the same time. How does a freight engineer handle his train? The same way a porcupine makes love— *very carefully.*

Keep to the Right

Where there is double track—that is, two tracks running parallel with each other—trains usually stay to the right. There are exceptions, as you will probably notice, but they are usually caused by track work of some kind.

Speed Limits

In most parts of the country, the maximum speed allowed for Amtrak trains is 79 mph. Why 79 and not 80, you ask? Well, federal regulations require that any train operating at 80 mph or faster must have a device in the locomotive cab that picks up and visually displays trackside signals for the engineer. Since most standard Amtrak locomotives are not so equipped, they hold their top speed to 79 mph.

This is certainly not to say that many trains don't go faster than 79 mph. Along the Northeast Corridor between Boston and Washington, D.C., Amtrak's Metroliners travel at 125 mph. In parts of Missouri, Pennsylvania, and a few other areas, passenger trains travel at 90 mph and higher. Apart from the speed limits, how fast the train goes depends on several factors, including track conditions, the weight of the train (meaning the number of cars), the type and number of locomotives pulling the train, and, as mentioned, whether or not that automatic signaling device has been installed in the engine cab.

Communication

In the old days, members of the train crew communicated among themselves with visual signals, waving their hands or, at night, lanterns. Today it's all done by hand-held radios, linking the conductors with the crew in the head end. The most powerful radio on the train is in the locomotive cab and with it the engineer can communicate with the dispatcher, who may be hundreds of miles away. The engineer can also receive radio messages from crews of other trains, from Amtrak personnel at stations they pass, and from other official sources using the railroad frequency.

When the need to communicate comes up among members of the service crew, they most often use the train's public address system.

Trackside Signs

During your railroad journey you'll see a lot of signs beside the track, obviously meant to communicate information to the crew in the head end. Once explained, the meanings are pretty obvious. I found that knowing what those signs mean added to the interest and enjoyment of my train trips.

While all railroads use signs to convey the same information to the engineer, the appearance of those signs differs somewhat from one railroad to another—just another reason why engineers have to qualify on each route. Here is a rundown on the most common railroad signs.

Mile Posts

Mile posts are the most common of all the railroad signs and, in many ways, the most important. Look for three-foot high white posts with black numerals located every mile along each route. They're positioned right next to the track, so you'll need to get close up to the window to see them.

You'll spot mile posts like this or small signs mounted on metal poles beside the track. They indicate the distance either to or from a major rail center and are used to pinpoint a train's location as it travels along its route. You can use mile posts to compute the train's exact speed.

Sometimes they're not posts at all, but signs on metal poles next to the track. Some are even attached to the electric poles running parallel to the tracks. In any event, you'll quickly be able to identify them because they're numbered in sequence, indicating the number of miles from that spot to a major terminus. Depending on which direction you're traveling, the numbers will get larger or smaller, one mile at a time.

Mile posts are important because they enable the railroad to pinpoint a location along a route. For example, before starting out on his run for the day, the engineer will be given train orders in which it may be noted that he can expect to find work crews on the track between mile posts 745 and 749. It works the other way, too. If the engineer notices any kind of problem en route, he can radio the dispatcher, referring to a specific mile post.

You can make use of the mile posts to figure out how fast the train is moving. There's a simple formula for that in Chapter 6: Life on Board. In some areas, curves in the track may have been straightened to permit higher speeds and, when that happens, the old mile posts might not be exactly one mile apart. So, if you want to be really accurate, check the speed several times over any given stretch of track.

Whistle Posts

You'll notice these right away, because there are a lot of them—a black "W" on a small white sign right at trackside. They tell the engineer to blow the whistle because there is a grade crossing ahead—that is, a place where automobile traffic crosses over the tracks. These signs are placed at varying distances from the grade crossing so that trains traveling at the maximum speed limit for that stretch of track will give adequate advance warning of its approach. Slower trains will either wait a few seconds after they pass the whistle post before sounding the whistle or whistle several times.

Flags

These come in four colors: red, yellow, green, and blue. Originally, flags were used as warning signals. Three of the colors mean exactly what you would think: red for "stop," yellow for "slow," and green for "resume normal speed." They're used to alert the engineer to something ahead on or near the track. Usually a work crew is involved, perhaps clearing a rock slide from the track or simply doing normal track maintenance. Whatever the reason, these flags are a visual warning to the engineer. Blue flags are placed at the front and rear of a single car, several cars, or an entire train, and they alert all concerned that people are working around or under the cars. Although still called "flags" by railroad people, these signs are usually colored squares of metal attached to a little metal pole. (They still *look* like flags.) At night, electric lanterns in the appropriate color are used. It's easy to miss these flags. They're pretty small, perhaps eight inches square. Usually you'll see them stuck into the ballast rock alongside the track just a foot or so from the rail. You *will* notice blue flags or lanterns placed by rail equipment in stations you pass through.

Speed Limit Signs

These are quite common and, as the name implies, they tell the engineer how fast he's allowed to travel. Most of the time there are two numbers posted. The top number is the speed limit for passenger trains; the bottom number applies to freight trains. An exact equivalent on many of our highways is where two speed limits are posted—one for passenger cars and another for trucks. The principal difference is that signs along a highway tell drivers what the speed limit is between that exact spot and the next sign, while most speed limit signs on a railroad tell the engineer how fast he can be traveling *two miles ahead*. The reason for that difference, of course, is that it can take that distance for the engineer to reduce his speed gradually from, say, 70 to 40 miles per hour. If the number shown on the sign means the engineer can *increase* the speed of the train, he may do so as soon as the entire train passes the sign. Train crews often refer to these signs as "speed boards." Just to confuse you, on some railroads there are two kinds of speed limit signs: Black numbers on yellow signs mounted diagonally on the pole indicate the speed limit two miles ahead; black numerals on white signs mounted level indicate the speed limit at that spot.

Exceeding the posted speed limit is a big no-no in railroading. Inspectors from the Federal Railway Administration are responsible for enforcing speed limits and other safety rules and do so by checking train speeds with radar guns. One or two speeding offenses by an engineer, even a few miles an hour over the limit, and he'll be looking for a new career.

Crossing Ahead

This black "X" on a white sign tells the engineer that your tracks will be crossing another set of tracks up ahead.

This speed limit sign (often called a "speed board") indicates that the limit for passenger trains is 70 miles per hour, while freight trains may not exceed 50 miles per hour.

Derail Signs

You'll often see these little derail signs, usually black letters on yellow or orange signs, along sidings as you're entering or leaving rail yards or stations. Near these signs, a metal device, often painted bright yellow or orange, is attached to a rail. It's designed to deliberately derail a freight car that might otherwise roll out onto the main line and become an obvious safety hazard.

Other Signage

Unfortunately, there is some variation in signage from one railroad to another. For instance, in some parts of the east you may see signs shaped like small yellow pyramids. These simply tell the head end crew that there's a "break in the rail" ahead—meaning a switch or another track crossing. In Canada, you'll see a lot of small black signs with two white dots. These tell the engineer to pay attention—there's something just ahead of which he should be aware. Most of the other signs you'll occasionally see along rail routes let the head end crew know when the method used by dispatchers to control their progress has changed. For instance, "Begin CTC" tells the engineer that his train is now under Centralized Traffic Control; "Begin ABS" means an Automatic Block Signal system is in use from that point on.

Signals

You can see a lot of these during any train ride, but you have to be looking for them because they're either placed right alongside or directly over the tracks. There are a number of different kinds, but, whatever the shape, almost all use green, yellow, and red lights to communicate with the engineer. These signals are used to keep trains running on the same track properly spaced and, in almost all cases, now operate automatically.

The track over which your train is running is divided into sections, called *blocks*. A signal located at the beginning of each block controls the rail traffic moving through it. Sometimes the distance between signals can be a number of miles, while other times it will be just a matter of a few hundred yards. How frequently the signals appear depends on how far ahead the engineer can see, where another track joins the main line, the location of a switch, and other factors. Generally, signals are set to keep a following train at least two blocks apart from the train up ahead.

For many years, signal lights were operated by electricity carried through wires strung on utility poles running alongside the track. You can still see those poles passing by outside the train window. More recently, especially since welded rail has become more commonly used, the electric impulses used to operate the signals are actually carried to them through the rails themselves.

In most cases it's pretty obvious, but here's what those signals mean:

Green (also called a *clear* signal): Proceed at normal speed.

Yellow: Approach (meaning pass) and be prepared to stop at the next signal.

Red: Stop and proceed at slow speed (usually 15 mph).

Absolute red: Stop and do not proceed.

There are a number of ways to distinguish an absolute red from a normal red signal—for instance a second red light will be illuminated as well.

Whistle Signals

If you're sitting close enough to the engine to hear the whistle, you'll soon notice that several different whistle patterns are used. Here's what they mean:

Long, long, short, long: This signal is used when approaching a grade crossing and is used when the locomotive passes a whistle post. (I've asked several engineers about the origin of this particular pattern, but none have known. The consensus seems to be: railroad tradition.)

Short, short: The train is about to move forward.

Short, short, short: The train is about to back up.

Long: This means the engineer is going to set—meaning to test—the brakes. This is done when the train is stopped and members of the train crew are outside to visually inspect the brakes once applied.

A series of long blasts: This indicates a serious emergency of some kind. Chances are extremely rare that you'll ever hear this signal.

By the way, "whistle"—both as a verb and as a noun—is still used, even though the term comes from the days of steam locomotives. Technically, it's an air horn.

Hot Box Detectors

These remarkable electronic gadgets are an important safety feature for our modern railroads. They're located in metal cases on either side of the track and equipped with sensors that look for overheated journal bearings, referred to as hot boxes by the railroads. Potentially, a hot box is big trouble. A bad bearing means steel in contact with steel at high speed. The axle and wheel become red hot and, left undetected, can fracture and cause an instant derailment.

As soon as the train passes over one of these detectors, an automated message is broadcast on the train's radio frequency then picked up by the crew in the locomotive and by the conductors. Here's a typical transmission from a detector, along with an explanation of what it all means:

SP detector: The detector belongs to Southern Pacific.

Pasco: We're in or near Pasco, Washington.

Temperature, eighty-seven: It's a warm day out there!

Speed, sixty-four: We're traveling within the 65-mph speed limit.

Track One: Where there's double track, this eliminates any confusion in case there's another train passing us on Track Two at the same time.

Number of axles, fifty-two: Yes, it's talking about us; and furthermore we're now sure the detector is functioning properly.

No defects: Good! Our train has no hot boxes and nothing is dragging on the track.

Repeat, no defects: Just making sure we got the critical information.

Detector, out: So we know the message is over.

Sometimes the detector will conclude its message by saying "Over," requiring the engineer to verbally acknowledge. That's so the dispatcher listening will know where we are and that we received the detector's message. Often there's another check. The conductor will radio the engineer following a detector's report just to be sure the message was heard in the head end. The following is typical:

"Good report, Number 7": Conductor telling the engineer that the detector reported no defects. The reference to the train number is to be certain the engineer knows the message is directed at him.

"Highball, 7": Engineer acknowledges conductor's message and tells him we're proceeding at track speed, the maximum permissible.

Although it's rare that a detector discovers a hot box on a passenger train, the electronic voice leaves little doubt about what to do: *"You have a defect. Stop your train! Stop your train!"*

If this does occur, there is almost always a *set out track*—you and I would call it a siding—near most hot box detectors where the train can be diverted while the crew assesses the problem. The car with the hot box is usually cut out and left on the siding while the rest of the train continues on its way. A minor inconvenience in the case of freight trains, but clearly a much bigger problem if it's a passenger car full of people. When *that* happens, Amtrak people really earn their pay. The on-board crew tries to accommodate the displaced people throughout the rest of the train. If that's not possible—and frequently it isn't—they'll arrange for alternate transportation and, if necessary, pick up the cost of meals and overnight lodging, too. But, let me emphasize, this is an extremely rare occurrence with passenger equipment, which is carefully inspected after each trip and periodically along the way.

High-Tech Equipment

Every so often, while passing through a rail yard, you may notice a pair of posts on each side of a track with what appear to be floodlights mounted on each. This is a good example of modern technology being used in the railroad industry. These lights are actually a scanner—pretty much like the one you're used to in the checkout line at the supermarket. As a freight train passes slowly between these posts, the scanner is used to identify, count, and sort specific freight cars from coded numbers on their sides.

Delays—Why They Happen

Unlike most of the railroads in Europe, passenger trains in North America are required to operate within a system primarily designed to handle freight trains. When an

Amtrak train is running on track owned by another railroad, that company and not Amtrak becomes responsible for the train's progress. Amtrak has incentive contracts with many of these host railroads, paying bonuses to the railroad for keeping Amtrak trains on time and withholding those payments for a poor record. In spite of these arrangements, Amtrak trains can be delayed when dispatchers for these host railroads give priority to their own freight trains. Unfortunately, that happens a lot . . . and with some railroads more than others.

The long-distance trains are more likely to experience delays than those on the shorter runs, and that's simply because there's more time for something to interfere with the train's progress. A Metroliner running between New York and Washington, D.C., is on 225 miles of track owned and controlled by Amtrak. It's far more likely to run on time than the *California Zephyr,* which travels the 2,400 miles between Chicago and Oakland over tracks controlled by three different railroads—Burlington Northern, Southern Pacific, and Union Pacific.

Delays are a fact of life in rail travel, but it will ease the aggravation if you know something about why they occur.

Amtrak makes a distinction between *in-bound* delays (late arrival) and *out-bound* delays (late departure), but they're closely related. In fact, the most common cause of an out-bound delay is the late arrival of an in-bound train. Amtrak will often hold up a departure if there are passengers on the arriving train who are expecting to make that connection. (You can see how this puts Amtrak in a no-win situation: Passengers on the *California Zephyr* will be unhappy if their departure from Chicago is delayed waiting for the *Lake Shore Limited* to arrive. But if Amtrak doesn't hold the *Zephyr,* forty or fifty passengers on the *Lake Shore* will miss their connection and then *they* will be unhappy.)

In-bound delays can cause other major problems for Amtrak, too. Arriving trains must be "turned" for the return trip, and, if they're significantly late, Amtrak crews have less time than they need for that process. And there's a lot to do. The train has to be cleaned, of course, and a mind-boggling variety of supplies have to be checked and re-stocked: food, fresh linen, and clean tableware for the dining car; ice, snacks, and drinks for the lounge car; fresh pillows for the coaches; clean sheets, pillowcases, and towels for the sleepers. Most of those beds have to be made up, too. There's also a lot going on outside the train, because every arriving train must be inspected before it can go out again. Of course this will no doubt be a day when the U. S. Postal Service shows up with an extra heavy volume of mail and, at the last minute, another mail car will have to be brought in and added to the consist.

Once en route, trains can be delayed for any number of reasons, and often are. An engine can break down with the closest replacement unit hours away. Perhaps there's an electrical problem in the dining car, and an Amtrak electrician has to come aboard somewhere along the way to fix it. If it's unusually hot outside, perhaps there are heat kinks in the rail caused by the steel expanding. Under those conditions, the train could be poking along under a "slow order." Maybe it's nothing more than unusually heavy freight traffic that slows the train's progress. Causes for delays seem to come in an endless variety. Here are just a few I've experienced over the past few years while gathering material for this book:

- Westbound *California Zephyr* delayed three hours when a freight ahead of us breaks a wheel and the track has to be repaired.
- Northbound *Silver Meteor* delayed thirty minutes in Savannah, Georgia, while paramedics come aboard to examine a sick passenger. (He's finally removed from the train and driven off in an ambulance.)
- Southbound *Silver Meteor*'s departure from Washington is delayed for four hours when a flash flood washes out a section of track south of the city.

- Eastbound *Empire Builder* delayed a total of two hours and forty minutes after waiting on sidings to allow four other trains to pass (three freights and the westbound *Builder*).
- Northbound *Montrealer* delayed forty-five minutes while train crew removes an old refrigerator and a mattress placed on the track by vandals.
- Westbound *Broadway Limited* delayed ninety minutes just outside Philadelphia when train loses head end power from locomotive.
- Northbound *Coast Starlight* delayed twenty minutes in Oakland where the tracks run down the middle of a main street fronting Jack London Square. Someone has parked a car on the tracks, locked it, and gone off shopping. (Yes, of course it's true. No one could make up something like that!)

It's interesting to note that of those seven delays, only one—the equipment failure near Philadelphia—can be laid at Amtrak's door. The others were caused by weather, equipment failure on another railroad, or quirky human beings. The delays experienced by the *Empire Builder* are fairly typical, and occurred because the Burlington Northern dispatcher gave priority to the other trains.

By the way, if the train is delayed for more than just a few minutes, the conductor should provide an explanation over the P.A. system. Don't bother asking one of the service crew—your car attendant or one of the servers in the dining car—they're usually too busy with their duties and almost certainly won't know why the train has stopped.

Hard-core railfans traveling with their scanners (see Chapter 6: Life on Board) can usually find out why the train has stopped by eavesdropping while the engineer and the conductor discuss the delay on their radios. Passengers without such electronic gizmos can still make educated guesses. Take a look out each side of the train. If there's another track, the odds are you're on a siding waiting for a train coming from the other direction; if you're on a single track, your train probably has a red signal—most likely because you've caught up to a slower train ahead of you.

Even when a train is late, it can still be considered on time. Most airlines record a flight as having left on time if the plane pushes away from the gate within fifteen minutes of its scheduled departure time. In much the same way, Amtrak determines if a train has arrived on time by establishing what are called on-time tolerances. They vary somewhat according to the length of the trip, but if a train's arrival falls within this grace period, it's still considered to be on time.

Amtrak On-Time Tolerances

Length of Trip	Grace Period
0–250 miles	10 minutes
251–350 miles	15 minutes
351–450 miles	20 minutes
451–500 miles	25 minutes
551+ miles	30 minutes

Making Up Time

Contrary to popular belief, it isn't possible to make up lost time by increasing the speed of the train since the schedule assumes the train will be running right at the posted speeds. Exceeding those speeds is just not done. For one thing, it's too easy to get caught and the penalties are severe.

Once a train falls behind schedule, there are only two ways to make up the time. The first is by hurrying up the loading and unloading of passengers and baggage at station stops along the way; the second is through *padding* in the schedule itself.

Padding is extra time built into the schedule. It's like a family having a little emergency stash in a savings account to cover unexpected expenses. So, if a train is delayed for twenty minutes because of track work somewhere along the route, a little padding in the schedule here and there helps get it back on schedule.

For example, take a look at this excerpt from a recent Amtrak timetable:

Train 48	Lake Shore Limited	Train 49
7:15P dp	Chicago, IL	12:58P ar
7:44P ar	Hammond, IN	12:04P dp

Train 48, the eastbound *Lake Shore Limited* en route to New York City, is scheduled to leave Chicago at 7:15 P.M. and arrive in Hammond, Indiana, at 7:44 P.M., a 29-minute trip. Train 49, the westbound *Lake Shore Limited,* originates in New York City and, according to the same timetable, requires *a full 54 minutes* to travel the exact same distance. That extra 25 minutes is padding to cover any delays that might have occurred somewhere in the 943 miles between New York City and Hammond.

Backing into the Station

Most of the time, trains simply pass through a station—pulling in on a specific track, stopping to load and unload passengers, then continuing on their run. At several of the major stops, however, trains back into the stations as a matter of normal procedure. This is done for two reasons.

First, to facilitate the train's departure, especially when the station is also a major junction. The train approaches from one direction, backs into the station, and departs in another direction. Look at a capital letter "Y" and imagine the station at the bottom. The train backs down the left branch to the station, then departs out the right branch. In fact, the arrangement of tracks which permits this maneuver is called—Surprise!—a "wye."

In other circumstances, there may also be environmental and safety reasons for backing into a station. This is the case at Chicago's Union Station, for example, where the platforms are on a lower level under the streets. Trains back in to keep the diesel-powered locomotives and their fumes as far from the terminal as possible. There's another consideration, too: In an enclosed area, those big locomotives are *loud!*

Weather Problems

Trains are usually bothered less by weather conditions than cars or planes; but rain, snow, or cold can and do cause problems for railroads. Heavy rain can wash out track or, more precisely, the roadbed on which the rails and cross ties have been laid. Drifting snow in mountain passes can slow or even stop a train. Steel rails contract and occasionally break in cold weather. Prolonged periods of sub-zero temperatures can freeze switches. Fog sometimes causes delays because it can severely reduce visibility for the head end crew.

Whatever the cause, and whether the train carries passenger or freight, railroads will go to great extremes to keep rolling or, failing that, to resume service as quickly as possible. Washed-out track can usually be repaired in relatively short time, but not always. The summer of 1993, for instance, brought such severe and widespread flooding throughout the Midwest that service on Amtrak's western trains was disrupted for several weeks. In winter, special locomotives equipped with snowplows or blowers are constantly on alert for use in the mountain passes.

There are also safety procedures that automatically go into effect. For instance, it's pretty much standard procedure for crews to reduce speeds once the temperature drops below zero degrees Fahrenheit for more than a few hours. Preventative measures are also taken. If you're traveling on a mountain route or in areas that are very cold in the winter, look for cylindrical propane tanks located next to switches. The propane is used to feed gas burners—very similar to the burners on the top of a gas stove—which heat the switches and prevent them from freezing in bitter cold weather. In some areas kerosene is used for the same purpose.

Delays or interruption in train service can also be caused by other natural events. Earthquakes can twist rails out of alignment and, in mountainous areas, rock or snowslides can obstruct tracks. Look for *slide fences* in many mountain passes. These are rather flimsy looking wire fences located beside the tracks in slide-prone areas. Their function is *not* to be a barrier for the rocks. When one or more of the wires is broken by a rock slide, a signal is automatically sent to the operating railroad. Trains are warned by radio about a possible obstruction at that location, and a crew is dispatched to clear the track.

Courtesy

The headlights of a locomotive, which are very bright as you might expect, can be dimmed in much the same way you dim the lights on your family car. Depending on circumstances, most engineers will dim their headlights when meeting or overtaking another train. Many will even dim their lights if they're directed into the eyes of motorists on a highway running parallel to the track.

Train crews help each other out and will look carefully at a passing train for any sign of a problem—smoke coming from a truck under one of the cars or a shifting load on one of the flatcars. If a freight train is waiting on a siding as your train goes by, the engineer of the freight will usually radio your crew after you pass to say something like, "Good run-by, Amtrak." The foreman of a track repair crew will do the same.

Split Trains

Some trains separate into two or more trains part way through their route. For instance, the *California Zephyr,* the

Pioneer, and the *Desert Wind* leave Chicago as one train. In Denver, the several cars comprising the *Pioneer* are split from the overall train, coupled to a new engine, and head off through Wyoming to Seattle. Some 15 hours later, when the original train reaches Salt Lake City, it splits again. Another new engine takes several cars, now called the *Desert Wind,* to Los Angeles via Las Vegas. Meantime, the *California Zephyr* continues on to the Oakland area. The entire process is reversed when the trains are eastbound, starting as three separate trains in Los Angeles, Oakland, and Seattle, linking first in Salt Lake City and then in Denver, and arriving in Chicago as three trains in one.

Passenger Manifest

A few hours before a train's departure time, Amtrak's computer prints out a list of all passengers booked on that trip. The printout provides the conductor and car attendants with the names of all passengers, the station where each will be boarding, their destination, and in the case of sleeping-car passengers, their car and room number. The manifest will also note if a particular passenger is elderly, handicapped, or might need some special service.

Clean Windows . . . Please!

Before each trip, most long-distance trains are taken through an automatic car wash . . . a super-sized version of the one around the corner where you take the family car. Some long-distance trains get their windows washed a second time at service stops along the way—the *Southwest Chief* gets this treatment in Albuquerque, the *California Zephyr* in Denver.

Keeping the windows clean is not easy, however. A brief rain squall followed by a dusty stretch of track can undo all those good efforts pretty quickly. So can passing through a lot of tunnels. You'll see a lot of blackened freight locomotives operating on the *California Zephyr's* route west of Denver. That's the result of the heat and smoke from the diesel motors in all those mountain tunnels. Finally, if a train is late arriving at its destination, there just may not be time to wash the consist before it gets serviced and sent off on its return trip.

Whatever the problems, clean windows should be a priority on *all* passenger trains. Amtrak justifiably sells itself as the best way to see America, but who wants to see the country through dirty windows? In recent years, Amtrak has started paying much closer attention to what had long been a nagging problem.

Private Rail Cars

Occasionally you'll find that a private rail car has been added to the rear of your Amtrak train. Most have been lovingly restored and refurbished by wealthy individuals who use them as land-going yachts. Others belong to railroads and other corporations that use them as rolling conference rooms. Traveling in a private rail car falls into the everyone-should-do-it-once category, and it may not be as far-fetched as you might think. A few travel companies who own this kind of equipment charter it for special excursions to individuals, groups, and organizations. On at least several occasions, inventive companies have used private rail cars as the venue for new business presentations to potential clients. The railroad expression for these cars is *private varnish,* a reference to the luxurious wood trim once commonly found in such equipment.

Amtrak charges $1.60 a mile for hauling these cars around the country and, although doing so is a source of additional revenue, it can sometimes turn into a major headache for the train crew. Most of these cars are 40–50 years old, sometimes even older than that, and Amtrak has

no control over how they're maintained. Mechanical problems do occur and can result in delays or other inconveniences for the entire train. Realistically, however, Amtrak
can't simply cut the car out of the consist and leave it on a
siding in the middle of nowhere. Owners of private rail cars
are, by definition, rich and influential.

For information on private rail car travel, call 202-547-
5696 or write to AAPRCO Charter Group, 106 North
Carolina, S.E., Washington, DC 20003.

Railfans

Finally, a word about the folks who have turned their fasci-
nation for trains into a hobby—sometimes a consuming
one. They call themselves railfans, but are often referred to
as foamers by railroad employees, meaning that they begin
to foam at the mouth whenever they see a train. For some,
the interest is broad and general; for others, it gets pretty
narrow. There are people who collect old railroad timetables, for example. Or dining car menus, tickets, posters, or
other memorabilia.

During almost any train ride, you'll see photographer/
railfans by the tracks taking your picture as you roll past.
Others are train spotters and spend their free time checking
off locomotive numbers in notebooks. The object is to have
spotted every locomotive of a certain series or owned by a
certain railroad.

Some railfans allow their passion to get in the way of
their good judgment. They'll be found wandering around in
areas of rail yards that are restricted to railroad employees
only. And some "collect" the builders' plates that are
attached to every rail car by the manufacturer. The sad fact
is, very few passenger rail cars still have the original plates
in place. Most have been—let's use the right word—*stolen.*

Largely because of these illegal or unauthorized activities
of the very few, railfans occasionally run into open hostility

from railroad people. More typically, they're treated with friendly, if maybe a bit weary, tolerance. More and more, railfans are genuinely appreciated. After all, as one veteran Amtrak road foreman pointed out, it's the railfans who write all those impassioned letters to their congressmen supporting rail travel in general and Amtrak in particular.

CHAPTER 11

What About All Those Freight Trains?

There are more than 500 railroad companies in the United States, although the vast majority—a total of 463 in 1993—serves very specific and usually very small geographical areas. In fact, these local railroads only operate an average of just over 50 miles of track. At the other end of the spectrum, we have what are called the Class 1 railroads. There are only a dozen of them, but their trains run over more than 123,000 miles of track and employ some 190,000 people. Class 1 railroads rang up almost $29 billion in revenues for the freight they carried in 1993. Here's a list of those companies (you'll see their identifying logos on locomotives and freight cars everywhere as you ride around the country):

Santa Fe (yes, its legal name is still the Atchison, Topeka & Santa Fe)
Burlington Northern
CN North America
Chicago and North Western
Conrail
CP Rail (which also includes the Soo Line)
CSX
Illinois Central

Kansas City Southern
Norfolk Southern
Southern Pacific (including the Denver & Rio Grande
Western)
Union Pacific

Many of these companies were formed from the financial wreckage of railroads that went through bankruptcy in the late 1960s. In fact, as this is being written, a merger of the Santa Fe and the Burlington is in the works. Unlike the circumstances of thirty years ago, however, both of those companies are sound and prosperous.

It really takes a cross-country train trip before most of us realize how extensive the country's system of freight railroads really is. Freight trains haul every conceivable type of commodity, but coal is still number one, accounting for some 21 percent of all freight revenues. From just one huge mine in Wyoming, a train pulling 110 cars loaded with coal to run midwestern power plants travels east to the Chicago area every single day of the year. You'll also begin to appreciate the immense capacity of the grain-producing areas of this continent when you pass one train after another, each pulling a hundred or more hopper cars filled with wheat or corn. Then there are the trains hauling chemicals, frozen food, fresh vegetables, motor vehicles, petroleum, minerals, lumber, paper, scrap metal, and . . . well, you name it, and it moves by rail.

Freight Locomotives

Pulling all those freight cars are some 18,000 diesel/electric locomotives. That may sound like a lot—and, of course, it is—but back in 1930 more than 57,000 locomotives were in service. (All but about 600 of those were steam engines.)

The appearance and design of freight locomotives varies tremendously—by weight, horsepower, number of axles, AC or DC traction motors, air-brake configuration, with or without dynamic brakes, and so forth. No matter, they're all fundamentally the same underneath: big, powerful diesel motors mounted on a rolling platform. (A more detailed description of how a locomotive operates may be found in Chapter 10: How It All Works.) Two factors determine the type of job for which any given locomotive is best suited: *horsepower* and *tractive force*. Horsepower is simply the common way of measuring how powerful the locomotive is—exactly the way we do with the family car. Another term for tractive force, certainly more familiar to the layman, would be *traction*. Whether it's a car or a locomotive, all that power can become almost useless if the wheels start slipping. That's what tractive force is all about, and that's why railroad locomotives are so heavy—to increase the tractive force and keep the wheels from slipping on the rails.

Depending on the gross weight of a train, additional "helper" locomotives may be added to provide more horsepower and more tractive force. The train's weight is determined by the number of cars in the consist and what's in those cars. Obviously, 100 cars loaded with coal will weigh much more than 100 cars loaded with wood chips, but the average capacity of a freight car is about 89 tons.

Passenger trains weigh much less than freight trains, but need to go faster, and that's why passenger locomotives can afford to sacrifice tractive force in favor of more horsepower. It's an oversimplification, but, generally speaking, freight locomotives are designed to pull very heavy weights at relatively slow speeds while passenger locomotives are designed to pull less weight, but go faster. Until Amtrak's new Genesis series, now called the P40, most of the locomotives used to pull passenger trains were freight engines that had been modified to operate at higher speeds.

Freight Cars

Almost 1.2 million freight cars of all types travel back and forth across the country. Almost exactly half of them are owned by the twelve big railroads, the rest by independent railroad car companies, the shippers themselves, and the small regional and local railroads.

As you might expect, railroad equipment can be expensive. The average price tag for all freight cars is now about $63,000. A brand-new refrigerator car right out of the box can cost $100,000 or more, and some cars, designed for carrying specific kinds of equipment or machinery, can be twice that amount. Every year, the Class 1 railroads buy about 30,000 new freight cars to either add to their fleets or replace worn-out equipment.

The average freight train is 66 cars long, and many will have well over 100 cars in the consist. In terms of the physics involved, there is almost no limit to how long a freight train might be given an adequate number of locomotives. There are a number of practical considerations, however. Probably the most obvious is how much of a train's capacity has been sold by the railroad's sales department. But very long freight trains can block busy city intersections for very long times and generate serious public relations problems. Extra-long trains can even cause the railroad itself problems if they block important switches in the rail yard.

You'll see thousands of freight cars from the window of your train. Part of what's interesting about a train ride is knowing what all those cars are for and what's inside them. There is an almost infinite variety of sizes and designs, but it all starts to take shape if we break them down into a few simple categories.

Boxcars

This is what most of us mean when we say "freight car." It's an enclosed car with a roof and sliding doors in the sides. It's used to carry a whole variety of general merchandise, particularly items that must be protected from the weather. If your local hardware store orders 200 power lawn mowers from a manufacturer, chances are those mowers rode across the country in one of these railroad cars.

The boxcar is the most basic of all freight cars. This one happens to be insulated to help minimize the effects of either cold or heat on whatever it is carrying. Numbers indicating the capacity of the car are stenciled on the side. Fully loaded, this car will carry almost 70 tons of cargo. (Photo courtesy of the Santa Fe Railway.)

A lot of boxcars are specially equipped in one way or another. For example, many are used to carry fresh produce from California all over the country. These refrigerator cars have to be equipped to maintain a constant, cool temperature so the fruits and vegetables inside won't spoil in the summer. In the winter, when shippers have the opposite problem, fresh produce crosses the country in heater cars to keep it from freezing.

Gondola Cars

Take a common boxcar and cut it in half horizontally and—*voila!*—a gondola car, or "gonnie" as the train crews call them. Gondola cars have low sides and ends, a solid

Pulling this train of gondola cars loaded with coal are three of the Burlington's new AC Traction locomotives. It's hard to tell because the camera's telephoto lens has "squeezed" the length of the train, but just the part we can see in this photo is a half-mile long. (Photo courtesy of the Burlington Northern Railroad.)

floor (meaning the contents can't be unloaded through a trap door in the bottom), and no top. Depending on the weight of the material they were designed to carry, some gondola cars have higher sides than others. You'll see all sorts of things being hauled in these cars—scrap metal for recycling, iron and steel products, and almost anything else that's heavy and doesn't need protection from the weather.

Hopper Cars

These look a lot like gondola cars, except they all have high sides and many are covered. But *all* hopper cars have one thing in common: The interior walls slope toward trapdoors

Covered hopper cars are used to haul bulk products: wheat, for instance, or potash, which is used to make fertilizer, glass, enamels, soaps, etc. The material is loaded from the top and unloaded through three trapdoors in the bottom of the car. (Photo courtesy of the Santa Fe Railway.)

in the bottom of the car through which the contents are unloaded. These cars are used to carry such things as coal and grain in bulk.

Tanker Cars

You can identify these cars very easily because they're basically long cylinders with a dome on top through which they are filled. Tanker cars are used for carrying liquids ranging all the way from milk to petroleum to some pretty dangerous materials—primarily chemicals. Many of these cars are pressurized to carry such things as carbon dioxide, which we think of as gas (providing the bubbles in soft drinks, for example), but which turns into a liquid when it's compressed.

Tank cars are used to haul liquids of all kinds. Each of these cars will hold almost 21,000 gallons. (Photo courtesy of the Santa Fe Railway.)

Flatcars

As the name implies, these cars are really nothing more than rolling platforms with no sides or top. The basic flatcar traditionally has been used to carry things such as logs (to a sawmill), lumber (from a sawmill), and other commodities that can be stacked flat and don't need to be covered from the weather. Some flatcars have high reinforced panels at each end, designed to keep loads—lumber, for example—from shifting either forward or backward with the movement of the train. The military uses flatcars to move tanks, trucks, and other heavy vehicles; and you'll often see very large pieces of machinery being carried in this manner.

An entire subgroup of flatcars are known as *intermodal cars*. They were first designed to carry truck trailers, which are hauled to the railroad yard by truck, unhooked, and simply swung aboard this special flatcar. At its destination, the trailer is lifted off the flatcar, hooked to the cab portion of a semi-trailer truck, and driven straight to its destination. Railroad people refer to this arrangement as TOFC (trailer on flat car) or *piggyback* and, to the everlasting confusion of the general population, the trains themselves are called *pig trains.*

Double-Stack Cars

These are a fairly recent innovation—actually a modified flatcar that features a sunken bed, which permits two shipping containers to be stacked, one on top of the other, yet still remain under the normal height limit of about 20 feet. The benefits to these *stack trains* are obvious: Trains that could formerly haul 120 trailers in a piggyback configuration can now carry up to 240 containers without adding to the length of the train. These cars are certainly easy to spot, and you'll see them almost exclusively on western routes. When these cars are loaded with two 9-foot-high containers, they're too tall to run on many eastern routes with their low bridges and tunnels. Many of these flatcars are now articulated—that is, permanently linked together—so that each set of wheels actually serves two flatcars. The net effect of this ingenious arrangement is to reduce the number of wheels touching the track by 50 percent, meaning there is a corresponding reduction in drag. That, in turn, translates into a significant savings in fuel costs.

Auto Rack Cars

You soon recognize Auto Rack Cars quickly. First of all, they're high—fully 16 feet. Automobiles and small trucks are driven inside and tied down into position on one of the two or three levels. The sides of these rail cars are very distinctive, too. They're made from panels of light-

These double-stack intermodal flatcars are the most cost-effective way to move goods across the country. After the train reaches its destination, each container is placed on a flatbed truck and delivered to the consignee's door. (Photo courtesy of the Burlington Northern Railroad.)

weight aluminum, which are designed to protect the cars and trucks inside from being damaged by material swirling up from the roadbed or—more common, I'm sorry to say—from stones thrown by youngsters from trackside.

Specialty Cars

If you want to ship some strange kind of cargo by rail, there will either be a specially built car that can accommodate it or, if you're going to ship a lot of these things, someone will build a car just for you. For instance, Boeing has some special "high-wide" cars they use to transport airplane fuse-

You'll see a lot of these auto rack cars on any cross-country train ride. They're also called "autoveyors" and are used for transporting cars and small trucks, which are carried on two or three levels inside. (Photo courtesy of the Santa Fe Railway.)

lages. There are even special rails inside these cars to make loading and unloading easier.

Etcetera, Etcetera

You'll see many different sub-types of rail cars during your rail travels, but most are variations of these basic types, modified in some way to meet a specific need.

It should also be noted that Canada's two largest freight railroads account for some very impressive numbers, too. Between them, CN Rail and CP Rail System (originally Canadian National and Canadian Pacific respectively) operate over 37,000 miles of road with 3,250 locomotives and more than 102,000 freight cars. The combined revenue for the two companies is about $5.3 billion annually.

Finally, I'm sure my friends with the various railroads who helped provide information for this and other sections of the book would like you to know that America's Class 1 railroads pay out somewhere between four and five billion dollars in taxes every year.

CHAPTER 12

Safety—Priority Number One

If you spend any time around railroad people, you'll soon become aware that safety is constantly on everyone's mind. And with good reason. With massive weights moving at high speeds, railroading is an inherently dangerous business. The consequences of poor safety practices can mean wrecks, which are hugely expensive—millions of dollars in damage to equipment and freight, not to mention additional millions when people are hurt or killed. The fact is, safety gets top priority because safety pays.

Every railroad employee is responsible for safe operations and, if necessary, is empowered to override orders from superiors if necessary. For example, if an engineer receives confusing or garbled radio instructions from a dispatcher, he can refuse to move the train until he's satisfied that he clearly understands what he's supposed to do.

Maintenance

Regular maintenance is just as important to a railroad as it is to an airline. Amtrak has several maintenance facilities around the country, usually located in or near major terminals. The Sunnyside Yard in New York City, formerly the principal repair and maintenance facility for the Pennsylvania Railroad, is one of Amtrak's busiest, servicing some 70 trains and providing maintenance for as many as 250 cars every day. Other major facilities are located at Beach Grove, Indiana, and at Wilmington and Bear, Delaware. Every locomotive is inspected every day to make sure it's functioning properly and, as with airplanes, locomotives are pulled out of service for preventive maintenance at regular intervals. The cars themselves go through similar checks and overhauls, although not as often as the locomotives.

Safety Procedures

Whether it's a railroad or an airline or a steel mill, the key to safety lies in establishing and rigidly sticking to prescribed systems and procedures. For every function or task in railroad operations, there is one right way to perform it. Railroad workers, regardless of their job, know that to deviate from proper procedures is to court disaster.

Some safety procedures are very obvious:

Speed limits. Individual railroads set the speed limits that apply to their tracks. How fast a train is permitted to go is determined by the "level of sophistication in the track," meaning the quality of the roadbed and the "super elevation." (That's what we would call the banking or tilting of the track, which counteracts centrifugal force and permits higher speeds around corners.) Once set by the railroads, speed limits are actually enforced by Federal Railroad Administration inspectors who monitor randomly selected areas of track with radar guns to make sure limits are observed. There are circumstances when a train might exceed the maximum authorized speed (going downhill, for example), but a horn will sound in the locomotive cab, and if the engineer doesn't use the brakes, they are automatically applied. In railroad lingo, that's called a *penalty application.*

Time off. Every member of the operating crew—the engineer, assistant engineer, and conductors—has a limit to the number of on-duty hours he or she is permitted to work. These crew members are not allowed to work for more than twelve hours without a break of at least eight hours. And that rule is strictly enforced. Once that limit is reached, engineers or conductors "go dead" and cannot continue to operate their train. That's true even if bad weather or mechanical problems have delayed the train so much that their time runs out before they reach a station. They must stop the train wherever they are and wait for a new engineer to be put aboard. Usually Amtrak will have been alerted to the problem in advance by radio and will arrange for a fresh crew to meet the train somewhere en route.

Drugs and alcohol. Railroads have always had strict rules against the use of alcohol or drugs, but they were always self-policed. That all changed a number of years ago when an accident occurred in Chase, Maryland. A Conrail engineer, Ricky Gates, ran his locomotive onto the main line and into an Amtrak train, killing a number of people. Gates tested positive for marijuana and, as a direct result, the federal government pressed for a universal policy of random drug testing. Those tests are now administered by the railroads to their conductors, engineers, assistant engineers, and dispatchers.

An additional and somewhat ironic benefit came from that accident. The railroad unions and the various companies realized they if they didn't work together closely and productively to find an acceptable and meaningful drug testing policy, the federal government would probably do it for them. From this improved relationship between the two traditional adversaries has come Operation Red Block, an anti-drug and alcohol program. It's run by the unions, supported by management, and considered effective by all concerned.

Also as a result of what railroad people refer to simply as "Chase, Maryland," every American railroad now meets specific federal guidelines for the certification of engineers. Prior to the accident, each company had its own standards and requirements for training, knowledge of rules, and physical exams. Today, however, minimum standards are constant throughout the industry and engineers are recertified every three years.

Many other safety procedures are unique to railroad operations, but here are a few typical examples to illustrate their variety and depth.

- When preparing to move a locomotive, the engineer will (1) start the bell ringing to indicate locomotive is about to move, and (2) blow the whistle to indicate direction of movement: two toots, forward; three toots, back.
- A road foreman must be present whenever a "civilian"— meaning you or me—rides in the cab of an Amtrak locomotive to minimize possible distractions for the engineer.
- Radio messages from dispatcher to engineer are acknowledged and carefully repeated to be certain that every detail of the message was understood.
- When a blue flag (or light) is placed at the end of a train to indicate that people are working under or around the train, the *only* person permitted to remove the flag is the one who put it there.
- When backing into a station, the train will come to a "safety stop" 50 to 100 feet from the bumper post, then continue backing slowly before coming to a final stop.
- The assistant engineer calls out passing signals to be certain they have been seen and noted by the engineer.
- A train may not depart without train orders, which provide the engineer with the latest information about track conditions and contain formal permission to depart.

Safety Equipment

Railroading is still very much a hands-on business, but more and more automation is being introduced, particularly in the area of safety devices. Again, it's impossible to list all of these gadgets, but a good sampling should give you the idea.

- As mentioned earlier, in every locomotive cab there's something called an *alerter,* which is designed to make sure the engineer is always in command of the train. If the engineer doesn't change the throttle position, touch the brakes, or blow the whistle—on some locomotives a special button must be pushed—for a period of 20–25 seconds, a strobe light will begin to flash in the cab and a horn will sound. At that point the engineer has just a few seconds to perform one of those tasks (to demonstrate "Yes, I'm still here and still in control"). If he doesn't, the brakes will be applied automatically, and the train will come to a complete stop.
- Electronic detectors are located beside the tracks which broadcast warnings to the train crew if they sense over-heated journal bearings (called hot boxes) or any kind of dragging gear. For more information about these devices, see Chapter 10: How It All Works.
- Every locomotive is equipped with an *event recorder* just like the "black box" carried in airplanes. It records the motion and speed of the train, and the use of controls by the engineer throughout the trip. In the event of an accident, the information from this device will be used to help determine the cause.
- Where trains traveling through mountain passes run close to canyon walls, wire fences are installed along sections where rock slides could obstruct the tracks. When you spot one you'll realize immediately that these flimsy *slide fences* couldn't hold back any falling rocks. On the contrary, they're *intended* to break, and when that happens a warning signal is triggered. The railroad's dispatcher is

immediately alerted and will notify the engineer of any train that may be approaching the area.

- Supplementing direct voice communication between the locomotive engineer and the railroad's dispatcher is an entire sophisticated and complex system of signals to control the movement and location of every train. A key element in all these systems is that each signal is automatically activated by the train itself, not by an individual at a distant location who may not be certain of the *exact* location of the train.

Grade-Crossing Accidents

This is without doubt the single biggest safety problem facing America's railroads. On city streets, main highways, and dirt roads, cars cross over train tracks at thousands of locations from one end of the country to the other. Every one is the site of a potential tragedy. Motor vehicles of all kinds are hit by trains with a frequency that is astounding—about one every ninety minutes! The circumstances vary, but the outcome doesn't: *The train always wins.* You want a comparison? A train hitting a car is roughly comparable to a car running over a mailbox.

Every year somewhere around 600 people are killed and 2,000 are seriously hurt in grade-crossing accidents. Most of these accidents occur during broad daylight, with good visibility, and with the warning signals working perfectly. Furthermore, most of the time the driver of the car involved is sober.

Even more surprising, in about a third of all the car/train collisions that occur at night, the car drives smack into the side of a moving train! Speed is almost always the critical factor in these accidents, because the driver of the car is over-driving his headlights—that is, by the time his headlights reveal the train, he's unable to stop before reaching the crossing.

It's sad but true that an unknown percentage of these incidents are actually suicides or attempts at suicide. Even so, I think we would agree that those deaths and injuries are all equally unnecessary.

It's rare to find a railroad engineer who hasn't been involved in a grade-crossing accident. Some handle it philosophically, realizing that they can't feel responsible for the death of someone who drove around a gate and into their path. For others, that's easier said than done. Recognizing that, most railroads make professional counseling available to crews involved in fatal accidents. For a few engineers, however, the experience is enough to force them out of their chosen profession. (More on this very serious problem can be found in Chapter 7: Who's In Charge Here?)

Several years ago, the nation's railroads joined other organizations to form *Operation Lifesaver,* a program of information and education aimed at reducing the number of these awful accidents. It has been working, although some of the credit goes to the railroads for installing warning lights and gates at more and more crossings.

Here are a few commonsense rules for drivers approaching train tracks:

- Always assume a train is coming, in the same way you would anticipate a car if you were crossing another road.
- Slow down, roll down the window, and listen. You can't hear the train if your car's closed in winter weather or the radio's blaring.
- Never *ever* ignore active warning signals or drive around lowered gates. (This isn't as obvious as it sounds. A driver may see a switch engine parked a hundred yards down the track to the left and assume that's what brought the gate down. Wrong. It's another train approaching at high speed from the right.)
- Where there's more than one track, watch out for a *second* train coming from the opposite direction behind the first one.

- Don't be tempted to race a train to the crossing, even if it looks like a safe bet. Because of their enormous size, trains appear to be traveling much slower than they really are. Ever watched a Boeing 747 on its final approach? It looks like it's floating lazily along when, in actuality, the plane is moving at 170 miles per hour.
- Don't ever stop your car on a track. If traffic's backed up, wait until there's room on the other side before you cross over. And, if your car happens to stall on the track, get everyone out immediately and call the police. They'll contact the railroad's dispatcher who will alert the engineer of any approaching train by radio.

Amazingly, in addition to grade-crossing accidents, more than 500 people are struck and killed by trains every year while trespassing on railroad property. (Technically, that includes railroad track wherever it might be—multiple tracks in a busy rail yard or a single track passing through midwest farmland.) Again, a few of these are probably suicides, but most often it's just a combination of curiosity and carelessness. No matter. Whether it's an auto/train collision or someone is hit while walking too near the track, they're all tough on the train crews.

Derailments

Technically, and as the term implies, a derailment occurs when the wheels of one or more cars come off the track. A number of things can cause derailments. If an overheated journal bearing (called a hot box, remember?) goes undetected long enough, the wheel and axle will get red hot and finally break. Sometimes very hot weather can cause "sun kinks," which push the rails out of alignment. Sometimes an obstruction on the track causes the train to slip off the rails. Whatever the reason, derailments are a major headache for railroads. When they do occur, particularly if it happens at high speed, there can be a lot of damage to track and equipment. Rail cars are very heavy, and it takes special know-how and equipment to get them back on the track. There could also be several hundred yards of track to repair. And all of this could be happening many miles from the nearest available manpower or equipment.

The chances of a rail passenger ever experiencing a derailment are remote. In freight operations, however, derailments are not so uncommon. Because they interrupt the flow of freight, derailments can mean big-time loss of revenue to a railroad. It's essential, therefore, that operations get back to normal as quickly as possible. Some railroads have their own crews and equipment on standby for this purpose. Others use one of several companies that are on call around the clock and specialize in handling derailments.

Safety Rules for You

Some of these warnings may not have occurred to you, and others may seem obvious, but you would be amazed at some of the dumb things people do around trains.

- When crossing tracks, step *over* the rails, not on them. They're slippery, particularly if wet, so it's a very easy way to twist or break an ankle.
- Don't walk right next to the locomotive, especially if it's off the station platform. Every so often an automatic "blow down" clears the air brake reservoir with 140 pounds of pressure. Accumulated water, sometimes mixed with just a tad of fuel oil, can spray on anyone who happens to be standing too close at the time. All that pressure can also cause small ballast rocks to fly. Please note that a blow down is an *automatic* function and is not controlled by the head-end crew. People standing close to the engine are startled when a blow down occurs and

sometimes, when they see an engineer laughing, mistakenly think it was done deliberately as a practical joke. Not so.

- Don't try to get to the other side of the train by crawling under it. (Yes, people really do.) The train could move unexpectedly or another train could be passing on the adjacent track. In either case, you're history. Don't walk around behind the train for the same reason.

- Once on board, don't leave your seat without shoes on and, for heaven's sake, don't let your kids run around without shoes. Amtrak makes an announcement about this but, in my opinion, it isn't given enough emphasis. The principal danger is the moving, overlapping metal plates that passengers walk across when passing between cars. Get one of your tootsies caught in there, and the next thing you know the conductor will be calling ahead for an ambulance to meet the train at the next station.

- Even with their shoes on, kids running around loose, whether on board or on the station platform, cause real heartburn for Amtrak people. A lot can happen to an uncontrolled youngster, and none of it is good. If you're traveling with kids, keep them on a tight leash. (See Chapter 6: Life On Board for some ideas on how to keep them occupied.)

- If you find yourself in the upper berth in a sleeping car, hook up the restraining straps designed to keep you from falling out. After all, you're sleeping in an unfamiliar bed five feet off the ground on a moving train.

- Most people don't think so, but it really can be dangerous to open the hinged window in a vestibule door to look out of the train or to take pictures—particularly at high speeds. Dust and debris from the track often flies up into the vacuum created by the moving train, and there can be very little clearance between the train and objects it passes. Oh yes, if someone in the car up forward chooses that moment to flush one of the toilets, you could be enveloped in a fine blue mist.

- As you should do on a plane or when spending the night in a hotel, be sure you know how to get out of the rail car in a hurry if you should have to do so. A number of windows in every car serve as emergency exits. Each is clearly marked and will have a red handle on it. Pull on that handle to remove the rubber gasket holding the window in place, then push the glass out.

Bottom line for all this talk about safety: The railroads have their act together pretty well. All it takes for the rest of us is common sense.

CHAPTER 13

Taking the Train in Canada

Several years ago, a two-hour television documentary called *Last Train Across Canada* was carried on PBS throughout the United States. It's about an inquisitive older gentleman who travels clear across Canada by train—an absolutely delightful presentation and, for that very reason, it has been rebroadcast periodically several times since. Most unfortunately, however, the program has given millions of viewers the mistaken impression that transcontinental train service in Canada no longer exists. Happily, that is not true. VIA Rail, Canada's equivalent to Amtrak, can still take you all the way from Halifax, Nova Scotia, in the east to Vancouver on the Pacific Coast in the west.

Although Canada is a huge country covering millions and millions of square miles, 90 percent of the country's population lives within 200 miles of its border with the United States. For that reason, Canada's passenger rail system is strung out more or less through the middle of this populated area—roughly 4,000 miles long and just 200 miles wide.

VIA Rail Canada Inc. is the company responsible for operating Canada's system of nationwide passenger trains. In some ways, its job is a lot less complicated than Amtrak's. Because of the long, narrow area it serves and the much smaller population, VIA operates fewer trains. Amtrak lists more than 100 trains in its timetables, of which nearly 20 run overnight and offer sleeping-car service. VIA Rail, on the other hand, operates some 33 trains, most running along sections of the 725-mile corridor between Windsor and Quebec City, where the population density is located. Of those, just five are overnight trains with sleeping-car accommodations. Don't let those comparisons give you the idea that VIA trains don't have something special to offer, however. To the contrary, they will take you through some of the most varied and magnificent scenery anywhere in the world.

The Canadian Rail Epic

The story of Canada's transcontinental railway has grown to something of epic proportions in that country, and not without good reason. There are many obvious similarities

VIA Rail Canada's System Map

with the American railroad, but one very significant difference. In America, people settled the west and the railroad followed; in Canada, the train came first. The idea was to link settlements on the far-off Pacific Coast with the growing cities of the east and, by doing so, encourage people to settle in the vast areas in between. Actually, British Columbia forced the issue by refusing to join the Canadian Federation until, in 1872, its leaders had secured the promise that a transcontinental railroad would be built within ten years.

And so indeed it was. In 1881, the Canadian Pacific Railway began construction of the railroad, which was finished just four years later, a tribute to the honest and able people who financed, designed, and built it. It passed through some extremely difficult terrain, in particular an area known as the Canadian Shield north of the Great Lakes, where engineers had to blast their way through hundreds of miles of some of the oldest and hardest rock on earth. Then it was across the prairies, through the Rockies, into the dense forests of the Pacific Northwest and, finally, to the sea. In terms of the difficulties involved, the Canadian Pacific overcame natural barriers and weather conditions at least as formidable as those encountered by the Americans twenty years earlier.

Two other railroads, the Great Northern and the Grand Trunk Pacific, came a few years later, and by the 1920s had completed another route farther to the north. The Grand Trunk struggled financially for many years and, for this and other reasons, the two companies were eventually combined and became the Canadian National Railway.

As had been expected, cities and towns sprang up along both of the transcontinental routes. The Canadian Pacific, in particular, took a decidedly paternal approach to the communities it had literally created. In fact, after deciding that the CPR's western terminus would be the town of Coal Harbour, a company official, who evidently felt the name was uninspired and dreary, decreed that the community should instead be named for the British seaman who first explored the area, George Vancouver. And so it was. By 1924, the Canadian Pacific was claiming to have settled 55,000 families on 30 million acres of land between the Great Lakes and the Pacific. While it's possible to argue those numbers, it is considered a fact that the CPR created some 800 cities and towns in three provinces along its route. Farther to the north, the Canadian National laid claim to 132 towns, although for many the word "town" was probably an exaggeration.

For many years, the CPR and the CN competed vigorously for passengers as well as freight. The CPR took the additional step of building what are to this day some of the finest hotels in the world in major cities along its route. Each railroad ran its "name" trains, many of which reached into the United States for business by terminating in major American cities such as New York, Chicago, and Detroit. Two of the Canadian Pacific's best were the *Mountaineer,* which ran during warmer months from St. Paul, Minnesota, through the famous resort town of Banff in the Canadian Rockies, to Vancouver. Another CPR train out of St. Paul was the *Soo-Dominion* to Calgary. The Canadian National focused on Chicago, with trains from there to Toronto and Montreal, among other cities. Both railroads ran transcontinental trains within their own country.

Along Comes VIA Rail

Canadian railroads struggled against many of the same problems that beset American trains in the decades after World War II, but held out a bit longer. Finally, in 1978, the Canadian Pacific and Canadian National merged their passenger operations. The result was VIA Rail Canada, a "Crown Corporation" wholly owned by the Canadian government. VIA Rail now provides passenger train service on a 9,000-mile system. It stretches from coast to coast and extends more than a thousand miles north to the town of Churchill on the shores of Hudson Bay. A number of VIA Rail's trains—the one to Churchill is a good example—provide the only link to the rest of the country for hundreds of isolated communities across the northern part of the country. Although operated at a loss, those trains are mandated by the Canadian government. As is the case with Amtrak, VIA Rail owns almost no track of its own, mostly operating instead over tracks belonging to the CN.

Also like Amtrak, VIA has not had an easy existence, waging a constant battle against those in the Canadian government who cannot or will not see the necessity if not the wisdom of a national rail transportation system. There have been periodic reductions in both personnel and service—the vogue term is "downsizing"—but still the system remains more or less intact. Furthermore, you'll find the equipment to be modern, the service good and, all things considered, the food really first rate.

What You Should Know About Canada's Trains

Basically, there isn't a great deal of difference between VIA Rail's operation and Amtrak's so there's no reason you can't include a trip on a Canadian train in a rail itinerary. Again, I would suggest you try putting together your own schedule as much as possible, turning everything over to a knowledgeable travel agent to double check what you've done and then handle the actual ticketing.

Most of the information contained elsewhere in this book will apply equally to either Amtrak or VIA Rail. A few things deserve mention, however, either because VIA does it a bit differently or because it bears repeating.

Reservations. Book as far in advance as possible, especially if your itinerary includes VIA's transcontinental train, the *Canadian,* during the summer months. For a few weeks every year, the *Hudson Bay* is often sold out, too. That train runs way up north to Churchill on the shores of Hudson Bay. Churchill becomes a tourist attraction toward the end of each September when polar bears come wandering into town. Whatever the train, if you choose to make reservations yourself, you can call either of VIA Rail's toll free numbers: 1-800-561-3949 or 1-800-561-9181. VIA will also accept collect calls from the United States. From Canada, call the VIA number listed in the local telephone book.

Timetables. Contact a knowledgeable travel agent or call VIA Rail's toll-free number for a free copy.

Discount fares. There are quite a few opportunities to cash in on special low fares. In fact, there are so many special rates, this is one area where a knowledgable travel agent can be a big help. Generally speaking, discounts from 25 to 40 percent are available if you travel during off-peak times. That can mean certain periods during the year (winter months except over the Christmas holidays), on certain days of the week, or on travel to remote areas. There are other discounts, too: 10 percent to seniors (60 and over) and "youths" (ages 12 through 24); 50 percent to children (ages 2 through 11). Infants under 2 travel free as long as they don't occupy a seat. Note that many of these discounts apply only to coach travel . . . but not all.

CANRAILPASS. This is VIA Rail's equivalent to the now-famous Eurail Pass and, like that one, it's a good deal as long as you plan to do a fair amount of travel. There are several versions of this pass depending on who's using it and for what time of year, but basically you get unlimited travel for a total of 12 days within a 30-day period. You can also arrange for additional days on a pass by paying a supplementary charge. A specific number of seats on every train is set aside for people using these passes, which means it's possible you won't be able to travel on a particular train even though you have already bought your CANRAILPASS. Even with the pass, you must have a ticket, however, so make your travel plans, get your pass, then buy your tick-ets. Once you have ticket in hand, no problem. The pass is good for coach travel, but you can still upgrade to VIA1 class or into sleeping-car accommodations by paying a sup-plement. Other benefits are added to the CANRAILPASS from time to time, so ask about those once your travel plans have taken shape.

Is the train on time? Maybe, but maybe not. If you're planning to board a VIA Rail train at a stop other than its point of origin, your best bet for correct information is to call the VIA phone number listed in the *local* telephone directory.

Parlez-vous français? No? Well, if you don't speak French, that's a pity, but don't worry about it. VIA employ-ees (indeed, most people you'll meet in the French-speaking parts of Canada) are quite fluent in English.

Baggage. As in Europe, you'll find free baggage carts in many stations. The Montreal and Toronto stations are two exceptions, but redcap service is available there. You may check heavy baggage if you wish, but be sure to find out in advance if that service is available at *both* ends of your trip.

Classes of service. It's pretty much the same as Amtrak, but VIA just gives different names to their various levels of service. *Sleeper Class* refers to the private accom-modations in sleeping cars on overnight trains, with two notable exceptions: To add some additional luster to what is already a first-rate experience, sleeper class on the *Canadian* (Toronto-Vancouver) is referred to as *Silver & Blue Class.* VIA now includes the cost of breakfasts and evening meals in the price of a Silver & Blue class ticket, leaving you to pay only for your own lunches. The equiv-alent class of service on the *Ocean* (Montreal to Halifax) is *Easterly Class,* although no meals are included in those fares. Within the Windsor to Quebec corridor, you can opt for *VIA1,* a first-class service provided on the shorter trips. If you board in Toronto, Montreal, or Ottawa, you'll get to wait for your train in a fancy lounge, and you'll be pre-boarded ahead of the regular coach passengers. The VIA1 cars are spiffy, and you'll get quite a good complimentary meal served to you at your seat. VIA1 includes specific seat assignments, so you can reserve either a window or aisle seat when you book. (I'm always disappointed if I can't sit by a window, so this one feature alone makes VIA1 a very attractive option for me.) There is, of course, an extra charge for this service. Coach Class, as on Amtrak trains, means you'll be in a standard rail car with rows of two seats on each side of a center aisle.

Paying for things. Cash, personal check (for exact amount and with two proper ID's), or the usual credit cards will be accepted either in railroad stations or on board. You may also use your American money, but don't let that lull you into thinking you can get by without having to exchange your dollars for Canadian currency. Once off the train or away from the major hotels, Canadian dollars are the coin of the realm, and you'll need them.

What to wear? Comfortable clothing is the standard for both VIA Rail and Amtrak. However, if you're traveling in Silver & Blue Class on the *Canadian* or Easterly Class on the *Ocean,* you will probably feel more at ease if you dress up a bit for meals in the dining car—especially for dinner. Because the service and the ambiance in the dining cars on those trains is very nice, a sport coat and tie is just more appropriate. Of course, you will not be tossed out into a passing snow bank if you show up in a polo shirt.

Tipping. Basically, it's just about the same as Amtrak—not necessary in coach unless your attendant provides some special service for you; $3 to $5 (Canadian) per night, per person in sleepers; and 12–15 percent of your tab in the dining car. Remember that if you're part of a package tour, tips are usually included in the cost of the tour.

Smoking policy. There's no smoking in any of the meal-service cars at any time. Nor is smoking permitted on any of the corridor trains running between Windsor and Quebec. On all other trains, smoking is allowed only in certain cars, both coaches and sleepers, so be sure to note your preference either way when making reservations.

Special needs. There are provisions on all VIA Rail trains to accommodate passengers in wheelchairs or who may have some other special needs. VIA Rail's only requirement, and it's a reasonable one, is that a passenger who will need special care during the journey (feeding, bathing, medication, etc.) must travel with an escort. The good news is that VIA will permit the escort to travel at no charge—an enlightened policy. Whatever your special requirements, please give VIA at least forty-eight hours advance notice.

What about pets? VIA is more flexible than Amtrak, but only seeing-eye and other service dogs are permitted to actually ride with their owners. Other pets, from parakeets to St. Bernards, ride in the baggage car where you, not the VIA people, are responsible for looking after them. On longer trips, you are permitted to take Rover for a "stroll" when the train reaches servicing stops.

Complaints or compliments. If you run into problems and can't get things straightened out on the spot, by all means pursue the matter later with a letter. Be concise, be unemotional, be polite. Write to: Customer Relations, VIA Rail Canada, P.O. Box 8116, Station Centre-Ville, Montreal, Quebec H3C 3N3. And—hey!—if you get some really excellent, genuinely friendly service along the way, as I rather suspect you will, send an "Atta-boy" to that same address, specifying the date, train number, and employee by name.

Railfans. Yes, Canada has its proportionate share of folks who are fascinated by trains, too. As noted elsewhere, these people are referred to as "foamers" by professional railroaders in the U.S., implying that they foam at the mouth upon catching sight of a train. That word is known north of the U.S. border, but, with a tact and gentility rather typical of the Canadians, the preferred term in that country seems to be "DRF" . . . for *Demented Rail Fan.*

On-Board Crews

Crew responsibilities are divided in almost exactly the same manner on VIA Rail trains as on Amtrak's. The only difference of note is that the person in charge of the crew on VIA's long-distance trains, comparable to Amtrak's chief of on-board services, is called a *service manager.*

Another point of possible interest: Compared to Amtrak, you'll see far fewer female conductors on VIA trains. In the past few years the company has made an effort to hire more women in nontraditional jobs. Unfortunately, when mandatory cutbacks came, the most recent hires were the first to be let go and, naturally, that meant most of the women.

Passenger Equipment

When it got started almost twenty years ago, a lack of quality rolling stock was one of VIA's biggest problems. Like Amtrak, VIA Rail went through a make-do period with the older traditional rail cars it inherited from both Canadian Pacific and Canadian National. They were refurbished a few at a time and many are still in operation—not very glamorous, but solid, comfortable, and reasonably reliable. These are the cars you'll ride in, for example, if you take that trip up to Churchill to see the polar bears, although they too will eventually be replaced with refurbished stainless steel cars.

But also included in that collection of equipment were 200 classic stainless steel cars originally built in the 1950s. Some sainted soul at VIA Rail decided these vintage cars were worth saving, and more than $200 million dollars was spent to rebuild the fleet completely from the wheels up. A number of structural and mechanical improvements were made in the cars, but the most important of these did away with the old steam heating systems in each individual car. Today the cars are all heated with head-end power, meaning with electricity supplied by a powerful generator in one of the diesel locomotives pulling the train. It's a far more reliable system and, if you're traveling across Canada in the winter, a reliable source of heat is a very good thing indeed! More about these wonderful cars a bit further on.

The trains operating in the Windsor-to-Quebec corridor are designated as LRC (light, rapid, comfortable) equipment, and indeed they are. These matched trainsets are quite sophisticated. A computer system actually tilts both locomotive and the cars as the train rounds curves, helping to neutralize the effects of centrifugal force on passengers and permitting higher average speeds. In fact, these LRC trains cover the 320 miles between Montreal and Toronto in a minute or two under four hours flat— fastest time in the world for conventional trains over that much distance. Furthermore, with modified technology and some track improvements, VIA expects to further reduce traveling time between those two major cities to 3 hours 15 minutes, which will be *averaging* close to 100 miles per hour.

Locomotives

All of VIA Rail's locomotives are diesel-electrics. The formal designation for the engines that haul the LRC corridor trains is GPA27, but VIA people refer to them simply as LRC locomotives. They're fast and powerful—capable of running at 125 miles per hour, although they won't be able to do so until all of the track in that stretch has been upgraded. For their long-distance trains, VIA uses good ol' F40s—the same locomotive that has been the bulwark of Amtrak's fleet for years. They're tough, durable, and reliable. They'd better be because, as you will hopefully see for yourself, all of those trains pass through long stretches of wilderness areas. Not a good place for breakdowns. (Don't worry, VIA uses twin locomotives on those trains . . . just in case.)

The Stainless-Steel Fleet

Even if you're not a true-blue train fan, the renovated and redecorated interiors of these cars—especially the sleepers—will make you think you've died and gone to heaven. They're neat, clean, are decorated in a very attractive color scheme, but still somehow haven't lost the feel of the 1950s when the cars were built. Both coaches and sleepers are now in use on four of VIA's trains: the *Canadian* and the *Skeena* in the west, and the *Ocean* and the *Chaleur* in the eastern part of the country. Here are some details on these wonderful cars.

Coaches

The layout is standard for most rail coaches—rows of seats, two on each side of a center aisle. There are seats for 62 passengers plus room for a wheelchair. Chairs recline and include leg rests. VIA provides both a pillow *and* a blanket for all coach passengers. There is a lavatory at each end of the car. There's space overhead for one or two small-to-medium-sized bags so plan to check anything more than that. Better yet, leave all that extra stuff at home.

Skyline Cafes

These cars include a food service area where a variety of sandwiches, hot meals, and drinks are available. Food may be taken back to your seat or you can eat in a large lounge area with tables and chairs. There is a panoramic dome with 24 seats on the upper level.

Sleepers

There are two lavatories and a real, honest-to-goodness shower in each of these stainless-steel sleeping cars. You can choose from three different types of accommodations, but all provide a call button, a reading light and, in roomettes and bedrooms, controls for heat and air-conditioning. *Sections* are two facing seats, which convert into a lower berth at night; an upper berth folds down from the wall above the window. Heavy zippered curtains are pulled across each section for privacy. (Remember the sleeping car scenes in the Jack Lemmon/Tony Curtis/Marilyn Monroe film *Some Like It Hot*? That's what a section looks like with the curtains pulled at night.) *Roomettes* are designed for one person and include a comfortable seat, a sink, a toilet, and a small closet where a few garments may be hung. At night, the bed folds down from the wall. It covers the toilet, however; so if you need to use the facilities during the night either get some instruction from the car attendant on how to raise the bed or be prepared to don a bathrobe and tip-toe to the lavatory at the end of the car. There are six bedrooms, each of which will accommodate two people and includes either a bench-type sofa or two chairs, a toilet, and a sink. The seating converts into two beds at night, a lower and an upper berth.

Sleeping car from VIA Rail's refurbished stainless-steel fleet.

Here are some additional observations about the facilities in these sleepers that may prove helpful:

- Bedroom F is about a foot larger than the others, and on a three-night trip you'll appreciate the extra space. Try to get this particular room when you book.
- Bedrooms A, C, and E are configured so that your seats are facing toward the *rear* of the train. Some people don't care, but I much prefer to ride facing forward. (Just to complicate things, these sleepers come in two slightly different configurations so, if these variables matter to you, double check with the VIA Rail reservations agent when the booking is made.)
- Some sleepers and Park cars (see illustration) also have drawing rooms that provide a sofa and two armchairs by day and three berths at night.
- Probably the best arrangement for a family of four traveling together would be to reserve Sections 1 and 2. They're located directly across from each other, so you'll be able to see out of both sides of the train during the day. The downside might be having other passengers walking by your seats as they pass through the car; but you'll quickly get used to that, and the reasonable cost of these accommodations should more than make up for it.

Park Cars

Several cars are named for Canada's national parks. They're certainly easy to spot, always being the last car of each train and with the distinctive bullet-shaped end. Park Cars are reserved for use by sleeping-car passengers only. There's a comfortable observation area at end of the car, a lounge toward the middle where passengers can get coffee and other beverages, and a dome on the upper level with two dozen seats. These cars also include sleeping accommodations: one

A "Park Car," which is used on three of VIA Rail's long-distance trains.

drawing room with three beds, and three bedrooms with two beds apiece.

Conventional Fleet

These are older cars and, while they have been refurbished, are still comparable to Amtrak's Heritage equipment, typical of coaches and sleepers manufactured during and after World War II. This equipment is used on the *Hudson Bay* between Winnepeg and Churchill and on the *Saguenay* and *Abitibi,* which run north and west from Montreal.

Coaches

There really isn't much difference from one railway coach to another—rows of seats, two on each side of a center aisle. Each car includes overhead baggage racks and lavatories with toilets and sinks.

Sleepers

The roomettes are designed for one passenger and include a toilet, a sink, and a bed that folds down from the wall for sleeping. Bedrooms will accommodate two people on a lower and an upper berth. There is an enclosed lavatory with toilet and sink. There are no showers in these cars.

LRC Fleet

VIA's LRC cars (which stands for "light, rapid, comfortable," as noted previously) are found in the Windsor-Toronto-Ottawa-Montreal-Quebec corridor. Trains operating along this route run quietly and smoothly at speeds up to 100 miles per hour. The cars are well designed with large windows and are tastefully decorated. Two types of service are offered in this central corridor.

Coach

The standard LRC coach will accommodate 74 passengers in rows of seats, two on each side of the aisle, and includes room for a wheelchair. Two lavatories are at the rear end of the car. A small food-service area is located at the opposite end, although passengers may purchase food and beverages right from their seats. Coffee, tea, and soft drinks are complimentary.

VIA1 Cars

These upgraded coaches have twenty fewer seats than the standard coach, which means more leg room. There are two lavatories at one end of the car and a fairly extensive food-service area at the opposite end from which the complimentary meals are served. The food in VIA1 class is quite good, rivaling first-class meals served by the airlines. Apéritifs, wine, and after-dinner drinks are all complimentary. Some conventional cars (that is, not the newer LRC equipment) are used for VIA1 class on some trains. They accommodate even fewer passengers because there are only three seats in each row, two on one side of the aisle, one on the other. Whichever car you get, it's a very pleasant way to travel—definitely worth the extra fare.

Bottom Line

Generally speaking, no matter which train you ride, you'll find VIA Rail's equipment modern, clean, and comfortable—especially those stainless-steel beauties. If you want a taste of the Golden Age, ride the *Canadian,* the *Skeena,* or the *Ocean.* You'll find a description of their routes, along with routes of most other VIA trains, in the following chapter.

CHAPTER 14

Now, Where Would You Like to Go?

This chapter contains information about many of the long-distance trains operated by Amtrak in the United States and VIA Rail in Canada. A few of the shorter routes are also mentioned, either because of their high ridership or because the scenery along the way is particularly noteworthy.

With the exception of the routes run frequently, I've provided both the name and number for each train. There will usually be two numbers—odd numbers for trains headed south and west, even numbers for those headed north or east. A third number given to a train probably means it operates at a different time on weekends. I've given you a few of the major stops along the route, but did not list all. Check an Amtrak or VIA Rail timetable for that.

Also shown is mileage from each train's point of origin to its ultimate destination and the approximate time it takes to cover that distance. You may notice that some trains take longer to travel in one direction than they do on their return trip, even though they cover exactly the same route. There are several explanations for that apparent discrepancy: a long grade that takes more time on the uphill run, more freight traffic encountered on one of the trips because it operates at a different time of day, or padding in the schedule. For details about specific arrival and departure times at all station stops en route, refer to current time-tables; or call Amtrak at 1-800-USA-RAIL or VIA Rail at 1-800-561-3949 or 1-800-561-9181.

In the comments that follow each listing, I've tried to tell you something about the scenery along the way and whatever else might make that trip different or interesting. In some cases, I'll tell you whether you'll see more or better scenery when traveling in one direction on a certain route as opposed to the other. This can indeed be the case since a train may pass through a particularly scenic area during daylight hours when traveling one direction, but through that same stretch during the night on its return trip. Occasionally I'll note from which side of the train you can best see special points of interest or particularly scenic areas. Between New York City and Albany, for instance, the westbound *Lake Shore Limited* travels for more than two hours along the east bank of the Hudson River. But if you're in a roomette on the right side of the train, you might never realize this. Of course, if you're traveling in the opposite direction—that is, eastbound toward New York City—the river will be on the right side. If you're rid-ing in coach, you'll be able to see out of both sides of the train, but would probably prefer to grab a seat on the side where the great scenery will be.

But—please!—remember that both Amtrak and VIA issue new timetables regularly and there are always changes. *Always.* Not just in the minor details either. For example, just weeks before sending the final manuscript for this book to the publisher, I got a phone call from an Amtrak official in Washington alerting me that a train I had included in this listing had been eliminated. So by all means, use the following information to help you plan a wonderful, scenic rail journey, but check all details with an Amtrak or VIA Rail reservations agent or a knowledgeable travel agent before your plans are set in concrete.

Amtrak

Adirondack (68, 69, 70, 71)

Between:	New York City and Montreal
Via:	Poughkeepsie, Albany, Ticonderoga, Lake Placid
Operates:	Daily
Distance:	381 miles
Duration:	Southbound, 10 hours; northbound, $9^1/_4$ hours
Equipment:	Heritage cars—coaches, cafe car

This is really a pretty trip and operates during daylight hours in both directions. The train runs along the eastern bank of the Hudson River for almost $2^1/_2$ hours between New York City and Albany, passing some magnificent old homes, the Military Academy at West Point, and Vassar College in Poughkeepsie. Northbound, the river will be on your left. Note that on Sundays only the southbound train has a later departure and consequently most of the scenic trip down the Hudson will be after dark.

Maple Leaf (63, 64)
Niagara Rainbow (62, 65)

Between:	New York City and Toronto
Via:	Poughkeepsie, Albany, Buffalo, Niagara Falls
Operates:	*Maple Leaf,* daily; *Niagara Rainbow,* Fri. (northbound) and Sun. (southbound)
Distance:	544 miles
Duration:	Northbound, 12 hours; southbound, 13 hours
Equipment:	Heritage cars—coaches, cafe car

The most scenic trip is northbound with the Hudson River on the left side of the train most of the way between New York City and Albany. You'll pass lots of wonderful old homes, the Military Academy at West Point, and Vassar

College in Poughkeepsie; but most of it is after dark during the southbound trip, except during the longest days of the summer months.

Vermonter (55, 56)

Between: Washington and St. Albans, VT (Montreal)
Via: Philadelphia, New York City, Hartford (CT), Springfield (MA), Montpelier (VT)
Operates: Daily
Distance: 606 miles
Duration: Northbound, 13¼ hours; southbound, 13¾ hours
Equipment: Heritage cars—coaches, cafe car

This train travels through some of the loveliest parts of Massachusetts and Vermont, although the last hour or so of the trip may be in the dark, especially during the fall and winter months. A connecting Amtrak bus will take northbound passengers over the border to Montreal—an additional two-hour ride. Likewise, passengers can board the bus in Montreal and be delivered to the St. Albans station for the southbound train.

Many Americans mistakenly think they can enter Canada with a wave of the hand. That's often true in some places, but not on the train. You'll need proof of identity such as a passport, a birth certificate, a citizenship certificate, or naturalization certificate. A driver's license is not acceptable. If there's anything out of the ordinary about your status, check carefully ahead of time to be sure you have the documentation you'll need.

International (364, 365, 366, 367)

Between: Chicago and Toronto
Via: Kalamazoo, East Lansing, Flint, Port Huron (MI), London, Kitchener (ON)
Operates: Daily
Duration: 12½ hours
Distance: 501 miles
Equipment: Amfleet cars—coaches, club coach, cafe car

The *International* runs every day, but I'd suggest avoiding the Sunday trains (366 and 367) if you have a choice. Monday through Saturday the trains leave either Chicago or Toronto bright and early, but on Sundays they depart closer to noon. As a result, the last part of the Sunday trip—a full four or five hours in winter months— is made after dark. That's a pity, because the train passes through quite a number of rather small towns, with some very attractive farms and wooded areas in between. This train is a joint operation between Amtrak and VIA Rail, with American and Canadian crews taking the train up to their own borders. As noted above, you will have to present proof of citizenship at the border in either direction.

Atlantic City Express, Bankers, Connecticut Yankee, Merchants Limited, Nathan Hale, Nutmeg State, Patriot, Senator, Yankee Clipper

Between:	Springfield (MA), and New York City
Via:	Hartford, New Haven, Bridgeport, Stamford
Operates:	Several times daily
Distance:	133 miles
Duration:	Approximately 3 1/2 hours
Equipment:	Amfleet cars—coaches, club coach (some trains), lounge/snack bar

This is a busy route with trains operating fairly often during the day. Southbound, the train crosses the Connecticut River after leaving Springfield and runs through some very attractive areas of rural Connecticut. In the summertime you'll see entire fields of tobacco covered by something that looks like white cheesecloth. The tobacco is a special variety used for cigar wrappers. Hartford's railroad station has had a facelift and now looks much the way it did around the turn of the century. The gold-domed State Capitol is on the left just as you leave the station. You'll get a new locomotive in New Haven, since only electric engines are permitted into the underground areas of New York City. (Headed north, of course, that's where they'll swap your all-electric locomotive for a diesel/electric.) New Haven is the home of Yale University, by the way, and from here to New York you're sometimes within sight of the ocean—actually, it's Long Island Sound. Once you reach Bridgeport, you'll be passing through communities from which lots of people commute to work into New York City. You'll cross the Hellgate Bridge onto Manhattan Island and, after passing some pretty depressing areas, dip underground and below the streets. These trains used to end up in wonderful old Grand Central Terminal (the commuter trains still do), but Amtrak now uses a bypass and goes straight to Pennsylvania Station. Some of these trains continue right on to Washington, D.C.

Bay State, Mayflower, Merchants Limited, Narragansett, New England Express, Patriot, Senator, Yankee Clipper

Between:	Boston, MA, and New York City
Via:	Providence, Mystic, New London, New Haven, Bridgeport, Stamford
Operates:	Several times daily
Distance:	231 miles
Duration:	Approximately 4¹/₂ hours
Equipment:	Amfleet cars—coaches, club coach (some trains), lounge/snack bar

This is really a nice ride. The southbound train passes through some typically New England areas after leaving Boston, coming within sight of the Atlantic Ocean soon after Providence, Rhode Island. For the next two hours, the ocean is frequently visible on the left. Also on the left, look for submarines as you cross the Thames River at New London. I'm not kidding—that's where they're built by the Electric Boat division of General Dynamics. The Merchant Marine Academy is also there. Along the Connecticut shore here, you'll see some wonderful old homes built early in the century, and pleasure boats by the hundreds. Approaching New York City, you'll get a good view of the city skyline.

Night Owl (66, 67)

Between:	Boston and Washington, D.C.
Via:	New London, New Haven, New York City, Philadelphia, Baltimore
Operates:	Daily
Distance:	457 miles
Duration:	9 1/2 hours
Equipment:	Heritage cars—coaches, sleepers, cafe car

Traveling from Boston to Washington for a business meeting? Well, go ahead and fly if you want, but this is surely the way I'd go. Board the *Night Owl* in Boston just before 10:00 in the evening and crawl into a comfortable berth for a good night's sleep, arriving in Washington just before 8:00 the next morning, all rested and ready to do battle with a bureaucrat. The schedule is almost exactly the same in the opposite direction. Trains depart a bit earlier on Friday and Saturday nights. For obvious reasons, scenery is not an issue with this train.

Metroliner Service

Between:	New York and Washington, D.C.
Via:	Newark, Philadelphia, Wilmington, Baltimore
Operates:	Daily
Distance:	226 miles
Duration:	3 hours
Equipment:	Amfleet cars—coaches, club coach

This is Amtrak's much-touted high-speed service. Several things differentiate Metroliners from conventional Amtrak trains running along the same route. Obviously they're faster, but in order to reach and sustain their top speed of 125 miles per hour, the consists are limited to either five or six cars. And, in order to cover the distance between New York and Washington in under three hours (schedule is actually 2:55), these trains necessarily make fewer stops. Finally, all seats on the Metroliners are reserved, so you are assured of a seat even if the train is full. You'll pay a hefty premium for choosing a Metroliner, however—as much as double the lowest possible fare for a conventional train. A good way to try out the Metroliner at a lower fare is to ride it on a weekend when the fares are quite a bit less. My suggestion is to take a Metroliner once for the experience, and after that, ride the conventional trains. They'll take a half hour or so longer, but still run at well over 100 miles an hour.

Broadway Limited (40, 41)

Between:	New York City and Chicago
Via:	Philadelphia, Harrisburg, Pittsburgh, Cleveland, Toledo, South Bend
Operates:	Daily
Distance:	915 miles
Duration:	Eastbound, 19 1/2 hours; westbound, 20 1/4 hours
Equipment:	Heritage cars—coaches, sleepers, dining car, lounge car

This train retains the name of one of the Pennsylvania Railroad's most prestigious trains. It passes through some very beautiful eastern scenery, particularly in the stretch between Philadelphia and Pittsburgh through Pennsylvania Dutch country, along the Susquehanna River and over the Allegheny Mountains. The ride also includes one of the best known spots in the country for railroad fans—the famous horseshoe curve near Altoona, Pennsylvania. The westbound train passes this spot after dark except in the summer months, but, traveling eastbound, be on the right side of the train to see this engineering marvel.

Amtrak's *Broadway Limited* climbs through the famous horseshoe curve near Altoona, Pennsylvania, on its way over the Allegheny Mountains. (Photo courtesy of Amtrak.)

Lake Shore Limited (48, 49)

Between:	Chicago and Boston or New York City
Via:	Cleveland, Buffalo, Albany
Operates:	Daily
Distance:	Chicago–Boston, 1,017 miles; Chicago–NYC, 959 miles
Duration:	Chicago–Boston, 21 hours; Chicago–NYC, 18 ½ hours
Equipment:	Heritage cars—coaches, slumber coach, sleepers, dining car, lounge car

The *Lake Shore* follows the same route as the New York Central's famous *Twentieth Century Limited*, skirting three of the Great Lakes—Michigan, Erie, and Ontario. The scenery will be quite different, however, depending on which direction you travel. The westbound train runs in daylight roughly from Cleveland to Chicago, while the sun follows the eastbound *Lake Shore* from Buffalo to either of its final destinations, Boston or New York. In my opinion, the eastbound train is the more scenic trip. Off and on between Buffalo and Schenectady you'll be following the old Erie Canal and can see a number of the canal locks from the right side of the train. When it was finished in 1825, the canal connected Buffalo on Lake Erie with the Hudson River at Albany, allowing people and goods to travel by water all the way from the Great Lakes to the Atlantic Ocean. The *Lake Shore* splits into two trains at Albany. The New York section runs due south along the Hudson River for several hours before reaching New York City, but only the eastbound train passes this way during daylight hours—one more reason why it's the more scenic of the two. Best viewing is on the right, by the way. After leaving Albany, the other section heads east to Pittsfield in the middle of the Berkshire Mountains, one of the choice skiing areas in the entire east. From there, you'll pass through Springfield and Worcester as well as a great many charming little New England towns before reaching Boston in the early evening.

Capitol Limited (29, 30)

Between:	Chicago and Washington, D.C.
Via:	Toledo, Cleveland, Pittsburgh, Harpers Ferry (WV)
Operates:	Daily
Distance:	780 miles
Duration:	Eastbound, 17 hours; westbound, 18 hours
Equipment:	Superliners—coaches, sleepers, dining car, lounge car

The eastbound trip is, I think, the more scenic of the two. The train leaves Chicago in the early evening and, by dawn, has reached Pittsburgh. You'll have daylight from there all the way into Washington, and it's a very pretty run—across the Allegheny Mountains in West Virginia, a stop at Harpers Ferry, into Maryland farm country, finally arriving in Washington by early afternoon. The westbound trip is very nice, too; it's just that you'll pass through that stretch around Pittsburgh in darkness. The *Capitol* is one of the first eastern trains to get Superliner equipment.

Pennsylvanian (42, 43, 44)

Between: New York City and Pittsburgh
Via: Philadelphia, Harrisburg
Operates: Daily
Distance: 444 miles
Duration: 10 hours
Equipment: Heritage cars—coaches, lounge/snack bar

The *Pennsylvanian* passes through the same beautiful countryside as the *Broadway Limited,* including the horseshoe curve near Altoona, Pennsylvania, but does so during daylight hours in both directions. This is definitely one of the more scenic trips among the eastern trains. Remember, for the best look at that famous horseshoe curve, be on the left side of the train if you're heading west.

Cardinal (50, 51)

Between: New York City and Chicago
Via: Philadelphia, Washington, D.C., White
             Sulphur Springs (WV), Cincinnati,
             Indianapolis
Operates: From New York—Sun., Wed., Fri.;
             from Chicago—Tues., Thurs., Sat.
Distance: 1,154 miles
Duration: 27 hours
Equipment: Heritage cars—coaches, slumbercoach,
             sleepers, dining car, lounge car

The eastbound *Cardinal* is one of my favorite trips. It will be dark, or close to it, when you leave Chicago, but the real scenery happens the next day almost from the moment you wake up and lasts all the way into Washington.

Probably the best part of the trip occurs as the train winds its way through the New River Gorge in West Virginia. About 25 minutes after leaving Montgomery, West Virginia, you'll see the New River Gorge Bridge from the right side. It's 1,700 feet long and almost 900 feet above the river. Remember the TV commercial when a Chevy Blazer was hooked to a king-sized bungee cord and shoved off a very high bridge? This is the spot! The *Cardinal* crosses the river more than once, but most of the time it will be on the right side. This is a lovely ride any time of the year, but it will really be something if you can manage to have your trip coincide with the fall colors.

FLORIDA TRAINS
Silver Meteor (97, 98)

Between:	New York City and Miami
Via:	Philadelphia, Washington, D.C., Richmond, Raleigh, Savannah, Jacksonville
Operates:	Daily
Distance:	1,391 miles
Duration:	26 1/2 hours
Equipment:	Heritage cars—coaches, slumbercoach, sleepers, buffet car, lounge car

You pretty much see it all on this trip: big cities and small towns, industry and agriculture, temperate and tropical. The first part of the southbound trip covers Amtrak's northeast corridor and is the high-speed part of the run. Because they're so long, none of the Florida trains can reach the 125-mph speed of a Metroliner, but you'll still be moving over 100 mph en route to Washington. You'll see some important rivers along here. Actually, you go *under* the Hudson right after leaving New York City, then over the Delaware, the Schuylkill, and the Susquehanna. Between the industrialized areas, you'll see some very pretty communities along here as the train passes through Philadelphia,

Wilmington, Baltimore and, finally, Washington. If you're breaking your trip here—and I'd certainly recommend it—be sure to spend some time right there in Union Station. It has been restored to its original grandeur and then some!

After leaving Washington the train crosses the Potomac River where the countryside gets very pretty indeed. You'll notice lots of familiar Civil War names through here. Unfortunately, unless you're traveling in the long days of summer, this part of the southbound trip will be after dark. For that matter, you'll miss the Carolinas, too. Early risers will be up in time to see Savannah, however, and it really is one of the South's most charming cities. By the time you've finished a leisurely breakfast, you'll be in Jacksonville. From here, the *Meteor* takes you through Orlando and Kissimmee, both stops for Disney World, then on down the eastern coast to Miami.

Silver Star (81, 82, 91, 92)

Between: New York City and Tampa
Via: Philadelphia, Washington, D.C., Richmond,
             Columbia (SC), Savannah, Jacksonville
Operates: Daily
Distance: 1,263 miles
Duration: 25¼ hours
Equipment: Heritage cars—coaches, slumbercoach,
             sleepers, cafe car, lounge car

This train covers mostly the same route as the *Silver Meteor*, but provides more in the way of scenery in either direction. Its mid-morning departure from New York means that you'll still have some daylight left for the very pretty countryside south of Washington. At Rocky Mount, North Carolina, the *Silver Star* heads inland for a stop in the wee hours at Columbia, South Carolina's capital. You'll get to Jacksonville early in the morning. From Jacksonville, the

Silver Star takes you through rural areas, mostly orange groves, to Tampa on the Gulf Coast.

Just before this book went to press, in an economy move by Amtrak, the full-service dining car was replaced with a cafe car serving airline-type tray meals. Not a critical issue, to be sure, but perhaps reason enough to opt for the *Silver Meteor* if your itinerary and schedule permit. Note, however, that the *Meteor* does not operate a Tampa section. Southbound passengers for Lakeland, Tampa, or St. Petersburg now leave the train in Winter Haven and are taken to their destinations by a connecting bus. Heading north, the process is reversed.

Auto Train (52, 53)

Between:	Lorton (VA) and Sanford (FL)
Via:	This train makes no intermediate stops.
Operates:	Daily
Distance:	861 miles
Duration:	$17\,1/4$ hours
Equipment:	Superliner cars—coaches, sleepers, dining car, lounge car, bi-level cars for transporting automobiles

The *Auto Train's* northern terminus, Lorton, Virginia, is a suburb of Washington, D.C. At the other end, Sanford, Florida, is just a few miles from Orlando and Disney World. This is really a classic case of finding a need and filling it. The train is operated for people who want to have their personal automobiles with them in Florida. Perhaps they just don't want to make the long drive south or maybe they'll be spending enough time in Florida to make renting a car an expensive proposition. Either way, the *Auto Train* is the perfect answer. Note that there are no intermediate stops—you board in Lorton and end up in Sanford, or the reverse. That's because special facilities are required to load and unload the cars—a fascinating operation to watch, by the way.

Automobiles are carried in specially designed bi-level rail cars while their owners ride up front in either coach or sleeping-car accommodations. *Only* passengers with cars can ride the *Auto Train*. (If you're heading for Florida without a car, the other Florida trains will be faster and more convenient, anyway.)

This is by far the longest train Amtrak operates, frequently consisting of as many as 44 cars and, because about half of those are basically freight cars, operationally that's the way this train performs—as a freight train. That only means you'll be traveling at somewhat slower speeds. Almost by definition, people who ride the *Auto Train* travel in both directions, but for what it's worth, the southbound

Automobiles are loaded aboard Amtrak's *Auto Train* in Loften, Virginia, for the overnight trip to Florida. (Photo courtesy of Amtrak.)

trip will be the most scenic—through Virginia and much of the Carolinas during daylight hours.

SOUTHERN TRAINS
Carolinian (79, 80)

Between: New York City and Charlotte, NC
Via: Philadelphia, Washington, D.C., Richmond,
             Raleigh
Operates: Daily
Distance: 702 miles
Duration: Southbound, $9^3/_4$ hours; northbound,
             $10^1/_2$ hours
Equipment: Amfleet cars—coaches, dinette car

The southbound train runs entirely during daylight hours, while much of the scenery between Washington and New York City will be after dark on the northbound trip. Essentially, for as far as it goes, the *Carolinian* follows the same route as the Florida trains.

City of New Orleans (58, 59)

Between: Chicago and New Orleans
Via: Urbana (IL), Memphis, Jackson (MS)
Operates: Daily (except Tue., Wed.)
Distance: 924 miles
Duration: $18^3/_4$ hours
Equipment: Superliner cars—coaches, sleepers, dining
             car, lounge car

I think I prefer the southbound trip because it offers a bit more daylight . . . although it may be because that's the direction Willie Nelson was headed. (If you don't get that reference, you're musically deprived. Buy his recording of *The City of New Orleans,* very possibly the best railroad song ever written.) Anyway, it's dark or close to it when the train leaves Chicago so you won't see much of all that Illinois farmland as you head south to Cairo. That's where you'll cross the Ohio River into Kentucky, although it happens in the early morning hours. About dawn, and just before you stop in Memphis, you'll see the 32-story Great American Pyramid. It's on the right and, believe me, you can't miss it. Then it's on through the Mississippi delta to the capital city of Jackson. By now, the river itself is well to the west. Another 80 miles or so, after passing through the town of— I wouldn't make this up—Magnolia, Mississippi, the train crosses into Louisiana. This is low country . . . Okay, *swamp* country. You can almost see the alligators and snakes out there, but it's very picturesque nevertheless. After a stop in Hammond, the train skirts around Lake Ponchartrain along the longest continuous railway curve in the world and into New Orleans. Let the fun begin!

Crescent (19, 20)

Between:	New York City and New Orleans
Via:	Philadelphia, Washington, D.C., Greenville (SC), Atlanta, Birmingham
Operates:	Daily between New York City and Atlanta; from Atlanta to New Orleans—Tues., Thurs., Sat.; from New Orleans to Atlanta— Mon., Wed., Fri.
Distance:	1,380 miles
Duration:	Westbound, 29$^3/_4$ hours; eastbound 30$^3/_4$
Equipment:	Heritage cars—coaches, slumbercoach (New York–Atlanta), sleepers, dining car, lounge car

This train, which was the pride of Southern Railway for years, still follows the same route—passing through all the major cities along Amtrak's northeast corridor to Washington, then swinging down through Virginia farm country before running along the edge of the Blue Ridge Mountains for several hours. Stay alert for the impressive Wells Viaduct after you leave Toccoa, Georgia. (Depending on the time of year, you may cross it after dark on the northbound trip.) After Atlanta—the *Crescent* operates between here and New Orleans three days a week—you'll travel west through impressive pine forests along the southern end of the Appalachian Mountains on the way to Birmingham. From there, the *Crescent* crosses into Mississippi, then turns and runs straight south. Just a few minutes after a stop at Slidell, Louisiana, you'll cross Lake Ponchartrain on a six-mile-long causeway. It's just one track wide and neither land nor any part of the causeway can be seen from either side of the train, creating the sensation that you're rolling right along on the water itself. From there you're just a half hour or so from arriving in New Orleans. If the *Crescent's* even close to being on schedule, you'll be there in plenty of time to enjoy some Creole cooking and maybe catch a set by the jazz band at Preservation Hall. What a town!

WESTERN TRAINS
California Zephyr (5, 6)

Between:	Chicago and Emeryville (CA)
Via:	Omaha, Denver, Salt Lake City, Reno, Sacramento
Operates:	Daily
Distance:	2,420 miles
Duration:	Westbound, 50 hours; eastbound, 52¼ hours
Equipment:	Superliner cars—coaches, sleepers, dining car, lounge car

This is arguably Amtrak's most scenic trip. It's spectacular in either direction, although if the eastbound train should be running more than an hour or so late (and it often does), you could miss some of the more impressive views coming out of the Rockies and into the Denver area.

Westbound out of Chicago, it's corn and more corn, then a dinnertime crossing of the Mississippi River at Burlington, Iowa. Omaha comes about midnight and you wake up in cattle country just east of Denver. The *Pioneer* splits off and heads north from there, so you'll have some time to get out and stretch your legs. Things start getting spectacular west of Denver as the *Zephyr* begins its climb into the Rockies, with best viewing from the right side of the train. In the next two hours, you'll pass through 27 tunnels, the last of which is the 6-mile-long Moffatt Tunnel. Before it was completed in 1928, the 10-minute trip you just took over Rollins Pass took five hours. For the rest of the day you'll follow the Colorado River through a series of canyons. The train crosses the river several times, but most of the best viewing will be from the left side. You should see lots of rafters, although it's not the real white-water stuff.

You'll cross Utah and enter Nevada during the night, getting to Winnemucca bright and early. Butch Cassidy once robbed a bank here. Following a mid-morning stop in

Superliner lounge cars provide panoramic views of the passing scenery. (Photo by the author.)

Reno, the *Zephyr* starts its climb into the foothills of the Sierra Nevadas. After a stop at Truckee—you're in California now—get a seat on the right side of the train for the ride along mountain ridges and past Donner Lake. It was named for 87 settlers led by George Donner who were trapped by snow in the winter of 1846–1847. Next comes the American River Canyon on the left side. The California Gold Rush took place in the 1850s and 1860s all through this area. After leaving the mountains and stopping at Roseville, you'll pass McClellan Air Force Base and enter the Sacramento Valley, known for producing almonds and rice. Next stop is Sacramento, capital of California and home of the very-much-worth-seeing California State Railroad Museum, followed by Davis, then Travis Air Force Base on the left. Next come the vineyards of Napa Valley and the Navy's "mothball fleet" in Suisun Bay on your left. After Martinez and Richmond, the *Zephyr* reaches what is now its final stop, Emeryville. The old Oakland Station, in a so-so part of town to begin with, was damaged beyond repair by an earthquake. Not to worry. An Amtrak bus will be at trainside to take passengers across the bay to San Francisco.

Pioneer (25, 26)

Between: Chicago and Seattle
Via: Omaha, Denver, Laramie, Ogden, Boise,
             Portland, Tacoma
Operates: From Chicago—Sun., Tues., Thurs; from
             Seattle—Sun., Tues., Thurs.
Distance: 2,662 miles
Duration: Westbound, $53\frac{1}{2}$ hours; eastbound, $54\frac{3}{4}$
             hours
Equipment: Superliner cars—coaches, sleepers, dining
             car, lounge car

The westbound *Pioneer* splits from the *California Zephyr* in Denver and heads off through Wyoming for the Northwest, roughly following the Oregon Trail. After stops for Cheyenne and in Laramie, the *Pioneer* crosses the Wasatch Mountains through Echo Canyon. A classic scene from the western novel *The Virginian* takes place in a dusty hotel bar in Wyoming, as the hero faces down a bad guy with the famous line, "When you call me that, smile." The incident was fiction, but the hotel bar is real enough. You can see it on the right side of the train about halfway from Laramie to Rawlins as you flash through the little town of Medicine Bow. By dawn, you're through Utah and Idaho and into Oregon. After climbing through the Blue Mountains, the *Pioneer* follows the Columbia River Gorge through some of the most beautiful scenery anywhere in Amtrak's system. You'll see a lot of the river itself, of course, but also Mt. Hood, Horsetail and Bridal Veil Falls, and a number of other points of interest. From Portland, the train turns north for a very scenic four-and-a-half-hour run to Seattle. The eastbound *Pioneer* originates in Seattle and joins the *Zephyr* in Denver for the balance of the trip to Chicago. You can ride this train in either direction and still catch most of the same scenery during daylight hours.

Desert Wind (35, 36)

Between:	Chicago and Los Angeles
Via:	Omaha, Denver, Salt Lake City, Las Vegas, San Bernardino
Operates:	From Chicago—Mon., Wed., Fri.; from Los Angeles—Mon., Wed., Fri.
Distance:	2,397 miles
Duration:	Westbound, 50¼ hours; eastbound, 52¼ hours
Equipment:	Superliner cars—coaches, sleepers, dining car, lounge car

Westbound, this train is a part of the *California Zephyr* from Chicago to Salt Lake City, where the *Desert Wind*'s cars are cut out and sent in a southwesterly direction to Los Angeles. That all happens close to midnight on the westbound trip; by the time you're up and about the next morning, the train is well into Nevada. Las Vegas comes around 8:00 A.M. and for the rest of the day, the *Desert Wind* heads southwest into California, across the Mojave Desert, over Cajon Pass and on into the Los Angeles area. You'll see most of the same country in daylight, regardless of which direction you travel; but if the eastbound train runs late (a real possibility), you could miss some of the best mountain scenery as you pass through the Rockies and head on down into Denver. So, all things being equal, I'd take the *Desert Wind* heading west.

Texas Eagle (21, 22, 521, 522)

Between:	Chicago and Houston or San Antonio (connecting for Los Angeles)
Via:	St. Louis, Little Rock, Dallas
Operates:	Sun., Tues., Fri.
Distance:	Chicago–Houston, 1,256 miles; Chicago–San Antonio, 1,308 miles
Duration:	Chicago–Houston, 28$\frac{1}{4}$ hours; Chicago–San Antonio, 30 hours Houston–Chicago, 29$\frac{1}{4}$ hours; San Antonio–Chicago, 30$\frac{1}{2}$ hours
Equipment:	Superliner cars—coaches, sleepers, dining car, lounge car

Southbound out of Chicago, you'll cross quite a number of rivers. There's the Chicago River first, followed by the Des Plaines and the Kankakee. You'll cross the Vermillion River just before a stop at Pontiac (Illinois, not Michigan, although both are named for the same Indian chief), followed by a number of other stops. It'll be close to midnight when you reach St. Louis, but stay awake if you can because the grande finale is the Mississippi, which you'll reach about 20 minutes after leaving Alton, Illinois. There's a great view of the city skyline on the left and several minutes later, the Gateway Arch on the right. Okay, *now* you can go to sleep.

You'll wake up in Arkansas, probably about the time the *Eagle* crosses the Arkansas River and pulls into Little Rock. You can see the dome of the State Capitol on the left. About mid-morning, you'll stop in Texarkana. The Arkansas/Texas state line runs right through the town. In fact, it runs right through the railroad station and, depending on whether you're sitting toward the front or the rear of the train, you'll either be in Texas or still in Arkansas.

By the time the train reaches Longview, you're in the middle of oil country. Then, as you follow along the Sabine River, it's cattle and horses. Dallas comes toward the middle of the afternoon and is where the *Eagle* splits into two trains—one section going due south to Houston, the other continuing through Fort Worth to San Antonio. The Houston train stops in Corsicana where, in the late 1800s, they were drilling for water and—darn!—hit oil instead. This is some of the prettiest country in Texas, and you'll see fields of wildflowers if the season is right. Lots of cotton and cattle, too. The route to San Antonio is also a nice one. Right after a stop in Austin, the state capital, the train crosses the Colorado River, reaching San Antonio just before midnight. Here in San Antonio cars from the *Texas Eagle* are coupled to the westbound *Sunset Limited* and continue on to Los Angeles. (If your trip began in Los Angeles, your car will be detached from the *Sunset Limited* here in San Antonio and become part of the northbound *Texas Eagle*.)

Southwest Chief (3, 4)

Between:	Chicago and Los Angeles
Via:	Kansas City, Dodge City, Trinidad (CO), Lamy (NM), Albuquerque, Flagstaff (AZ), San Bernardino
Operates:	Daily
Distance:	2,259 miles
Duration:	41 1/4 hours
Equipment:	Superliner cars—coaches, sleepers, dining car, lounge car

This is another of my favorite trips because it passes through some truly beautiful parts of the country. After a late-afternoon departure from Chicago, you'll head west across Illinois farmland for several hours, finally reaching and crossing the Mississippi River into Iowa around 9:00 P.M. Kansas City and Topeka come and go during the night and, by the time you wake up the next morning, you'll be just about in Dodge City. Boot Hill is a bit up the way from the old brick station.

The country will stay fairly flat for a short while, but by mid-morning the *Chief* has crossed into Colorado and is climbing up toward Raton Pass and the New Mexico border. You've been following the original route of the Santa Fe Trail for quite a while by now, and off and on all through here the trail is still plainly visible from the right side of the train. Once through the pass, the third stop is Lamy, New Mexico, which is the station serving Santa Fe. Santa Fe is a very old town and much worth visiting for a few days. This was the final destination on the old Santa Fe Trail, but the *Chief* still has almost a thousand miles to go.

Next comes Albuquerque. The train stops for almost a half hour here for servicing and window-washing, so you'll have time to get off and look at some of jewelry being sold by Native Americans on the platform. During most of the year, someone from the New Mexico Historical Society boards the train here and provides commentary over the lounge-car P.A. system about the history and geology of the area all the way to Gallup. (Other volunteers do the same thing on the eastbound train.) The *Chief* gets to Flagstaff around 10:15 P.M. and, if you're making a side trip to the Grand Canyon, this is where you'll leave the train. Otherwise, you'll probably sleep through all of Arizona, waking up in time for a leisurely arrival into Los Angeles.

It's close to a toss-up, but I think the westbound trip is a bit better, only because the eastbound train may run late. In that eventuality, passengers will miss some of those really beautiful mountains in Colorado because of darkness.

Empire Builder (7, 8)

Between:	Seattle or Portland and Chicago
Via:	Spokane, Glacier Park (MT), Fargo, Minneapolis–St. Paul, Milwaukee
Operates:	From Chicago—Mon., Wed., Fri., Sat.; from Seattle or Portland—Mon., Wed., Fri., Sat.; daily between Chicago and Minneapolis–St. Paul
Distance:	2,209 miles
Duration:	Portland–Chicago, 45 hours; Seattle–Chicago, 45 1/2 hours
Equipment:	Superliner cars—coaches, sleepers, dining car, lounge car

Another of my favorite trains! I've taken the *Builder* in both directions, but prefer the eastbound train because you see more of both the Cascades in Washington and the Rockies in western Montana—especially if the westbound train should run late.

The run from Seattle to Spokane is very pretty—first north along the shores of Puget Sound to Everett, then east into the magnificent Cascade Mountains. In summer months it'll still be light when you reach Wenatchee, justifiably called the Apple Capital of the World. Then on through farm and ranch land toward Spokane. Sit on the left for this part of the trip. The Portland section heads north, crosses the Columbia River into Vancouver, Washington, then it also heads for Spokane, turning east and passing through the Columbia River Gorge for more than 50 miles. Most everything, including a look at Mt. Hood (weather permitting), will be on your right. These two sections meet in Spokane well after midnight, becoming one train for the rest of the trip to Chicago.

If you can, wake up early the next morning because you'll be in Montana, skirting the southern edge of Glacier National Park. These are the Rockies now—less forested, but more rugged than the Cascades. About 30 minutes past the West Glacier stop is the little community of Essex. It's a flag stop so chances are you'll just go right on by, but watch for the Isaak Walton Inn on the left side of the train. This little hotel sits right on the Burlington Northern's busy main line and is a favorite train-watching spot for railfans. At least two or three of them will be out in front of the hotel taking your picture—guaranteed!—so get up close to the window and wave as you go by.

In the middle of the morning, you'll leave the Rockies and begin learning firsthand what the phrase "Big Sky Country" means. It will take all day to cross Montana, but don't let anyone tell you this is a boring ride. It's a rolling terrain with vast fields of grain, grazing cattle, and, later on, oil wells. You'll stop at Cut Bank, just 25 miles below the Canadian border. Two stops later it's Havre. Get off the train and take a look at the magnificent steam locomotive on display at the station. You'll begin to see the Missouri River during the afternoon, and will cross it several times.

The *Empire Builder* passes through North Dakota during the night, turning at Grand Forks and following the Red River south. Breakfast will be in Minnesota, perhaps somewhere between St. Cloud and Minneapolis–St. Paul. Just before lunch, the train will cross the Mississippi, quite wide here, and stop at La Crosse, Wisconsin. For the next few hours, it's dairy country. Then comes Milwaukee and, just 90 minutes later, Chicago. What a ride!

Coast Starlight (11, 14)

Between:	Los Angeles and Seattle
Via:	Santa Barbara, San Jose, Oakland, Sacramento, Klamath Falls (OR), Eugene, Portland, Olympia
Operates:	Daily
Distance:	1,389 miles
Duration:	35 hours
Equipment:	Superliner cars—coaches, sleepers, dining car, lounge car

You really get to see a bit of everything on this train, especially on the northbound run, which provides a bit more daylight for some of the scenic highlights. Heading north out of Los Angeles, most of the interesting scenery will be on the left since the train runs along the shoreline part of the way. After the stop at Oxnard, you should be able to see the Channel Islands about 20 miles off shore . . . the big platforms for the offshore oil wells, too.

In mid-afternoon, the *Starlight* stops at the old mission town of San Luis Obispo, then begins climbing up toward Cuesta Pass. If you've followed my suggestion and are sitting on the left, you'll see the entire train as it goes through two horseshoe curves, not to mention the California Men's Colony, a state penitentiary. The train is now entering the Salinas Valley, appropriately called "the Country's Salad Bowl" and will be following the Salinas River, too. At the northern end of the valley you'll pass through Castroville. Take note if you like artichokes, because this is where most of them come from. By the time the sun goes down today, you'll have a good idea how important agriculture is to California.

The *Coast Starlight* doesn't go into Oakland anymore because of severe earthquake damage to the station there so passengers now leave the train at nearby Emeryville. If your destination is San Francisco, Amtrak will have a bus waiting to take you there when the train pulls in at the Emeryville station.

Get to bed early tonight, because you'll want to be awake early in the morning for a stunning view of Mt. Shasta from the left side of the train soon after you leave Dunsmuir, California. In fact, this second day aboard the *Coast Starlight* is one wonderful panorama after another. (By the way, most of the truly spectacular views will be on the *right* side of the train today, after the train leaves Chemult, Oregon.)

From Klamath Falls north is a big logging area so you'll be traveling though forests of Douglas fir. After Chemult, the train climbs to the Cascade Summit—that's Odell Lake down there, and Maiden Peak beyond—and, on a single track, runs along the western side of Willamette Pass and Salt Creek Canyon, giving you a constantly changing vista for many miles. Building this railroad was quite a project. You'll pass through 22 tunnels between here and Eugene! After a stop in Salem, Oregon's capital, the train heads through the Willamette Valley toward Portland.

Hope for a clear day, because as you get closer to Portland, Mount Hood and Mount St. Helens will be on your right. You'll be able to tell which is Mount St. Helens; the violent eruption in 1980 blew away a large part of the peak. It's quite obvious, even from this distance. Leaving Portland, the "City of Roses," the train crosses the Columbia River and stops again in Vancouver. (Okay, everyone . . . back over to the left side of the train!) From here on you'll follow the Columbia River, then run along the edge of Puget Sound through Tacoma and right past the Kingdome into Seattle. It is, as you will find, a wonderful city.

San Joaquins

Between: Emeryville (CA) and Bakersfield
Via: Martinez, Stockton, Merced, Madera, Fresno
Operates: Four times daily each way
Distance: 312 miles
Duration: 6 hours
Equipment: Amfleet cars—coaches, cafe car

These trains run up and down through the middle of California, and since three of the four daily *San Joaquins* complete their runs during daylight hours, viewing opportunities will be the same in either direction. The trains stick pretty much to the huge San Joaquin Valley, with the Sierra Nevada off to the left on the southbound trip; but Amtrak provides connections at stops along the rail route with buses heading in a number of directions. For instance, you can step off the train in Stockton and onto a bus that will take you to San Jose and Monterey. From the Amtrak stop at Merced you can take a bus to Yosemite National Park; and buses from Bakersfield fan out to destinations all over Southern California, including Los Angeles, Palm Springs, Santa Barbara, Disneyland, and even Las Vegas, Nevada.

San Diegans

Between:	Santa Barbara or Los Angeles and San Diego
Via:	Fullerton, Anaheim, San Clemente, Del Mar
Operates:	Several times daily
Distance:	Santa Barbara–San Diego, 232 miles; Los Angeles–San Diego, 129 miles
Duration:	Santa Barbara–San Diego, 6 hours; Los Angeles–San Diego, 3 hours
Equipment:	Amfleet cars—coaches, club coach, lounge car

The *San Diegans* run right along the coast for most of the way between Los Angeles and San Diego, and on most days you'll see lots of swimmers and surfers. You can pick from among several trains that run during daylight hours to enjoy the great scenery in either direction. Just try to get a seat on the right side of the train if you're heading southbound because that's where the ocean will be. There are also some offshore oil platforms visible several miles off the coast. This train is a "push-pull" operation—that is, if the locomotive pulls the train from L.A. to San Diego, it will push it from San Diego back to L.A. This eliminates the need to turn the entire train around in San Diego. The engineer simply moves from the locomotive cab to a little room at the end of what had been the last car. From there he operates the locomotive with a duplicate set of controls during the return trip. It can be a bit startling to see one of these trains go whizzing "backwards" through a grade crossing at 70 or so miles per hour, but it's really a more efficient operation. The engineers are not overly fond of this configuration, feeling (quite correctly, I think) that they are much more vulnerable in the event of a grade-crossing collision should it occur while they're operating from the auxiliary cab.

TRANSCONTINENTAL TRAIN
Sunset Limited (1, 2)

Between:	Los Angeles and Miami
Via:	Phoenix, El Paso, San Antonio, Houston, New Orleans, Mobile, Tallahassee, Jacksonville, Orlando, Fort Lauderdale
Operates:	From Los Angeles and Miami—Sun., Tues., Fri.
Distance:	3,066 miles
Duration:	Eastbound, 69½ hours; westbound, 68¾ hours
Equipment:	Superliner cars—coaches, sleepers, dining car, lounge car

The *Sunset Limited* was a very ambitious undertaking for Amtrak. It is, in fact, the first true transcontinental train in the nation's history since other cross-country trips always required either the passenger or the rail car to change trains somewhere along the way. It's hard to say whether the eastbound or the westbound train offers the most or the best scenery since you'll miss some nice areas in either direction. On balance, I think you'll get to see a bit more on Train 1, the westbound *Sunset,* although the best solution to that dilemma would be a round-trip.

You'll have a nice afternoon run due north from Miami through some of the swank resort communities of Florida's east coast. Your first on-board sunset will occur somewhere south of Jacksonville, where the train swings to the west and heads across the state's panhandle through the night.

Mobile, Alabama, arrives with morning (ask for grits with your eggs and bacon in the dining car), and you can see

Mobile Bay on the left. This is a gracious city and worth taking some time to explore. Angling a bit more to the south, the *Sunset* will nip across that little "tab" at the bottom of Mississippi, stopping at Pascagoula (bird-watching area to the left after leaving), Biloxi (shrimp boats), and Gulfport (big seaport). Last stop in Mississippi is Bay St. Louis, an art colony and very large recreation area. About a half hour after leaving Bay St. Louis and before the New Orleans skyline comes up on the left, you'll pass through Honey Island Swamp. Yes, there are indeed alligators in there, and you'll probably see them sunning themselves if the sun's out.

Just after leaving New Orleans, you'll pass the Superdome, then cross the Mississippi River on the Huey Long Bridge. This bridge is four and a half miles long, some 200 feet high, and must be seen to be believed! The eastbound *Sunset* crosses after dark, which is one more reason I recommend taking this one. For the next several hours the train moves through bayou country. Since the ground is pretty soggy through much of this wetland, most of the tracks were built on pilings. As a matter of fact, you'll notice that the cemeteries all through here are above ground because the water table is so high. Sunset number two happens right about the time you cross into Texas.

Houston and San Antonio come and go during the night, and by morning you'll be near Del Rio. The Rio Grande is to the left and, on the other side, Mexico. About 45 minutes after leaving Del Rio, you'll cross the Pecos River on a very high bridge—320 feet down to the river. This is pretty dry country and lots of cacti and mesquite can be seen now. About 20 minutes farther on, the *Sunset* rolls through the town of Langtry, once the home of the legendary Roy Bean. He wasn't really a judge, but nevertheless proclaimed himself the "only law west of the Pecos" and dispensed his own unique version of justice here for a number of years. Somewhere along the way, Ol' Roy became infatuated with Lily Langtry, a famous British actress, and named the town for her—a dubious honor at best. The *Sunset* heads a bit more to the north now, climbing into the Del Norte Mountains. Just after a stop in Alpine, Texas, you'll cross Paisano Pass, over 5,000 feet in elevation and the highest point of the entire trip. It's after lunch when you reach El Paso, located on the Rio Grande and surrounded by the Franklin Mountains. The railroad station here dates back to 1904 and has been handsomely restored. You'll cross the Rio Grande and into New Mexico just a few minutes after leaving El Paso. It's here that the *Sunset* passes literally within a few feet of the Mexican border, which is marked by a white post just to the left of the train.

You'll cross the Continental Divide shortly after leaving Deming, New Mexico, around mid-afternoon, and will reach the Arizona border an hour later. Mining is big in these parts—gold and silver and copper. Your third sunset on board comes as Amtrak's Train 1 heads for Phoenix.

During the night the *Sunset Limited* crosses the Arizona/California border and, if it's running close to on time, there'll be an early morning arrival into Los Angeles. Three sunsets, three time zones, three thousand miles. Quite a journey!

VIA Rail Canada

WINDSOR-QUEBEC CORRIDOR
VIA Rail's heaviest traffic occurs in the busy 725-mile central corridor between Windsor (just across the Detroit River from Detroit) and Quebec City. VIA trains run at speeds up to 100 miles per hour on much of this track. LRC equipment is used on these routes, and both standard and VIA1 class service is available on all trains. For these corridor trains, I've provided a listing of major routes and travel times to help in planning an itinerary. For specific train numbers, along with departure and arrival times, refer to a VIA timetable or contact VIA Rail directly at their toll-free numbers.

Trains Between	Distance	Duration
Montreal and Quebec	169 miles	2½ hours
Montreal and Ottawa	116 miles	2 hours
Montreal and Toronto	335 miles	4–4½ hours
Ottawa and Toronto	277 miles	4 hours
Toronto and Windsor	223 miles	4 hours

EASTERN TRAINS
Ocean (14, 15)
Between: Montreal and Halifax
Via: Lévis, Mont-Joli, Matapédia, Campbellton, Moncton
Operates: Daily except Tues.
Distance: 840 miles
Duration: 18 hours
Equipment: Coaches, dome/cafe/lounge car, sleepers, dining car, observation car

The *Ocean* leaves Montreal in the early evening, immediately crosses the St. Lawrence, and then swings due east along the river's southern banks. The St. Lawrence is really a major waterway. It will be on the left side of the train for nearly eight hours and, by the time the train turns south at Mont-Joli, the St. Lawrence is nearly 30 miles wide. Unfortunately, because of the train's schedule, it will be dark through most of this area. About the time you wake up, you'll be crossing into the Province of New Brunswick. After making a stop at Campbellton, the train runs south along the coastline with the Gulf of St. Lawrence off to the left. The famous Bay of Fundy is much farther south, but this entire region is known for its extraordinary tides, which rise and fall as much as 50 feet twice a day. At Bathurst, the *Ocean* turns inland, passing through forests and farming country. After leaving Newcastle, the train crosses the upper part of Miramichi Bay, a mecca for fisherman looking for Atlantic salmon, then continues south across country to Moncton and into the Province of Nova Scotia. The *Ocean's* final destination, the city of Halifax, was the jumping-off point for many convoys heading across the North Atlantic for England and Russia during World War II, and it's still a busy seaport. If you're into seafood, you've come to the right area! Like the *Canadian,* this train features VIA's refurbished stainless-steel cars. What a treat.

Chaleur (16, 17)

Between:	Montreal and Gaspé
Via:	Lévis, Mont-Joli, Matapédia
Operates:	From Montreal—Sun., Wed., Fri.; from Gaspé—Mon., Thurs., Sat.
Distance:	654 miles
Duration:	16 hours
Equipment:	Coaches, sleeping cars, dining car

After leaving Montreal at 7:00 P.M., the *Chaleur* follows the St. Lawrence River on the same route as the *Ocean.* During summer months, whales are often seen in the river, which is very wide along here. In the wee hours after a stop at Mont-Joli, the train turns south, then swings east again at Matapédia and heads along the southern shore of the Gaspé Peninsula. That big body of water you'll see off to the right when you wake up will be Chaleur Bay. (*Chaleur* is French for "warm." Personally, I'll take their word for it.) By the time you get to Chandler, Chaleur Bay has become the Gulf of St. Lawrence. This area is heavily forested, with many lakes and rivers, and is a very popular area for hiking, camping, hunting, and fishing. Just in time for lunch, the *Chaleur* reaches the centuries-old town of Gaspé itself. There are several wilderness parks in the immediate area, and many tours are available. This is a great place to hole up and write a novel.

WESTERN TRAINS
Hudson Bay (692, 693)

Between:	Winnipeg and Churchill
Via:	Dauphin, The Pas, Wekusko, Wabowden, Thompson, Gillam
Operates:	From Winnipeg—Sun., Tues., Thurs.; from Churchill—Tues., Thurs., Sat.
Distance:	1,055 miles
Duration:	33½ hours
Equipment:	Coaches, sleepers, dining car

Winnipeg, the *Hudson Bay's* southern terminus, has a population of some 600,000 people and is one of Canada's major cities. Churchill is at the far end of the train's route and at the opposite end of the urban spectrum as well. It's a community of 1,200 souls located on the shores of Hudson Bay and just 600 or so air miles below the Arctic Circle. Between Winnipeg and Churchill, the train passes from prairie into dense forests and finally onto the tundra before reaching Hudson Bay itself. Along the way, it makes 26 scheduled stops, although the timetable lists another 55 "flag stops," where the train will stop if someone wants to get on or off.

There usually aren't many passengers on the *Hudson Bay,* but every year in late September when polar bears appear in and around Churchill, the train runs full for four or five weeks. Compared to the *Canadian* or the *Ocean,* this train is strictly basic transportation. While the cars are old, they're comparable to Amtrak's Heritage fleet and quite serviceable. Just don't expect something new and shiny.

Because it is the only practical way in or out of many very small communities in the northern part of Manitoba, VIA Rail is mandated to operate this train by the Canadian government.

The Canadian (1, 2)

Between:	Toronto and Vancouver
Via:	Sudbury, Sioux Lookout, Winnipeg, Saskatoon, Edmonton, Jasper
Operates:	From Toronto—Tues., Thurs., Sat.; from Vancouver—Mon., Thurs., Sat.
Distance:	2,776 miles
Duration:	Westbound, 71 hours; eastbound, 70 hours
Equipment:	Stainless-steel cars—coaches, dome/cafe/lounges, sleepers, dining car, observation car

This is VIA's premier train and deservedly so. In my opinion, the westbound trip is the one to take because the scenery keeps getting more spectacular as you go. From the rich farmland around Toronto, the *Canadian* travels north before turning west to cross above Lake Superior through a wilderness of lakes, each surrounded by birch and pine forests. Then it's across the vast plains—cattle and wheat country—and into the Canadian Rockies to Jasper before reaching Vancouver and the Pacific. It's an absolutely sensational trip and is really enhanced by the quality of the train itself. The stainless-steel cars have been completely refurbished and the dome cars—there are three on each train—are the best possible way to enjoy the scenic beauty. During the very busy times of year, meaning roughly May through September, this train runs quite full and, as a result, the dining car is reserved for the use of sleeping-car passengers only. Meals for coach passengers are served in one of the two glass-domed Skyline lounge cars that are part of the consist. During other times of the year, there is no food service in the lounge cars, and all passengers are served in the dining car.

Skeena (5, 6)

Between:	Jasper and Prince Rupert
Via:	Prince George, Smithers
Operates:	From Jasper—Wed., Fri., Sun.; from Prince Rupert—Tues., Fri., Sun.

Distance: 721 miles
Duration: 20 1/2 hours
Equipment: Stainless-steel cars—coaches,
             dome/cafe/lounge, sleepers, dining car

The *Skeena* connects with the cross-country *Canadian* in the resort town of Jasper, which is located in the middle of the Canadian Rockies. I have the feeling I've overused the word *spectacular* in describing some of these train rides, but the word certainly applies to the area surrounding Jasper. It's well worth stopping here for a few days. From Jasper, the *Skeena* heads northwest through the Rockies, crossing into British Columbia and continuing through the Bulkley Valley to meet the Skeena River, which it follows all the way to the Pacific Ocean and its destination, Prince Rupert. Gorgeous all the way!

Malahat (198, 199)

Between: Victoria and Courtenay
Operates: Daily
Distance: 140 miles
Duration: 4 1/2 hours
Equipment: Self-propelled rail diesel cars

Vancouver Island is the largest island in the Pacific Ocean off the coast of North America—roughly 300 miles long—and this train is an excellent way to see a good part of it. In fact, very few train rides pack as much fabulous scenery into such a short period of time as this one does. From the town of Victoria, the *Malahat* passes through some heavily forested areas before beginning to climb up toward Malahat Pass. The train will be crossing some deep gorges and a VIA Rail booklet suggests that anyone who gets a bit queasy from heights might prefer sitting on the left side of the train. (They aren't kidding, folks!) After descending from the pass, the train passes a number of lakes followed by some very picturesque farming country. You'll be crossing a number of rivers for the next several miles. If you're a fisherman, just get off anywhere along here. Whatever spot you pick will be the right one. About halfway through the trip, the train will cross the Nanaimo River. There's another bridge, higher and off to the west— a favorite spot for those who hook themselves to a big rubber band and jump off. If a bungee-jumper happens to be poised on the railing as you go by, the *Malahat* will stop on the bridge to give everyone aboard a ringside seat. From many spots along here you can look east, off to the right, and see Washington State across the Strait of Georgia and, to the left, the mountain range running down the center of the island. Fishing has always been important to the local people and, for that matter, to the wildlife, too. Keep your eyes peeled for bald eagles in this area, by the way. The last stop is Courtenay, a town of 10,000 and a jump-off point for hikers and skiers. If you want to, on most days you can leave Victoria fairly early in the morning, spend an hour in Courtenay, then catch a return train that will get you back before 8:00 P.M. But consider at least an overnight in Courtenay. You can savor the prospect of that return train ride over a nice dinner.

CHAPTER 15

Is There a Train in Our Future?

M ost Americans are surprised to learn that people in other parts of the world are riding trains in comfort and safety at speeds approaching 200 miles per hour. What's really amazing is that it's all being done with traditional technology: electric locomotives taking power from an overhead wire to pull cars with steel wheels along steel rails. That's the way railroads have been running their fastest trains for 50 years and, although exotic new technology is well on the way, that's probably how we'll be doing it for a while to come yet. It's equally amazing to many that, so far, the United States is not part of this train renaissance. After all, we've been a leader in the transportation field for 200 years, dating back to John Fitch's steamboat and including the Wright brothers, Henry Ford, Neil Armstrong, and a thousand others in between.

Is Everyone Else Wrong?

The fact is that every other industrialized country in the world has seen the advantages of a rail passenger system that moves people rapidly and efficiently. Most countries have already built such systems and are now busy expanding and updating them. The rest are planning and building high-speed rail lines as fast as they can.

Japan began its famous "bullet train" service in 1964. The first trains ran at 125 miles per hour along a 320-mile route between Tokyo and Osaka. That original system has since been expanded to more than 1,300 miles and carries 400,000 passengers every day at speeds up to 170 miles per hour. The on-time performance of the Japanese trains is extraordinary, to say the least. In his definitive book, *Supertrains,* Joe Vranitch notes that in 1989 the Japanese compiled figures for all trains for which late arrivals had been reported. The average was 28 *seconds*.

In France, the famous TGV (*train à grande vitesse*—literally "high-speed train") now routinely operates at speeds up to 186 miles per hour with trains running as close as ten minutes apart during busiest times. A ride on the TGV is quite remarkable—smooth, quiet, and without any real sensation of traveling at such speed. On-time performance is 98 percent. By the way, neither the French nor the Japanese system has ever experienced a passenger fatality.

High-speed trains are also running in Germany, Great Britain, Spain, Austria, Sweden, and Denmark, among other countries—all at speeds of 140 miles per hour and up. New high-speed rail lines are being planned in Portugal, Russia, Turkey, Greece, Taiwan, Australia . . . almost everywhere. Except here.

Have you ever made that grueling four-plus-hour drive across the desert from Los Angeles to Las Vegas? A train like the TGV could get you there in *two* hours. It's an idea that makes sense and has been discussed. There's been talk about high-speed trains for other areas, too—in the Northwest, connecting Portland, Tacoma, Seattle, and Vancouver; back east, linking Philadelphia with Harrisburg and Pittsburgh; in Florida, taking people from either Tampa or Miami to Disney World in Orlando; and in Canada, along the corridor from Windsor through Ottawa and Montreal to Quebec. Several other areas are being considered, too.

The trouble is, until there's real commitment from Washington, D.C., or from the Canadian government in that country, it's not going to happen. Certainly not in the United States as long as influential voices in Congress still seem willing to let Amtrak wither and die. It's a position that's hard to understand, given the obvious success high-speed trains have had in all these other countries. Under similar circumstances within his own field, I've often heard a shrewd and successful banker/friend of mine ask, "What do they all know that I don't know?" It's a sensible and obvious question. Why aren't we asking it about high-speed rail?

Do We Really Need High-Speed Trains?

Let's start with what would seem to be two safe assumptions: First, our population will continue to increase. Second, all those people will want the same kind of mobility we enjoy now. If those assumptions prove to be true—and they will, of course—it will invariably mean more cars on more highways. It will also mean more airplanes flying around, but in the *same* amount of sky. In other words, more congestion, more pollution, and more safety concerns.

But what if we didn't commit those mega-billions to support and expand our auto/plane transportation habit? What if, as a nation, we threw our resources into building a nationwide passenger rail system instead, with high-speed trains operating in and around 15 or 20 of the major urban areas? The answer is, people would travel just as efficiently, just as fast, and in greater safety. Furthermore, we could stop and probably reverse the degradation of our environment caused by our out-of-balance addiction to the automobile and the airplane. The catch is, it can only be done if people can be convinced that the high-speed train is indeed a reasonable transportation alternative.

Trains Are as Fast as Planes

Well, all right, a train certainly won't get you from New York to California as fast as a passenger jet, but it quite possibly will be comparable for a trip under 300 miles. That's a two-hour run for a high-speed train, and from city-center to city-center it will give the commercial jet a run for its money.

It's hardly state-of-the-art, but consider Amtrak's Metroliner service between New York City and Washington, D.C. Even today, those trains will take you from Washington's Union Station (just a few hundred yards from the Capitol itself) to mid-town Manhattan in just a tad under three hours. Try doing that by air! You'll be hard pressed to make it any quicker—taxi from the Capitol to the airport; wait to check in, to board, to take off; and after the actual flight, it's another very long cab ride into Manhattan. No wonder almost half of the people traveling between New York and Washington are now doing so relaxed and in comfort on the train. And running over the same tracks, a European-style high-speed train could cut the time between those cities by another 20 to 40 minutes.

The fact is, 300–400 miles is the distance most of us travel most often. That's certainly the case at Chicago's O'Hare Airport, busiest in the nation, where over 40 percent of the arriving flights are from destinations 300 miles away or less. (O'Hare is typical, not unique, by the way. The number is almost the same for Los Angeles International and is over 50 percent at San Francisco International and New York's Kennedy Airport.) Proponents of high-speed rail have long argued that trains could carry people between Chicago and other nearby cities in the midwest—Milwaukee, St. Louis, Indianapolis, Ft. Wayne, Toledo, Detroit, Cincinnati, and a host of smaller towns— faster, cheaper, and safer than planes. They're already doing it in Europe, after all. Alas, because of crowded skies around Chicago from air traffic at O'Hare and Midway airports, and because of pressure to provide even more flights, a third major airport south of that city is still a possibility. The cost would be staggering—in the billions of dollars, in the thousands of acres of land, in the displacement of homes and businesses, and in the impact on the environment.

High-Speed Rail Is Cheaper to Build

Yes, it is! Depending on the terrain, it costs anywhere from $50 million to $200 million per mile to build a typical interstate highway. New modern airports are currently costing $2 billion to $5 billion each and, depending on which expert you talk to, this country supposedly "needs" from ten to twenty new ones. You and I will be paying for those airports, of course, either with our tax dollars or in the form of higher air fares, which the airlines must charge to cover the increased landing fees they'll be forced to pay. The cost for building a high-speed rail system? Again depending on the terrain, about $30 million per mile—and that's including the trains themselves. Even exotic new maglev (magnetic levitation) systems are cheaper to build than highways or airports.

Trains Are Better for the Environment

This one is a slam dunk for rail. New highways and airports gobble up thousands of acres of land (land that never again generates property taxes for the local governments, by the way). Particulate pollution from automobiles and jet planes fills the air in most of our major cities, where it's measured and actually calculated by the *ton*. In his forward to *Supertrains,* author Tom Clancy offers an extreme but illustrative example. He points out that "the *Concorde* . . . weighs 400,000 pounds when it takes off from the United States and 200,000 when it lands in England, having left 100 tons of fuel in its supersonic wake." Then there's the whole problem of noise pollution.

Electrically powered high-speed trains, on the other hand, have no exhaust and therefore emit no pollution. The amount of land used by two parallel tracks is obviously a great deal less than would be required for an interstate highway—in fact, in many instances, the rail line would be built along the existing highway's right-of-way. As far as noise is concerned, a high-speed train is roughly as loud as a stream of traffic, the difference being that noise from the automobiles is virtually continuous, while the train passes quickly once every 20–30 minutes.

Trains Are More Energy Efficient

Another easy one. Calculated on a per-passenger-mile basis, a high-speed train uses less than two-thirds the energy consumed by an automobile and only about *one-fifth* as much as a jet plane. We can really begin to see the potential benefits by comparing energy consumption in the U.S. with areas in Europe where high-speed rail is a viable alternative to the private automobile. On a per capita basis, Americans use almost 450 gallons of gasoline a year, while residents of a typical European city use just over 100 gallons.

And Safer, Too

Most of us are painfully aware of the carnage that occurs year after year on our highways—roughly 40,000 killed and many times that number injured. Statistically, planes are many times safer than automobiles, but there are serious concerns about our ability to maintain that high standard. The airlines of the world are now using about 12,000 planes to carry their passengers, but over the next ten years industry experts say about 7,000 new planes will be added to those fleets. The lion's share will be flying around in American skies. If there is legitimate concern about aviation safety now, how safe will we be with a 60 percent increase in the number of commercial aircraft? And if safety *isn't* a serious concern, why all the pressure for so many new multi-billion-dollar airports?

So how safe are trains . . . really? Well, if done right, a high-speed rail system is perfectly safe. Certainly in the case of the French and Japanese systems, we can take that statement literally—neither system has ever experienced a serious accident. Here at home, it's quite true that Amtrak has been less than perfect, although I know of no serious accident involving a passenger train where responsibility has been laid at Amtrak's doorstep. In the worst incident, when some 40 people were killed, a barge collided with a bridge in dense fog, knocking the tracks out of alignment just moments before the train started across. Over its 24-year history, Amtrak has compiled an excellent safety record, and the fact remains that you're many times safer on a cross-country train ride that you are driving your own car to the local convenience store for a bottle of aspirin.

Ideally—and it's the way they do it in Japan and France—passenger trains should operate on their own exclusive rights-of-way. Except for most of the Northeast corridor, however, Amtrak is forced to share tracks with freight trains, meaning increased traffic operating at vastly different speeds. It's a safe arrangement, but one that often requires slower speeds or lengthy delays for Amtrak trains.

Small Towns Need Trains

Often overlooked in the plane-car-train argument are the thousands of communities all over the U.S. and Canada for which the train is the *only* public transportation link to the rest of the country. Canada's VIA Rail, for instance, runs a thrice-weekly train that passes through more than eighty tiny communities on its thousand-mile journey north from Winnipeg to Hudson Bay. Amtrak also serves countless little towns all over America that have no airports and are bypassed even by buses. Obviously, high-speed trains will never be a realistic option for most of these communities, but people in these small towns will be more than glad if they can simply keep their existing service—1950s technology and all.

Maglev Is Coming . . . Fast!

Just when we're beginning to grasp the idea of traveling up to 200 miles per hour on land, along comes yet another new transportation technology: *magnetic levitation.* Think it's some kind of exotic, pie-in-the-sky science fiction? Wrong! Maglev is already here, and it really works. As with so many great ideas, the basic concept is quite simple.

We've all held a magnet in each hand and, by turning them one way or another, felt them either attract or repel each other. In a nutshell, that's how maglev works. Large electrically powered magnets are built into both the train and the guideway and, by using their pushing and pulling forces, the train can be lifted free of its track and moved forward. As I said, this is not futuristic stuff. Maglev vehicles are currently being run on test tracks in several parts of the world, and one, in Japan, has reached a speed of 323 miles per hour. Engineers in Japan say that there is no reason why a speed of 600 miles an hour can't be achieved. (Perhaps *passenger terror* would be considered a valid reason. Clearly, there must come a point when, no matter how smooth the ride might be, extreme speeds at ground level become fearful for anyone without the psyche of a test-pilot.)

Because the maglev train has literally no contact with the guideway, there is no friction and virtually no sound. Witnesses at a maglev test track in Germany reported being able to hear a pair of crows cawing nearby while the train was racing by.

Although potentially able to travel much faster than today's bullet trains and France's TGV (see figure), a maglev system offers virtually the same benefits: It's energy efficient, pollution free, and quite safe. Furthermore, once all testing and certification have been completed and maglev trains can be ordered up "off the shelf," best estimates now say that the cost of building a maglev system will be about the same as for high-speed rail. Even if you have just a casual interest in this futuristic stuff, stay tuned . . . because we ain't seen nothin' yet!

First, Some Little Steps

Maglev is all well and good, but the more immediate problem is to keep our conventional rail system up and running until a few more people in power see the light. To that end, Amtrak has some modest plans for the near future, which could mean some significant improvement in rail service for at least a few parts of the country. The short-term goal is to find a way to increase the average speed of their trains along some of the busier eastern routes. Too many curves along some stretches of track are now preventing trains from going faster; where the track is straighter, the existing equipment is already operating at top speed.

Within the past few years, Amtrak has tested two European trains for possible use in this country. First was the Swedish X-2000, which features computer-controlled cars that tilt as the train rounds curves, helping to neutralize the effects of centrifugal force on passengers and allowing the train to travel at higher average speeds. Soon after the X-2000, Amtrak tested a German ICE (Intercity Express), which is now operating at speeds up to 186 miles per hour on some of the new rail lines in that country. Amtrak put both the Swedish and the German trains into service on regular runs

France's high-speed trains, the TGV, now routinely operate at speeds approaching 200 mph.

in several areas. The results, including reaction from passengers, have been analyzed and will be used to prepare specifications for high-speed equipment to be built specifically for Amtrak's needs. The problem, as always, will be money.

What About the "S" Word?

That's "S" for *subsidy,* which is still considered a dirty word by many. Strangely, there are those who see nothing wrong with heavy government support of municipal bus systems, but are opposed to any subsidy where Amtrak is concerned. Yet in one way or another government subsidizes *every* form of public transportation. There are no exceptions. Government builds highways for cars and buses; government builds airports for planes; government even builds bike paths and sidewalks.

But wait, you say, government doesn't subsidize American or Delta or United Airlines, so why should the taxpayers assist Amtrak? Ah, but government *does* subsidize the airlines. There are lots of examples, but the most obvious is our nationwide air traffic control system, which is run by the FAA, an agency of the federal government. Amtrak and all the other private railroads have traffic control systems, too, but pay all the costs themselves. Cities and states float bonds to build and expand airports. (Honolulu International Airport has been under construction to one degree or another without interruption since the early 1960s.) And remember, too, that you and I pay a special tax on every airline ticket we buy. That money goes into a separate trust fund and is spent to advance the aviation industry.

Not one rail system in the world, which is intended for the use of the general public, is *not* subsidized by government. So why do some politicians continue to insist that Amtrak should be able to provide a nationwide rail transportation system without assistance from the government? Why, especially, when it's so clear to many of us that for some very important reasons—environmental, economic, and social—rail should be the one means of transportation government *en*courages, not *dis*courages.

Amtrak's Going to Make It

There are those in this country—people who know a great deal about trains and the transportation industry—who are worried about the future of rail travel in North America. And well they should be. After all, for twelve years it was a stated goal of the Reagan and Bush administrations to do away with any subsidy for Amtrak, and there are plenty of anti-rail people left in Congress at a time when budget-cutting is on everyone's mind. Still, in spite of it all, there is some cause for hope if not optimism.

First and foremost, I suppose, given even passable equipment and service, Americans have made it abundantly clear that they *like* trains. Long-distance trains in particular run full much of the year, particularly in the sleeping cars. During the summer months, even Amtrak critics agree that the company could double the number of trains and still fill them up.

Second, in spite of tremendous handicaps, Amtrak is getting its act together little by little. In fact, Amtrak can actually lay claim to being the most cost-efficient national rail system in the world by at least one very important yardstick: The company's revenue now covers a full 80 percent of its operating costs. No other public rail system anywhere can come close to that. By comparison, VIA Rail Canada recovers about 60 percent of its operating costs from revenues.

Make no mistake, however: Amtrak will always need support from federal and state governments. Indeed, several states already subsidize certain Amtrak trains operating within their borders because they recognize that those trains are providing essential transportation links for their citizens.

What Amtrak really needs—in fact, all Amtrak has *ever* needed—is a stable source of adequate funding. The key words are *stable* and *adequate*. How can Amtrak be expected to plan for the orderly replacement of worn-out equipment, for example, if they have no idea from one year to the next how much support they'll be getting from the federal government?

With stable and adequate funding, however, Amtrak *could* do what it *wants* to do: buy new equipment, reduce mechanical breakdowns, provide more trains on its popular routes, run them at more convenient times, improve on-time performance, and—Okay, so this is my own personal addition to the list—wash every window on every train every day. Sound like a good program? Well, an equally good plan for funding it has been floating around in Congress for some time.

A Penny for Amtrak

It's such a simple idea: earmark one cent per gallon of the gasoline tax for Amtrak. That one penny would provide a reliable, adequate, and predictable source of revenue, roughly $1 billion a year, which would be about double what Amtrak now receives in support from the federal government. Even more important, that one penny would signify America's long-term commitment to rail transportation, with all the positive implications that holds for energy consumption and the environment. There's also a wonderful element of justice in having the automobile, our biggest single source of pollution, provide the means of saving and perpetuating the passenger train, which is environmentally benign.

What Can Be Done?

Several things, none very difficult.

Write letters. We all get to vote for (or against) one member of Congress, two U.S. senators, and the president. Letters from constituents are effective. Nothing will have more impact. Keep each letter short and to the point. Tell them you think the United States should have a decent passenger rail system and that the Penny for Amtrak would be a good way to make it happen.

Join the club. There are many nonprofit groups around the country that actively promote rail transportation at the state and local levels. I've included a list in the back of this book. The organization focusing on Congress and the current administration in Washington, D.C., is the National Association of Railroad Passengers. If you're interested in supporting Amtrak and advancing the cause of high-speed rail, I would certainly encourage you to join. For more information, call 202-408-8362. NARP's annual dues are $25. Mail a check to:

National Association of Railroad Passengers
900 Second St., NE
Washington, DC 20002

Take a train ride! Amtrak needs the money. For that matter, VIA Rail does, too. Besides, now that you've read this book, you'll certainly know how to get the most possible enjoyment from the trip.

So . . . All Aboard!

A Few Suggested Itineraries

Here are some examples of long-distance train trips that will provide plenty of great scenery plus an opportunity for some sightseeing along the way. You won't need many suggestions from me before you begin plotting your own. It will help if you refer to Amtrak and VIA Rail system maps on pages 39–39 and 215. You can begin these trips from any of the principal cities included in the itinerary. For instance, in the Big City Tour listed on the next page, you can start your trip from New York just as easily as you can from Chicago.

For more detailed information about specific trains mentioned here, refer to Chapter 14. A number of these itineraries have been specifically suggested because they include only three stopovers and therefore qualify for an All Aboard America fare. Don't worry too much about meeting the three-stop criteria, however. A knowledgeable travel agent can often figure out ways to minimize any extra charge. In fact, I'll show you one of the best ways in a couple of the itineraries following.

Finally, you should also get ahold of the latest edition of Amtrak's Travel Planner, which includes a good variety of preplanned rail tours. You can obtain a free copy by calling Amtrak's Great American Vacations at 1-800-321-8684.

Big City Tour

CHICAGO–WASHINGTON, D.C.–
NEW YORK–BOSTON–CHICAGO

Take the *Capitol Limited* from Chicago to Washington, because it's the most scenic train between those two cities. Plan to spend at least several days in Washington, then head up to New York City. Take a Metroliner so you can experience a 125-mile-per-hour train ride. New York is worth several days, too—museums, Broadway shows, great restaurants. The *New England Express* is a good choice when you go up to Boston. It's a more scenic choice because it runs along the Connecticut shoreline and has a nice mid-afternoon arrival. Italian food in the North End, the Red Sox at Fenway Park, or colonial history all over town. Boston's got it! From here, it's the *Lake Shore Limited* across New York State, along three of the Great Lakes, and back into Chicago.

This trip stays entirely within the eastern zone and includes three stopovers, thereby qualifying for the lowest fare.

Glaciers to Glitz

SAN FRANCISCO–SEATTLE–GLACIER
PARK–CHICAGO–TRUCKEE–SAN FRANCISCO

If you want variety, this itinerary certainly has it. First, hop the northbound *Coast Starlight* for one of the more scenic rides in the Amtrak system, through the Cascade Mountains on up to Seattle. From there, board the *Empire Builder* and, after more of the Cascades, get off at either Essex or Glacier Park in Montana while you're still in the Rockies. Catch the same train a few days later, whenever you're ready, and head east to Chicago. See the sights in the Windy City, then head west on the *California Zephyr* through the Rockies and across the desert to Truckee, a wonderful little town in the Sierra Nevadas. After a day or so, catch the *Zephyr* once again and continue on into San Francisco. (Actually, the train terminates in Emeryville, near Oakland, and an Amtrak bus will take you into San Francisco.)

Sharp eyes will note that this itinerary includes *four* stops—Seattle, Glacier Park, Chicago, and Truckee—which is not permitted on an All Aboard America fare. The answer? Use that special fare from San Francisco as far as Truckee, which includes most of the itinerary. Then buy a coach seat on a regular fare for the relatively short daytime ride from there back to San Francisco. That's one of the tricks of the trade a smart travel agent can help you with.

A Western Triangle

LOS ANGELES–SAN FRANCISCO–PORTLAND–DENVER–
LAS VEGAS–LOS ANGELES

Here's another one-zone itinerary. Start in Los Angeles and take the *Coast Starlight* up to San Francisco for a few days of fine dining and sightseeing. Then catch the *Starlight* again and continue on up the coast to Portland. From here, head southeast through the Columbia River Gorge and all the way to Denver on the *Pioneer.* Now you go west, young man, on the *Desert Wind*—through the Rockies, across the desert to Las Vegas. Two or three days is more than enough time to see a few shows and lose the rest of your money. Just don't sell your train ticket, because you're taking the *Desert Wind* again, back to L.A.

Once again, use the All Aboard America fare to get you from L.A. all the way around to Las Vegas. From there, buy your return ticket to Los Angeles at regular price.

Big Mountains, Little Towns

LOS ANGELES–SANTA FE–GALESBURG–GRANBY–LOS ANGELES

This trip starts with the *Southwest Chief,* which takes you from Los Angeles to Santa Fe and, after a few days there, on over Raton Pass and across the plains to Galesburg, Illinois. This is a small town except for a long weekend in June when it hosts an annual event called Railroad Days. Worth seeing! From Galesburg, head west on the *California Zephyr,* hopping off in the little town of Granby, Colorado, for a few days of fishing or riding or just gazing at those mountains. Then it's the *Desert Wind* straight back to Los Angeles—this time *without* a stop in Las Vegas.

Oh, Canada!

CHICAGO–TORONTO–VANCOUVER–SEATTLE–
SAN FRANCISCO–CHICAGO

Let's plug VIA Rail into this itinerary, specifically that famous ride across the Canadian Rockies. From Chicago, take the *International* through Battle Creek (home of the cornflake) to Toronto. Try the glass elevator to the top of the CN tower, or see a baseball game at Sky Dome. Then settle into those great sleeping-car accommodations on the *Canadian* for the 3,000-mile trip across Canada to Vancouver. From there you'll take an Amtrak bus back across the U.S. border to Seattle, where you can spend a few days before catching the *Coast Starlight* down through the Cascade Mountains to San Francisco. Then it's the *California Zephyr* back through our own Rockies and across the Corn Belt to Chicago.

The Santa Fe Trail

CHICAGO–DODGE CITY–SANTA FE–GRAND CANYON–
LOS ANGELES–CHICAGO

Here's one that takes advantage of the special air/rail fares Amtrak has worked out with United Airlines. It also involves just one train, the *Southwest Chief,* but what a trip it is. You'll leave Chicago in the late afternoon, crossing the Mississippi just after dark. Western history buff? Spend a day in Dodge City and visit Boot Hill. Then on to Santa Fe where you'll be dazzled by the silver jewelry made by Native American craftsmen. Two or three days here is a must. Back on the *Chief* again, this time getting off at

Flagstaff, Arizona. The Grand Canyon is just 80 miles away, and an Amtrak bus will be waiting at the station to take you there. (Do they think of everything, or what!) It'll be bedtime when you reboard the train a day or so later, so get a good night's sleep and be ready for an early morning arrival in Los Angeles. Take your time seeing the sights in L.A., then fly straight back to Chicago—it's all part of your air/rail fare. If you live on the west coast, you can take this same trip in reverse order. The one thing you can't do, of course, is begin this itinerary somewhere in the middle.

The Grand Tour

NEW YORK–WASHINGTON, D.C.–ORLANDO (DISNEY WORLD)–
NEW ORLEANS–LOS ANGELES–SAN FRANCISCO–
SEATTLE–CHICAGO–BOSTON–NEW YORK CITY
With this trip you can say you traveled around the country and mean it literally. You'll see the Atlantic Ocean from the *Silver Meteor* and the Gulf of Mexico from the *Sunset Limited,* which will also take you within a few feet of the Mexican border. The Pacific Ocean will be in plain sight off to your left as the *Coast Starlight* travels north, and, heading east across Big Sky Country, the *Empire Builder* comes within 25 miles of Canada. You'll run along the shores of three of the Great Lakes on the *Lake Shore Limited,* and end up back at Long Island Sound on the *Yankee Clipper.* When you stop and think about it, that's really quite remarkable, isn't it? Especially when you consider the variety of people and cultures and activities you'll encounter in all those cities along the way.

Semi-Grand Tour

SEATTLE–CHICAGO–NEW ORLEANS–LOS ANGELES–
SAN FRANCISCO–SEATTLE
For this abbreviated version of our 'round-the-country trip, we just lop off the eastern part of the country. We start in

Seattle, heading east on the *Empire Builder* to Chicago. There we take the *City of New Orleans* due south to that very same city. After at least several days of good food and great music, we take the *Sunset Limited* to Los Angeles, connecting with the *Coast Starlight* for the run up the California coast to San Francisco, then on up through Oregon and back to Seattle.

Fall Colors I

PHILADELPHIA–PITTSBURGH–CHICAGO–WASHINGTON, D.C.–
PHILADELPHIA

If you can time things so you hit the peak of the fall colors, this will be a sensational trip. Take the *Pennsylvanian* from New York to Pittsburgh because the entire ride is done during daylight hours. Stay over there for a day or so if you wish, or have a nice dinner while waiting for the *Broadway Limited,* which comes through later in the evening en route to Chicago. From there, take the *Cardinal* or the *Capitol Limited* back to Washington. It's a glorious trip at any time of the year, but really something special in the fall. After a few days in Washington, zip back to Philadelphia on a Metroliner.

Fall Colors II

NEW YORK CITY–SARATOGA SPRINGS–
TICONDEROGA–MONTREAL–NEW YORK CITY

You can wait until the foliage is at its peak, then do this trip on a weekend with just a shoulder bag. Take the *Adirondak* north out of New York City up the Hudson River to Albany, then cross country into Canada. Spend the night in Montreal—there's an excellent hotel that's actually part of the station complex—and take the same train back to New York the next day.

Take this same train during the summertime if you have a week or ten days, and it becomes quite a different trip. First stop is Saratoga Springs, quite the spot during racing season. Next, soak up some history in the museum at Fort Ticonderoga and spend a day or two in the Lake George area. Lake Placid is just a few miles away, too. Then meet up with the *Adirondak* again and head on up to Montreal. While there, since you're interested in historical sites, you might as well visit Quebec City, too. It's less than three hours away by Via Rail's Train 24, the *Chaudière.* This eighteenth-century city will keep you fascinated for at least two or three days. Then it's back to Montreal to catch the *Adirondak* home to New York.

Southern Comfort

WASHINGTON, D.C.–ATLANTA–NEW ORLEANS–MOBILE–
JACKSONVILLE–CHARLESTON–WASHINGTON, D.C.
You start this tour of our southern states aboard the *Crescent,* which leaves Washington at dinner time and reaches Atlanta just after breakfast. Stop for a visit here if you wish, or stay aboard all the way to New Orleans. When you're finally ready to leave (it could be several days), catch the eastbound *Sunset Limited.* You can either get off in Mobile—they say the Deep South is actually north of this city!—or stay aboard across the Florida panhandle to Jacksonville. As long as you're here, you really should take an extra day for a visit to St. Augustine, just 30 miles to the south. Back in Jacksonville, you catch the *Silver Meteor* north for Charleston, South Carolina, then reboard the *Meteor* a few days later for the overnight ride back up to Washington.

Travel with a Reason

Somehow, train trips seem to be more successful if there's a specific purpose woven into them. Think about putting together a rail itinerary based on a special interest or hobby: the Old West, the Civil War, major league baseball, rail museums, prospective colleges for your 16-year-old son or daughter, visits to old friends, and so on and so forth. As you can see, the opportunities and possibilities are almost endless. Take your time. The only thing more fun than the planning is the doing.

APPENDIX B

Good Places to Stay

Elsewhere in this book I've warned against trying to make close connections when changing trains on long-distance trips. For many different reasons, trains can be late—sometimes very late—and missed connections are often the unpleasant result. If that happens, at the very least you will be inconvenienced and your carefully planned train excursion badly disrupted. It's just much safer to break up your trip with an overnight stay.

You can choose to stop and spend a few nights anywhere along the way during a rail journey, of course, but the cities included here are the most common connecting points in rail itineraries. A look at the system maps for Amtrak and VIA Rail will show you at a glance how the routes intersect. All hotels mentioned are close to the railroad station and, while only a few are what I would call "ritzy," you will find them all clean, well appointed, and quite satisfactory. Some even offer rather special experiences, which have been so noted. Please bear in mind that the principal criteria here is convenience to the railroad station. To me, that's of primary importance if you're overnighting in a city—perhaps arriving in the afternoon on one train and leaving the next morning on another. If you're going to be in one of these cities for several days, however, proximity to the station could be of less importance than being more centrally located.

I have provided only a general indication as to what you might expect to pay at any of these hotels. For one thing, rates can change dramatically depending on the day of the week or the season. Furthermore, it's all relative, anyway. A room rate of $100 might be expensive in one city and very moderate in another. As a general rule, however, you can expect to pay somewhere between $75 and $150 per night at most of these hotels.

Chicago

THE MIDLAND HOTEL
172 West Adams at LaSalle
Chicago, IL 60603
312-332-1200

If you're traveling by rail from almost anywhere in the east to almost anywhere in the west, you'll probably have to change trains in Chicago, which explains why more rail connections occur here than at any other point in the Amtrak system. Consider that a real plus, because Chicago itself is all the reason you need for breaking your trip for a day or so. Union Station, which has recently undergone extensive renovation, is smack downtown on Canal Street, literally in the shadow of the Sears Tower. Also nearby on the shore of Lake Michigan is an outstanding aquarium, not to mention a galaxy of shops and stores and museums. Then, of course, there are the Cubs, the White Sox, the Bears, the Bulls, the Blackhawks. . . .

The Midland Hotel is closest to Union Station and, happily, it's a delightful one—reasonable rates, not too big, and recently re-done in original art deco, which seems to fit well with the Golden Age of train travel. The staff is genuinely friendly, from the hotel's telephone operator to the general manager. Guests get a complimentary full-on breakfast buffet (includes made-to-order omelettes) and a free drink during afternoon cocktail hour. The hotel's other restaurant, called The Exchange, is really outstanding. It's a bit of a walk to the station, but the hotel will take you there free in their own English taxi as long as you give them some advance notice.

Denver

The Oxford Hotel
1600 17th Street
Denver, CO 80202
800-228-5838

One of Amtrak's biggest and most popular trains, the *California Zephyr,* passes through Denver and, in fact, a lot of people elect to get off here and continue their journey after a few days of touring in and around the Mile High City.

The Oxford Hotel itself is, in my humble opinion, worth an overnight stay in Denver. Located literally a few hundred yards from the main entrance to Denver's Union Station, it's undeniably the city's oldest hotel, first opening in 1891. And, if it's possible for a small hotel to be *grand* at the same time, this one is. The owners spent a great deal of money restoring the Oxford in the 1980s, and the result is a wonderful tasteful elegance. For example, sherry is served to hotel guests every afternoon at 4:00 P.M. in the lobby. No two rooms are alike, each being decorated individually, and many come with very nice antique furniture. Oh, yes, there are real down pillows on the beds—always the mark of a hotel that goes a step or two beyond the cosmetic. The rates are reasonable, too, starting at around $80.

Essex, Montana

Isaak Walton Inn
Isaak Walton Inn Road
Essex, MT 59936
406-888-5700

Okay, so this isn't one of the great railroad centers of our country. But Essex is a kind of Mecca for rail enthusiasts because it's located right on the Burlington Northern's main line and a lot of rail traffic, including Amtrak's *Empire Builder*, goes through here all day long. And by the way, Essex is located on the southern edge of Glacier National Park, which means it's smack in the middle of some truly glorious country.

The Isaak Walton Inn is perfectly situated just a 100 yards or so from the tracks and railfans/guests hang out at the hotel watching, waving, and clicking away with their cameras as the trains rumble by. The hotel staff gives new meaning to the word "friendly"; the rooms are rather plain, but spotless; and the price is right. Several "deluxe" units have been created from old cabooses. Clearly, this hotel isn't for everyone, but I do think most folks who spend a day or so here will agree that it was worth doing.

Los Angeles

THE NEW OTANI HOTEL & GARDEN
120 South Los Angeles St.
Los Angeles, CA 90012
800-421-8795

No less than four of Amtrak's long-distance trains originate here in Los Angeles: the *Desert Wind* and the *Southwest Chief* to Chicago, the *Coast Starlight* to Seattle, and the transcontinental *Sunset Limited* to Miami. In addition, the *San Diegans* depart several times daily on their three-hour trip to the south. All this rail activity means you may well have need to spend a night or two here between trains. Of course Los Angeles is so sprawled out, it makes even more sense to pick a nice hotel as near as possible to Los Angeles Union Passenger Terminal. (By the way, while you're there, take a few minutes to enjoy a look around this great old station.)

The New Otani is just 4¹/₂ blocks away and an easy walk from the station unless you're weighed down with baggage. I'd also recommend taking a taxi from the station to the New Otani late at night. The hotel is in an area known as Little Tokyo, and there's a spot quite close by with shops and open-air booths selling clothing, food, jewelry, and many other items mostly with a Latin American flavor. The hotel itself features excellent restaurants and a Japanese Garden.

Montreal

THE QUEEN ELIZABETH
900 René Levesque Blvd.
Montreal, Quebec H3B 4A5
Canada
514-861-3511

This is a wonderful city in which to find yourself between trains. Many Americans are surprised to discover that it is very much a French city. In fact, Montreal is the second largest French-speaking city in the world. (Yes, Paris is number one.) Coming into Canada by train from the U.S., you'll either end up here or in Toronto. And, whether your rail itinerary has you going from here to Toronto and points west, or east to New Brunswick and Nova Scotia, you'll probably want to layover here.

The Hotel Queen Elizabeth is actually part of the huge Montreal railroad station complex, and you can literally walk from your hotel room to your train or the local subway without going out-of-doors. (For four or five months a year, that's a distinct advantage!) In fact, the hotel sits right above an 18-mile network of underground promenades, with a large variety of shops and restaurants. The hotel is well furnished, offers two quite excellent restaurants, and has every amenity you would expect from a top quality hotel. Royalty from many countries have stopped here—yes, including Queen Elizabeth II. The hotel has quite a spread of rates so you can opt for the very plush if you wish. Rates for the rest of us begin at about $100 (U.S.).

New Orleans

MAISON DUPUY HOTEL
1001 Rue Toulouse
New Orleans, LA 70112
800-535-9177

I've included New Orleans on this list of cities because this is where you will get off the *Sunset Limited* coming from Los Angeles and other cities in the southwest before connecting with the *City of New Orleans* (for Chicago and other cities along the Mississippi) or with the *Crescent* (for Atlanta, Washington, D.C., Philadelphia, and New York City). I trust it's not necessary to talk about why you should consider a stopover here.

The Maison Dupuy (pronounced doo-PWEE) is a small hotel smack in the heart of the French Quarter. It will be a bit pricey for some, but there really isn't a hotel that I would recommend within walking distance of the Amtrak station. This hotel is just a bit over a mile from the station—a quick taxi ride—and it's a charming place for an overnight stay in what is certainly one of America's more delightful cities.

New York City

HOTEL PENNSYLVANIA
401 Seventh Ave.
New York, NY 10001
212-736-5000

Lots of rail connections are made here, too, since New York is the terminus for trains originating in Boston, Montreal,

Toronto, Chicago, New Orleans, and Miami. For years, trains from the north and west arrived in New York at Grand Central Terminal, while Florida trains and those from other southern cities ended up at Pennsylvania Station. More often than not, passengers making connections in New York City had to deal with a cross-town cab ride as they transferred bag and baggage from one station to the other. No more. After a bypass was completed in 1994, all of Amtrak's long-distance trains now use Penn Station. It's certainly more convenient, but a magnificent era ended when Grand Central was relegated to serving only north-bound commuters, and veteran rail travelers still suffer real pangs at that thought.

The Hotel Pennsylvania is probably the best choice for rail travelers coming to New York City, especially if you'll be continuing on to another destination the following day. It's neither new (it was built in 1919) nor swank (although a $20 million renovation is underway), but the rates are reasonable and it does have a wonderful kind of brassy ambiance that's somehow just right. The hotel is also directly across the street from Penn Station and if, like me, you put a high value on convenience, this is where you should land for a night or two in New York City. There are two restaurants in the hotel—one an Irish pub—and the Penn Bar, a popular local hangout for years. A number of other restaurants are nearby. It's a stone's throw to the new Madison Square Garden, home of the Rangers and the Knicks, and not much farther to the Broadway theaters. Fans of the big bands from the 1940s and 1950s will find it easy to remember the hotel's phone number: *PEnnsylvania 6-5000!*

Oakland, California

The Oakland station was damaged beyond repair by an earthquake, and Amtrak trains are now stopping at Emeryville. Most passengers getting off here—either from the *California Zephyr* or the *Coast Starlight*—grab a cab, or are met by someone. If your final destination is San Francisco, your train will be met by an Amtrak bus which will take you right into San Francisco.

Portland, Oregon

THE BENSON HOTEL
309 SW Broadway
Portland, OR 97205
503-228-2000

Here is another of America's very nice cities and a good place for a stopover—perhaps connecting from the *Coast Starlight* to the *Empire Builder* or the *Pioneer.* The Benson Hotel is about ten blocks from the Amtrak station, so you'll probably want to take a taxi if you're toting any more than a shoulder bag. (As in Seattle, taxis are very inexpensive and city buses in the downtown area are free.)

The hotel was built by Simon Benson, one of the areas great lumber barons. When it opened in 1912, the Benson was the tallest building in the city, as well as the first to boast electric lights and elevators. A major renovation just a few years ago did a wonderful job of restoring the hotel's original luster. The hotel has two very good restaurants, particularly the London Grille. Best of all, the rates are affordable, which makes it the obvious choice for an overnight stay if you're making rail connections in Portland.

Salt Lake City, Utah

SHILO INN
206 South West Temple
Salt Lake City, UT 84101
801-521-9500

A short while after Amtrak located in the old Rio Grande Depot, the city fathers decided to locate two or three shelters for some of the less fortunate among us in the immediate vicinity. What timing! The station itself is perfectly safe, however, and includes the Utah Historical Society and a decent restaurant. Nevertheless, you should take a taxi to wherever you're going.

There are any number of perfectly adequate hotels in the general area, the Shilo Inn being one. It's only three blocks from the station, but—if you've been to Salt Lake City you already know this—they are *long* blocks. The hotel has recently been refurbished, and offers a very central location in Salt Lake City, near Temple Square (heart of the Mormon Church), the Salt Palace, and the Delta Center, as well as plenty of shopping.

Seattle, Washington

INN AT VIRGINIA MASON
1006 Spring St.
Seattle, WA 98104
800-283-6453

Seattle is a wonderful place to layover between trains for a few days. For example, you could come up from Southern California on the *Coast Starlight* and, after spending a few days here, head east on the *Empire Builder*. In any event, there's a lot to see and do in a fairly compact area. It's easy to be a tourist in Seattle, too, because cab rides are very inexpensive and buses operating in the downtown area are free.

The Inn at Virginia Mason isn't within walking distance from Seattle's railroad station, but it is quite close—not more than a five-minute cab ride. I found it quite by accident several years ago and wouldn't stay anywhere else in Seattle. Everything is very tastefully done in a style that's a bit 1920s. The rooms are comfortable, quite spacious, and reasonably priced. There's a very nice restaurant—small, but the food is well prepared and presented. If you want glitz and glamour, you should probably stay someplace else, but something about this little hotel makes you feel at home right away.

Toronto

THE ROYAL YORK HOTEL
100 Front Street West
Toronto, Ontario M5J 1E3
416-368-2155

This is Canada's second largest city and, we're told, the most ethnically diverse city in North America. This is where you can board VIA Rail's premiere train, the *Canadian,* for one of the world's great train rides—through the wilderness and across the western mountains en route to Vancouver on the Pacific Coast. What could be more fitting than to spend a night or two in a wonderful hotel before embarking for a wonderful ride on a wonderful train?

The Royal York Hotel is one of several magnificent hotels built by the Canadian Pacific Railroad along its route across that country. The hotel is very dignified, very elegant, and—Yes, I'm afraid so—pricey. It is, however, an experience worth having at least once. The Royal York is located smack across the street from Toronto's cathedral-like train station. In fact, when you check out of the hotel, the bellhops will place your luggage on a brass cart and roll it right across the street for you, setting your bags down where you check in for your train.

Washington, D.C.

THE BELLVUE HOTEL
15 E Street, NW
Washington, D.C 20001
800-327-6667

If you travel by train, chances are you'll pass through Washington, D.C., sooner or later. It's the logical place to make connections when you're traveling between the Midwest and the South or from New Orleans to anywhere in the Northeast. For goodness sake, take advantage of that! This city is worth a visit of at least several days. The renovation and restoration of Union Station has been completed, and it is once again a magnificent edifice! In its own right it has become a gathering place for Washingtonians working on the Hill—and justly so. There are numerous shops and several excellent restaurants. From the station, you can also walk to the Capitol and the buildings that house the Congressional and Senate offices. Before you leave home, contact the office of your congressman or senator. One of his or her staff people will be glad to take you on a tour of the Capitol and can also arrange for visits to the White House, FBI Headquarters, and other interesting places. Then, of course, there's the Smithsonian Institution, which alone is worth several days of your time.

The Hotel Bellvue is by far the most convenient place to stay if you're passing through Washington on the train. It's just a two- or three-minute walk from the front of Union Station. This is not a big hotel, but the staff is friendly and the rooms are clean, spacious, and nicely decorated. Most important, in a city known for outrageous hotel rates, the Bellvue is, by comparison, reasonably priced. Furthermore, a complimentary breakfast is included in the room rate.

APPENDIX C

Golden Spike Travel Agents

A s noted in the chapter on planning your rail trip, most travel agents are not familiar with the intricacies of booking a long-distance train trip. To help you find a knowledgeable one, I've included here a list of travel agencies that earned Amtrak's Golden Spike Award in 1994. These awards are given to travel agencies who reach a specified volume of sales in Amtrak tickets. Use this list as a guide only. Many of the travel agencies along the Northeast corridor achieve their high volume of Amtrak sales simply by selling a lot of Metroliner tickets so they still may not know a great deal about long-distance train travel. If your hometown travel agent flunked the simple one-question test suggested in Chapter 5, and there isn't a Golden Spike agency near you, you might wish to contact one of the following three travel agencies. Each is a rail travel specialist and has a toll-free number for just that purpose.

Ted or Sylvia Blishak, Accent on Travel, 112 N. 5th St. Klamath Falls, OR 97601 (800-347-0645)

Stan Barriger, Ascutney Travel, 44 Pleasant St., Claremont, NH 03743 (800-872-4674)

Carl Fowler, Rail Travel Center, 9 Congress St., St. Albans, VT 05478 (800-458-5394)

I'm sure that most of the Golden Spike agencies listed below are fully capable of booking any rail itinerary you might have in mind, and no doubt some of them also have toll-free telephone numbers for their clients. Unfortunately, I was not able to get that information. I will, however, be delighted to include them in future editions of this book.

Don't worry if the travel agent you settle on isn't in your hometown. The entire transaction can be handled over the phone, and they'll mail your tickets to you. So plan as much of the trip as you can yourself, then have the travel agent you select double check your efforts and take care of the ticketing.

Arizona

PHOENIX
American Express, 20023 N. 31st Ave.

G.E. Travel Center, 3200 N. Central Ave.

California

ALISO VIEJO
XpoAmerica, 101 Columbia

FULLERTON
Slotsy Tours & Travel, 1821 W. Commonwealth Ave.

RIVERSIDE
Let's Travel Tours, 5510 Osburn Pl.

SAN FRANCISCO
Golden Vacations, 350 8th St.

SIMI VALLEY
Peters Travel Service, 1750-D Los Angeles Ave.

WALNUT CREEK
Key Holidays, 1390 S. Main St.

Colorado

AURORA
CUC Travel Services, 3033 S. Parker Rd.

DENVER
RMA Travel & Tours, 1660 S. Albion

WINTER PARK
Winter Park Resort Travel Service, 677 Winter Park Dr.

Delaware

NEWARK
Travel One/MBNA, 400 Christiana Dr.

U.S./Charlie B. Travels, 77 E. Main St.

WILMINGTON
Delaware Travel Agency, 4001 Concord Pike

Hercules Travel, 1313 N. Market St.

Holiday Travel Agency, 1100 N. Market St.

Rosenbluth Travel Agency, 1001 Jefferson St., P-20 Plaza Square

Zeneca Travel, 1800 Concord Pike

District of Columbia

WASHINGTON
AAA World Wide Travel Agency, 701 15th St., NW

ACT Travel, 1722 Eye St., NW

American Express Travel Service, 2201 C St., NW, 1150 Connecticut Ave.

Cal Simmons Travel, 1200 18th St., NW

Carlson Wagonlit Travel, 10th & Pennsylvania Ave., Museum of Natural History, Pentagon

Connections the Travel Company, 1901 L St., NW

Dimensions Travel Company, 1850 K St., NW

Lawyers Travel Service, 1350 Connecticut Ave., NW

McCabe Bremmer Travel, 1730 K St., NW

Metro World Travel Service, 1330 Connecticut Ave.

Omega World Travel, 200 Constitution Ave., NW, 600 Maryland Ave., SW

Passport Executive Travel, 1025 Thomas Jefferson St.

Premier Travel Service, 1300 I St., NW

Rosenbluth Travel Agency, 1025 F St., NW

Travel Inc., 1331 Pennsylvania Ave.

Travel On, 800 21st St., NW

Travelogue Tours, 1201 New York Ave., NW

West End Travel, 1001 22nd St., NW

Florida

BRADENTON
AAA Travel Agency, 6210 Manatee Ave. West

DELRAY BEACH
AAA Travel Agency, 3075 S. Federal Hwy.

Kings Point Travel & Tours, 6626 W. Atlantic Ave.

Oriole Travel Station, 7431 W. Atlantic Ave.

FORT LAUDERDALE
VIP Tours/Hollywood, 2699 Stirling Rd.

FORT MYERS
AAA Travel Agency, 2516 Colonial Blvd.

HOLLYWOOD
GAT Marketing & Travel, 3325 Hollywood Blvd.

JACKSONVILLE
Cosmopolitan Travel, 3630 Rogero Rd.

Ground Transportation, Naval Air Station

LAUDERHILL
AAA Travel Agency, 4800 N. University Dr.

PALATKA
Great Escape Travel, 400 Highway 19 North

PALM BEACH GARDENS
AAA Travel Agency, 9123 N. Military Trail

POMPANO BEACH
AAA Travel Agency, 601 E. Atlantic Blvd.

PORT CHARLOTTE
AAA Travel Agency, 21229-A Olean Blvd.

PORT RICHEY
AAA Travel Agency, 10532 Devco Dr.

ST. PETERSBURG
AAA Travel Agency, 800 Second Ave. South

SARASOTA
AAA Travel Agency, 3844 Bee Ridge Rd.

SEMINOLE
AAA Travel Agency, 9200 Seminole Blvd.

SUNRISE
Prestige Travel Agency, 7783 NW 44th St.

VENICE
AAA Travel Agency, 2100 Manatee Ave. West

Georgia

NORCROSS
American Express Travel, 400 Pinnacle Way

Illinois

CHICAGO
Vacation Village Travel, 1424 West 95th St.

LINCOLN
House Travel, 419 Broadway

MACOMB
Macomb Travel Center, 120 E. Calhoun St.

QUINCY
Bergner's Travel Headquarters, 3121 Legion Blvd.

SCHAUMBURG
Signature Travel Services, 200 N. Martingale Rd.

Indiana

GOSHEN
Menno Travel Service, 210 S. Main St.

Maine

PORTLAND
AAA Travel Agency, 425 Marginal Way

Maryland

ANNAPOLIS
Omega World Travel, 2521 Riva Rd.

BALTIMORE
Ramsay Scarlett Travel, 19 South St.

Safe Harbors Business Travel, 25 South St.

T. Rowe Price Travel, 100 E. Pratt St.

Thomas Cook Travel, 32 South St.

Travel One, 10 N. Calvert St.

World Travel Planners, 111 S. Calvert St.

BETHESDA
American Express Travel, 10400 Fernwood Dr.

Travel Coordinators, 7316 Wisconsin Ave.

CHEVY CHASE
Ober United Travel Agency, 5420 Wisconsin Ave.

COLUMBIA
Corporate Travel Concept, 7165-A Columbia Gateway

HANOVER
Carlson Travel Network, 1327 Ashton Rd.

HUNT VALLEY
American Express Travel, 11050 York Rd.

Travel One, 225 International Circle

JOPPA
Travel Destinations Management Group,
3330 Fashion Way

Linthicum
American Express Travel Services, 1306 Concourse Dr.

Owings Mills
American Express Travel, 10461 Mill Run Cir.

The Travel Connection, 11433 Cronridge Dr.

Travel Destinations Unlimited, 110 Painters Mill Rd.

Potomac
The Travel Place, 11325 Seven Locks Rd.

Towson
Maritz Travel, 7720 York Rd.

Wheaton
AAA World Wide Travel Agency, Wheaton Plaza
North Bldg.

Massachusetts

Cambridge
Thomas Cook Travel, 39 John F. Kennedy St.

Michigan

Detroit
KeyTours, P.O. Box 517

Southfield
Can-Am Travel, 3000 Town Center

Minnesota

Owatonna
Travel Headquarters, 143 W. Bridge St.

Missouri

FENTON
Maritz Travel Company, 1385 N. Highway Dr.

Montana

GLASGOW
Scottie Travel, P.O. Box 191

KALISPELL
Flathead Travel Service, 500 S. Main St.

New Jersey

BASKING RIDGE
American Express Travel Service, P.O. Box 53889

CAMDEN
Rosenbluth Travel Agency, 1 Campbell Pl.

CHERRY HILL
Rosenbluth Travel Agency, 57 Haddonfield Rd.

EAST HANOVER
American Express Travel Services, 59 Rt. 10 at Ridgedale

ELIZABETH
Rosenbluth Travel Agency, 1201 Corbin St.

FLORHAM PARK
New Jersey Automobile Club, One Hanover Rd.

FRANKLIN LAKES
Becton Dickinson Travel, One Becton Dr.

Stratton Travel, 795 Franklin Ave.

HAMILTON SQUARE
Graycar Travel Agency, 3672 Nottingham Way

ISELIN
Rosenbluth Travel Agency, Woodbridge Pl.

JERSEY CITY
Astral Travel Service, 895 Bergen Ave.

LAWRENCEVILLE
American Express Travel Services, 989 Lenox Dr.

LONG BRANCH
American Express Travel, 121 Monmouth Pkwy. Rt. 36

MOUNT LAUREL
Travel One, 921 Pleasant Valley Ave.

NEWARK
American Express Travel, 745 Broad St.

VTS Travel, 570 Broad St.

NORTH BRUNSWICK
J & J Travel, Rt. 1 N. and Aaron Rd.

NORTHFIELD
World Wide Travel Agency, 901 Tilton Rd.

NUTLEY
Travel Forum II, 54 Windsor Pl.

OCEAN
AAA Travel Agency, Ocean Plaza Shopping Center

ORADELL
North Jersey Auto Club, 505 Kinderkamack Rd.

PENNINGTON
Kriegner Travel Service, 11 N. Main St.

PISCATAWAY
American Express Travel, 220 Centennial Ave.

PRINCETON
American Express/Revere Travel, 36 University Pl.

American Express Travel Service, 10 Nassau St.

Maritz Travel, Mobil Technical Center

TOMS RIVER
AAA Travel Agency, 864 Rt. 37 West

WILDWOOD CREST
Festival Travel & Tours, 5501 New Jersey Ave.

New York

ALBANY
Argus Travel, Stuyvesant Plaza

CTN/Albany Travel Unlimited, Albany County Airport

Fort Orange Travel, 90 State St.

Hudson Valley Auto Club, 618 Delaware Ave.

New Scotland Travel, 269 New Scotland Ave.

Travel Management Services, 23 Computer Dr., East

BRONX
Liberty Travel, 1385 Metropolitan Ave.

BROOKLYN
Calendar Travel Agency, 227 Utica Ave.

D L & W Travel, 530 Norstrand Ave.

Fan Fare Travel, 299 Livingston St.

Liberty Travel, 180 Montague St.

Me Again Travel, 66 Court St.

CATSKILL
Empress Travel, 388 Main St.

CLIFTON PARK
Phillips World Travel, Clifton Country Mall

FAR ROCKAWAY
Town & Country Travel, 21-35 Mott Ave.

GARDEN CITY
Automobile Club of New York, 1415 Kellum Pl.

GLEN COVE
Hillside Travel, 51-A Forest Ave.

JAMAICA
Pleasure Travels, 122-25A Guy R. Brewer Blvd.

LATHAM
CTN/Albany Travel Unlimited, 3 Cornell Rd.

MANHATTAN
American Express, 380 Madison Ave.

American Express Travel, 65 Broadway,
1 Chase Manhattan Plaza, 37 Wall St.

American Express Travel Related Services, 1120 6th Ave.,
100 Church St., 200 Vesey St.

Bear Stearns Travel, 245 Park Ave.

Capital Cities/ABC Inc. Travel Dept., 77 West 66th St.

Carlson Travel Network, 757 3rd Ave., 225 Liberty St.,
555 Madison Ave.

Carrier Travel, 1040 6th Ave.

Continental-American Travel, 770 Lexington Ave.

CTN/Aviron Travel, 110 Church St.

Direct Travel, 1180 6th Ave., 1515 Broadway

Empire Blue Cross & Blue Shield/USTravel, 622 3rd Ave.

Harlem Travel Bureau, 2002 5th Ave.

Humbert Travel Agency, 400 Madison Ave.

Japan Travel Bureau, 787 7th Ave.

Journeycorp Travel Management, 488 Madison Ave.

Kintetsu International Express, 1325 6th Ave.

Let's Go Travel, 107 West 86th St.

Liberty Travel, One 5th Ave., 2280 Broadway,
260 East 72nd St., 120 Fulton St.

Linden Travel Bureau, 41 East 57th St.

MSW Columbia Travel Group, 630 5th Ave.

MacPherson Travel, 352 7th Ave.

Maritz Travel Company, 140 Broadway,
330 Madison Ave., 153 East 53rd St.

Mark Allan Travel/American Express, 880 3rd Ave.

Morgan Stanley Travel Dept., 1251 6th Ave.

Nippon Travel Agency Pacific, 120 West 45th St.

Park Avenue Travel Service, 60 East 42nd St.

Pisa Brothers, Inc. Travel Bureau, 630 5th Ave.

Protravel International, 515 Madison Ave.

Radler Travel Services, 355 West 52nd St.

Rosenbluth Travel Agency, 1 Chase Plaza, 104 West 40th St., 99 Wall St.

Sea Gate Travel Agency, 450 7th Ave.

Stevens Travel Management, 30 East 33rd St.

Thomas Cook Travel, 779 Broadway, Two Penn Plaza, 72 Wall St.

Travel Planners, 114 East 25th

Tzell Travel & Tours, 70 West 36th St.

Ultramar Travel Bureau, 3 West 51st St.

USTravel, 1140 6th Ave., 10 Hanover Square, 90 John St., 7 World Trade Center

Valerie Wilson Travel, 475 Park Ave. South

VTS Travel Enterprises, 55 John St.

World Travel Specialists, 461 Park Ave. South

Zenith Travel, 16 East 34th St.

ROCKVILLE CENTER
Time To Travel, 100 N. Village Ave.

SCHENECTADY
Woodside Dorp Travel Agency, 426 Franklin St.

TROY
Woodside Dorp Travel Agency, 277 River St.

North Dakota

WILLISTON
Daryle's Travel, 407 Main St.

Oklahoma

NORMAN
Travel Service, 2500 S. McGee

Oregon

KLAMATH FALLS
Accent on Travel, 112 N. 5th St.

Pennsylvania

ALLENTOWN
Lehigh Valley Motor Club, 1020 Hamilton St.

Rosenbluth Travel, One Windsor Plaza

ARDMORE
Travel One, 6 Greenfield Ave.

BENSALEM
Center Travel, 1943 Street Rd.

COLLEGEVILLE
American Express, 500 Arcola Rd.

DOUGLASSVILLE
World Travel, 1724 W. Schuylkill Rd.

HUNTINGTON
Gateway Travel Center, 606 Mifflin St.

KING OF PRUSSIA
American Express Travel Related Services,
200 N. Warner St.

Carlson Wagonlit Travel, 150 Allendale Rd.

KINGSTON
Kingdom Tours, 300 Market St.

MALVERN
Cherry Hill Travel, Travel One, 40 Great Valley Pkwy.

World Travel, 10 Great Valley Pkwy.

PHILADELPHIA
American Express Travel Management Services,
Two Penn Center Plaza

CTN/South Street Travel, 217 South St.

CTN/Squires Travel Service, 200 S. Broad St.

Cherry Hill Travel, 30 S. 17th St.

Get A Way Travel, 111 Township Line Rd.

Lawyers Travel Service, 1717 Arch St.

McGettigans Corporate Planning Service,
100 Penn Square East

Monarch Travel Services, 2100 Walnut St.

Premier Travel Services, 217 S. 20th St.

Rosenbluth Travel Agency, 1601 Chestnut St.,
One Franklin Plaza, 1515 Walnut St., 2401 Walnut St.

Thomas Cook Travel, 3728 Spruce St.

Travel One/Reliance Insurance, 4 Penn Center

Uniglobe/Sampson Travel Agency, 10 Penn Center

Uniglobe/The Traveling Man, 1107 Walnut St.

VTS Travel Enterprises, Broad & Walnut Sts.

Whole World Travel, 2 Logan Square

PLYMOUTH MEETING
Rosenbluth Travel, 1 Plymouth Meeting Hall

RADNOR
Uniglobe/Sampson Travel, 100 Matsonford Rd.

RIDLEY PARK
American Express Travel/Boeing, Rt. 29 West

WAYNE
IVI Travel, 680 E. Swedesford Rd.

WEST CHESTER
World Travel, 1365 Enterprise Dr.

South Carolina

KINGSTREE
Kingstree Travel Agency, 133-A E. Main St.

Tennessee

NASHVILLE
CUC Travel Services, 49 Music Square West

Texas

HOUSTON
Triumph Travel, 16225 Park Ten Place

Vermont

ST. ALBANS
Rail City Travel, 9 Congress St.

Virginia

ALEXANDRIA
Thomas Cook Travel, 1340 Braddock Pl.

UTSC Travel Resources, 1500 King St.

FAIRFAX
AAA World Wide Travel Agency, 12600 Fair Lakes Cir.

FREDERICKSBURG
Fredericksburg Travel Agency, 105 William St.

MCLEAN
Cahan Travel Management, 6721 Curran St.

VIENNA
AAA Travel Agency, 8300 Old Courthouse Rd.

Rosenbluth Travel Agency, 1604 Springhill

Washington

FORT LEWIS
Fort Lewis Bus Depot, 12th & Liggett

KIRKLAND
Schwartz Tours, 204 Central Way

Wisconsin

NEW RICHMOND
Travel Now, 225 S. Knowles Ave.

British Columbia

SURREY
Skyway Travel Service, 12845 96th Ave.

APPENDIX D

Excursion Trains and Railroad Museums

Scenic Railway Excursions

In preparing this list of scenic train rides throughout North America, every effort was made to be complete and accurate. Nevertheless, it should be used as a guide only, since fares, schedules, and other details of an individual railway's operations can and do change frequently. All of these excursion trains have up-to-date printed material available at no cost so call or write for current information before making plans for a visit. It should also be noted that this is not a complete list. A number of companies were contacted and asked for information, but either did not respond or did not do so in time to meet publication deadline. A more detailed list of excursion trains and rail museums may be found in the Steam Passenger Service Directory, which can be ordered through local bookstores or by calling the publisher direct at 802-434-2351. You may also write to Great Eastern Publishing, P.O. Box 246, Richmond, VT 05477.

Alaska

ALASKA RAILROAD
P.O. Box 107500
Anchorage, AK 99510
907-265-2494

The Alaska Railroad provides both scheduled passenger and freight service. Since other railroads offer either one service or the other, but not both, that makes Alaska Railroad the only full-service railroad in North America. The railroad is also unique because it's a private corporation owned by the state of Alaska. The company operates from the deep-water port of Seward through Anchorage to just beyond Fairbanks, a distance of some 500 miles. The railroad offers more than a dozen one- and two-day rail/tour packages, which originate in one of those three cities and include a choice of hotel accommodations where appropriate. The departure days and times of these rail tours are so varied, the only practical way to get valid up-to-date information is to call and ask for one of their comprehensive brochures. In addition to offering tours for visitors to this spectacular state, the trains of Alaska Railroad also provide transportation links for local residents. Equipment is modern and includes coaches, observation dome cars, and dining cars.

Operates: All year; daily from mid-May to mid-September. Winter hours and operations vary so call for details.

Features: Tour guides travel aboard many trains.

Reservations: 800-544-0552

WHITE PASS & YUKON RAILROAD
P.O. Box 435
Skagway, AK 99840
907-983-2217

Train runs from Skagway at sea level, to 2,865-foot White Pass summit, and beyond to Lake Bennet, a total distance of 41 miles. Considered an engineering marvel, the route features spectacular mountain scenery, crossing several impressive trestles. At Fraser (mile 28), the train connects with a bus for White Horse, another 83 miles inland.

Location: Depot is at 2nd and Spring streets in
                  Skagway, next to the Klondike National Park
                  Service Visitor Center.

Operates: May 16–Sept. 22

Departures: To Lake Bennet, Sun.–Fri., 8:05 A.M.; to White
                  Pass summit, daily, 8:50 A.M. and 1:20 P.M.

Duration: Round-trip to Lake Bennet, 5½ hours;
                  round-trip to White Pass summit, 2¾ hours.

Fares: Lake Bennet excursion: adults, $119; children
                  12 and under, $59.50; infants free; includes
                  box lunch. White Pass summit excursion:
                  adults, $72; children 12 and under, $36;
                  infants free.

Features: Gift shop at depot.

Reservations: From US: 800-343-7373; from NW Canada,
                  800-478-7373

Arizona

GRAND CANYON RAILWAY
518 E. Bill Williams Ave
Williams, AZ 86046
602-635-4000

Steam locomotives pull fully restored 1920-vintage passenger cars. This trip begins at the Fray Marcos Hotel &
Depot in Williams, Arizona, and terminates at the Grand
Canyon Log Depot. Both buildings are on the National
Register of Historic Places. The route covers 64 miles of
high desert plateau country, beginning in the tall pon-
derosa pine forest around Williams at an elevation of 6,700
feet. From there the train descends 1,500 feet to the desert
grassland area of Willaha then climbs a 3 percent grade
into the forests of Coconino Canyon, finally reaching the
6,800-foot level and its destination at the South Rim of the
Grand Canyon.

Location: Go west from Flagstaff on I-40, take 163
                  exit, go south for ½ mile.

Operates:	Fri., Sat., Sun. in Feb.; Wed.–Sun., Mar. 1–14; daily, Mar. 15–Jan. 1 (except Christmas Eve and Christmas Day).
Departures:	Dep. Williams, 9:30 A.M.; arr. Grand Canyon, 11:45 A.M.; dep. Grand Canyon, 3:15 P.M.; arr. Williams, 5:30 P.M.
Duration:	One way, 2¼ hours; round-trip, 8 hours. (includes 3½ hr. stopover at Grand Canyon).
Fares:	One way—adult, $45.23; teen (13–19), $24.62; child $12.48. Round-trip—adult, $55; teen (13–19), $29.50; child $15.73. Fares include tax and park admission fee.
Features:	Gift shop, railroad museum, breakfast cafe, wild west entertainment, strolling musicians.
Reservations:	800-843-8724

California

CALIFORNIA WESTERN RAILROAD
P.O. Box 907
Fort Bragg, CA 95437
707-964-6372

More commonly known as the Skunk Train, steam or diesel locomotives haul passengers from Fort Bragg on the California coast some 40 miles inland to Willits. Trains may be boarded at either terminus. The route passes through two deep mountain tunnels, follows the Noya River, and crosses some 30 bridges and trestles as it climbs up through the giant redwood forests. Trains feature coaches and an open observation car. Most trips during winter months are made in restored 65-passenger motorcars from the 1920s and 1930s.

Location:	To Fort Bragg—North from San Francisco on Rt. 1; in Fort Bragg, turn left at Laurel Ave., go straight to depot. To Willits—north from San Francisco on US 101; in Willits, turn right on Commercial St., turn left into depot parking lot at railroad tracks.

Operates: Year-round.
Departures: Schedule varies according to season; call for
                 departure times.
Duration: Full day for Fort Bragg–Willits round-trip;
                 half day for trip to Northspur (mid-point)
                 and return from either terminus.
Fares: Full day trip—adults, $26; children 5–11,
                 $12. Half-day trip—adults, $21; children
                 5–11, $10. Children under 5 free unless occu-
                 pying revenue seat.
Reservations: 707-964-6371

PORTOLA RAILROAD MUSEUM
P.O. Box 608
Portola, CA 96122
916-832-4131

Visitors to the museum may ride in diesel-powered caboose
train on a one-mile loop track around the facility. Museum
includes 25 locomotives and more than 50 rail cars. With
prior arrangement and at additional fee, visitors can "rent"
and operate diesel locomotives under instruction from a
qualified engineer.

Location: Portola is northeast of Sacramento. From
                 Hwy. 70 in Portola, go south on Gullnig St.,
                 cross bridge and turn right on Commercial
                 St., follow signs to museum entrance on 1st
                 Ave.
Operates: Museum open daily all year; train rides,
                 Memorial Day to mid-September.
Departures: Continuous, 11 A.M.–4 P.M.
Duration: 15 minutes
Admission: All day passes—$2 per person; $5 for family;
                 additional donations to museum are appreci-
                 ated.
Features: Gift shop, snack bar, artifact displays.
Reservations: Not required.

NAPA VALLEY WINE TRAIN
1275 McKinstry St.
Napa, CA 94559
707-253-2111

Passengers enjoy a non-stop gourmet dining experience aboard lavishly restored 1915 Pullman dining and lounge cars while following a 36-mile route through the heart of the picturesque Napa Valley.

Location: From San Francisco take Oakland Bay Bridge to I-80 East; exit onto Hwy. 37 (Marine World Parkway) and continue to Hwy. 29; turn right on Hwy. 29 and continue to Napa/Berryessa junction; keep right and proceed to downtown Napa; turn right on McKinstry and into train parking lot.

Operates: Daily, year-round.

Departures: Brunch: Sat., Sun., holidays, 8:30 A.M.; lunch: Mon.–Fri., 11 A.M.; Sat., Sun., holidays, 12:10 P.M.; dinner: Tues.–Fri., 6 P.M.; Sat., Sun., holidays, 5:30 P.M.

Duration: 3 hours

Cost: Train fares, $24–$30; meals, $22–$39.50 (Wine not included.)

Features: Wine shop, art gallery, and boutique at Napa Station.

Reservations: 800-522-4142

ROARING CAMP & BIG TREES NARROW GAUGE RAILROAD
P. O. Box G-1
Felton, CA 95018
408-335-4400

Several different steam locomotives haul trains through a giant redwood forest, past a logging town dating back to the 1880s, to the top of Bear Mountain. Route includes the steepest narrow-gauge railroad grade in North America and some of the tightest turns.

Location:	Highway 17 to Santa Cruz; exit at Mt. Herman; stay right approximately three miles; turn left at Graham Hill Road; Roaring Camp is one-half mile on right.
Operates:	Daily except Christmas; may vary Jan.–Mar.
Departures:	One to five times daily between 11 A.M. and 4 P.M. depending on time of year and day of week.
Duration:	1¼ hours
Fares:	Adults, $12; children $8.75, under 3 years free.
Features:	1880s general store, chuck wagon barbecue, country music; other special activities scheduled periodically.
Reservations:	408-335-4484

SANTA CRUZ, BIG TREES & PACIFIC RAILWAY
P.O. Box G-1
Felton, CA 95018
408-335-4400

These trains operate during the summer months carrying passengers along the San Lorenzo river between the redwood forest near Felton, California, (Roaring Camp) and Santa Cruz on the coastline. Passengers may ride in coaches or on open flatcars. Railroad also hauls freight along the same route.

Location:	Highway 17 to Santa Cruz; exit at Mt. Herman; stay right approximately three miles; turn left at Graham Hill Road; Roaring Camp is one-half mile on right.
Operates:	Mid-May through late Nov., plus special excursions.
Departures:	From Roaring Camp, 10:30 A.M., 2:30 P.M.; from Santa Cruz, 12:30, 4:30 P.M.
Duration:	1 hour each way.

Fares: Round-trip—adult (16 years and older), $14; children (3–15), $8.95; 3 years and under, free.
Reservations: 408-335-4484

SIERRA RAILWAY CO.
(Railtown 1897 State Historic Park)
P.O. Box 1250
Jamestown, CA 95327
209-984-3953

Several steam locomotives haul the "Mother Lode Cannonball" on a 12-mile ride through the heart of California's Gold Rush country. Company also offer two extended rides: the *Twilight Limited,* with snacks and drinks aboard and a western BBQ upon return; and the *Wine & Cheese Zephyr,* serving a variety of cheeses with selected California wines during the trip.

Location: About 2 hours east of the San Francisco area. Take Rt. 108 to Jamestown, turn south on 5th Ave. to Railtown 1897.
Operates: Sat. and Sun. only, Mar.–Nov.
Departures: 10:30 A.M., 12 noon, 1:30, 3 P.M.; BBQ train, 5 P.M. (Saturdays in June, July, Aug.).
Duration: Mother Lode excursions, 1 hour; BBQ Train, *Wine & Cheese Zephyr,* 2 hours.
Fares: Excursions: adults, $9; children 3–12, $4.50. *Wine & Cheese Zephyr:* adults, $24.50; children 3–12, $12.50. BBQ Train: adults, $34.50; children 3–12, $16.
Features: Roundhouse, repair and maintenance shop complex, turntable.
Reservations: 209-984-3953 (No advance sales for excursion trains.)

WESTERN RAILWAY MUSEUM
560 Railroad Ave.
Hercules, CA 94547
707-374-2978

Rides are confined to antique electric railway cars, but a variety of elegant Pullman cars are on display along with steam and diesel locomotives.

Location:	Midway between San Francisco and Sacramento on I-80; take Rio Vista Exit (Rt. 12); go east 13 miles.
Operates:	Sat., Sun.—all year; Wed.–Sun. during summer months.
Departures:	Continuous, 11 A.M.–5 P.M.
Admission:	Adults, $5; children 4–12, $2; families, $15.
Features:	Carbarns, volunteer guides, bookstore, picnic areas.
Reservations:	Not required.

YOSEMITE MOUNTAIN SUGAR PINE RAILROAD
56001 Highway 41
Fish Camp, CA 93623
209-683-7273

From 1899 to 1931 the Madera Sugar Pine Lumber Company used wood-burning Shay locomotives to haul logs to the sawmill at Sugar Pine. The line has been restored and runs through the scenic Sierra Nevadas at 5,000 feet elevation, winds down a 4 percent grade into Lewis Creek Canyon, and passes through several horseshoe curves. Restored locomotives haul passengers in both open and covered cars; Jenny railcars (self-propelled trolley-like cars) are used on most weekdays. From June through early October, the railroad operates an evening excursion called the Moonlight Special, which includes a barbecue dinner and music.

Location:	Twelve miles below the south entrance to Yosemite National Park on Hwy. 41.

Operates: Jenny railcars—daily, Mar.– Oct.; special
                   occasions during the rest of the year. Steam
                   train—daily from mid-May through Sept.;
                   weekends only in Oct.
Departures: Jenny railcars—every ½ hour, 10 A.M.–3:30
                   P.M. (departs as late as 4:30 P.M. in summer
                   months). Steam train—11 A.M. and 12:30
                   P.M. on most days, with increased after-
                   noon schedule in summer months. Call for
                   details. Moonlight Special—Sat. nights,
                   June through first week of Oct.
Duration: 45 minutes
Fares: Steam train—adults, $9.50; children (3–12),
                   $4.50. Jenny railcar—adults, $6.25; children
                   (3–12), $3.25; Moonlight Special—adults,
                   $27.50; children (3–12), $15.
Features: Museum, bookstore, gift shop.
Reservations: 209-683-7273 (Required for Moonlight
                   Special only.)

Colorado

CUMBRES & TOLTEC SCENIC RAILROAD
P.O. Box 668
Antonito, CO 81120
719-376-5483

(Complete listing can be found under "NEW MEXICO.")

DURANGO & SILVERTON NARROW GAUGE RAILROAD
479 Main Ave.
Durango, CO 81301
303-259-3372

This coal-fired, steam-powered narrow-gauge railroad has
been in continuous operation since 1881. The spectacular 45-
mile route between Durango and Silverton crosses valleys

surrounded by red rock cliffs, climbs along mountain ridges with rushing Animas River 400 feet below, and offers vistas of the million-plus-acre San Juan National Forest. Overnight layovers in Silverton may be arranged. Additional train makes one round-trip each day between Durango and Cascade Canyon at special times during the year.

Location: At intersection of Highways 160 and 550, go north one block and turn right on College Drive (6th St.); go one more block and turn right on Main St.; depot is located at 5th St. and Main Ave.

Operates: Mid-Apr. through Oct.; Thanksgiving Day through Jan. 1 (except Christmas Day).

Departures: Schedule varies with time of year; call for details.

Duration: One way, 3 ¼ hours; round-trip, 9 hours (including 2 hours in Silverton).

Fares: Round-trip—adults, $42.70; children under 12, $21.45; parlor car, $73.40 (adults only). Private cars available for groups.

Features: Yard tours (additional fee), gift shop, concession car on train.

Reservations: 303-247-2733 (Recommend making reservations 4–6 weeks in advance.)

GEORGETOWN LOOP RAILROAD
P.O. Box 217
Georgetown, CO 80444
303-670-1686

Powered by a steam locomotive, the train runs between the towns of Georgetown and Silver Plume, both rich in mining and railroad history. Route passes through spectacular scenery of pines, aspens, and mountain vistas, including a crossing of the Devil's Gate High Bridge.

Location:	One hour west of Denver on I-70; exit 228 to 15th Street; right on Rose Street to Old Georgetown Station at corner of Rose and 11th Street.
Operates:	June 1–Sept. 30. (Dates vary slightly, year to year.)
Departures:	Every 80 minutes between approximately 9:20 A.M. to 4 P.M. from Silver Plume and Devil's Gate locations. Number of departures may vary depending on date.
Duration:	1¼ hours
Fares:	Adults, $10.95; children, $6.50; 3 years and under free when not occupying seat.
Features:	Gift shop, restaurant at Old Georgetown station; optional silver mine tour.
Reservations:	303-670-1686

LEADVILLE, COLORADO & SOUTHERN RAILROAD
P.O. Box 916
Leadville, CO 80461
719-486-3936

Train leaves from the Leadville depot and travels through Colorado's high country, following the headwaters of the Arkansas River to a spectacular view of the Fremont Pass and on to a view of Mt. Elbert, highest peak in Colorado.

Location:	From Denver, take I-70 west; exit at Copper Mountain (Rt. 91); go south on Rt. 91 through Climax to Leadville. From Grand Junction, take I-70 east; exit at Rt. 24; go south on Rt. 24 through Minturn to Leadville.
Operates:	Memorial Day weekend through first weekend in Oct.
Departures:	Memorial Day–mid-June, 1 P.M.; mid-June through Labor Day, 10 A.M., 2 P.M.; Labor Day–first weekend in Oct., 1 P.M. on weekdays and 10 A.M., 2 P.M. on Sat. and Sun.

Duration:	Round-trip, 2½ hours.
Fares:	Adult, $18.50; children (4–12), $9.75; children 3 and under, free.
Features:	Historic depot, museum/gift shop, concessions.
Reservations:	719-486-3936

MANITOU & PIKE'S PEAK RAILWAY
Box 351
Manitou Springs, CO 80829
719-685-1045

This is the world's highest cog railway, operating for more than 100 years from Manitou Springs to the 14,110-foot summit of Pike's Peak. Route follows a rushing stream through steep canyons, finally emerging onto Alpine vistas above the timberline.

Location:	Go west from Colorado Springs on I-25; take exit #141 (US 24) and go 4 miles to Manitou Springs exit; go west on Manitou Ave. 1.5 miles to Ruxton Ave.; left on Ruxton Ave. for ¾ mile to depot.
Operates:	Last week of Apr.–Oct. 31
Departures:	Every 80 minutes from 8 A.M. to 5:20 P.M. (Number of daily trips varies according to time of year.)
Duration:	1¼ hours each way.
Fares:	Adults, $21; children 5–11, $9.50
Features:	Gift shop, restaurant at summit.
Reservations:	719-685-5401 (Advance reservations strongly advised.)

Connecticut

THE VALLEY RAILROAD COMPANY
Railroad Ave., P.O. Box 452
Essex, CT 06426
203-767-0103

Steam and diesel locomotives haul passengers through the Connecticut River Valley in old-fashioned comfort, including a vintage parlor car. At Deep River, passengers can opt to extend their trip by transferring to a river cruise on a multi-decked riverboat.

Location:	From Hartford, take I-91 to Exit 225; go south on Rt. 9 to Exit 3; follow signs. From shore points, take I-95 to Exit 69; go north on Rt. 9 to Exit 3, follow signs.
Operates:	Apr. 30–June 8: Wed., Sat., Sun.; June 11–Sept. 5: daily; Sept. 7–Oct. 30: Wed.–Sun.; Nov.–Dec.: occasional special events.
Departures:	Number of departures varies with time of year; call for details.
Duration:	Train only—1 hour; train and boat—2½ hours.
Fares:	Train only—adults, $8.50; children 2–11, $4.25. Train and boat—adults, $14; children $7.
Features:	Gift shop, working rail yard, exhibits; snacks available in parlor car en route.
Reservations:	203-767-0103

Delaware

QUEEN ANNE'S RAILROAD
730 King's Hwy.
Lewes, DE 19958
302-644-1720

This company operates an excursion train and the *Royal Zephyr Dinner Train* through the southern Delaware countryside over what used to be Pennsylvania Railroad track. The excursion trains use open-air heavyweight coaches; the dinner train treats passengers to former New Haven Railroad coaches which have been completely refurbished. Both diesel and steam locomotives are used.

Location: South from Milford on Route 1; exit on
                 Route 404 and go east to Lewes; follow
                 signs to Cape May Ferry.
Operates: Mid-May–Oct.
Departures: Excursion train—Mon., Thurs., Sat. at 2 P.M.;
                 Wed., at noon and 3:30 P.M. *Royal Zephyr*
                 schedule varies considerably, so call for details.
Duration: Excursion train, 1 ½ hours; *Royal Zephyr*—2 ½
                 hours.
Fares: Excursion train—adult, $7; children (3–12),
                 $5; Dinner train—adults, $39.95; children,
                 $32.95.
Reservations: 302-644-1720

Hawaii

LAHAINA, KAANAPALI & PACIFIC RAILROAD
P.O. Box 816
Lahaina, Maui, HI 96767
808-661-0089

This steam-powered train carries passengers between the
old whaling town of Lahaina and the resort area of
Kaanapali on the Island of Maui. The 6-mile route passes
through sugar plantations with the ocean on one side and
the mountains of West Maui on the other.

Location: Puukolii Boarding Platform—Hwy. 30 at
                 Puukolii Rd.; Kaanapali Station—mountain
                 side of Hwy. 30 opposite Kaanapali resort
                 area; Lahaina Station—near Pioneer Sugar
                 Mill at Hinau Street.
Operates: Daily except Thanksgiving and Christmas.
Departures: Every hour and 20 minutes between 8:55
                 A.M. and 5:20 P.M.
Duration: 30 minutes each way.
Fares: Round-trip—adults, $12.; children 3–12
                 years, $6.

Features: Singing conductor, narration, sightseeing
                 packages.
Reservations: 808-667-6851

Illinois

ILLINOIS RAILWAY MUSEUM
Union, IL 60180
815-923-4000

Visitors can see a variety of rail equipment, including steam
and diesel locomotives, electric streetcars, and "L" trains.
Other historic railway equipment is on display, from vintage passenger coaches to modern streamliners.

Location: From Chicago, go west on I-90 to Marengo
                 Exit; go northwest on Rt. 20 about 4.5 miles
                 to Union Road; turn right on Union and fol-
                 low signs to museum.
Operates: Daily, Memorial Day–Labor Day; weekends
                 only during May and from Labor Day
                 through first week of Oct.; Sun. only during
                 Apr. and last three weeks of Oct.
Departures: Regularly between 11 A.M. and 5 P.M. (4 P.M.
                 on weekdays).
Duration: Trains—45 min.; trolleys—15 min.
Admission: Adults, $7; children 5–11, $5 when trains are
                 operating.
Features: Bookstore, museum shop, refreshments.
Reservations: Not required.

MONTICELLO RAILWAY MUSEUM
P.O. Box 401
Monticello, IL 61856-0401
217-762-9011

This attraction features not only a rail museum and a rail yard,
but a train ride that includes wooded areas and farmland.
Passengers may board or layover at either the Illinois

Central Depot (museum site) or at the Wabash depot in Monticello, which was built in 1899. Visitors may walk through the display cars at the museum and are permitted to walk through the Camp Creek Yard where there are numerous pieces of equipment.

Location: From I-72, take Exit 63, which is midway between Champaign and Decatur; follow signs.

Operates: Weekends and some holidays, the first weekend in May–Oct.

Departures: From the museum site: 1, 2, 3, 4 P.M. from Wabash Depot in Monticello: 1:30, 2:30, and 3:30 P.M.

Duration: Round-trip, 50 minutes.

Fares: Adults, $5; seniors (62+), $3; children (4–12), $3.

Features: Gift shop in the Illinois Central Deport, light snacks.

Reservations: None required.

Iowa

BOONE & SCENIC VALLEY RAILROAD
Box 603
Boone, IA 50036
515-432-4249

A 12-mile route through the Des Moines River valley, crossing two bridges (one 156' high). Railroad features diesel and steam locomotives (latter operates weekends and holidays only).

Location: 20 miles west of Ames on US 30; go north on Story St., through business district; go left on 10th St. for six blocks.

Operates: Memorial Day weekend–Oct. 31.

Departures: Mon.–Fri., 1:30 P.M.; Sat., Sun., holidays, 11 A.M., 1:30, 4 P.M.

Duration: Round-trip, 1½ hours.

Fares: Adult, $10 (steam) $8 (diesel); children 5–12, $4.
Features: Museum (free), gift shop, snack bar.
Reservations: 800-626-0319

Kentucky

BLUEGRASS SCENIC RAILROAD & MUSEUM
P.O. Box 27
Versailles, KY 40383
606-873-2476

The 5½-mile route runs between Versailles and the Kentucky River, passing through horse, cattle, and tobacco farms and over three wooden trestles. Passengers may detrain at the Kentucky River where there is an overlook that includes the Wild Turkey Distillery, the Kentucky River Valley, and Young's High Bridge, a railroad bridge built in 1889 by the Louisville Southern Railroad.

Location: Located in the Woodford County Park of US 62; enter the park via Beasley Road, cross railroad tracks and turn left into parking lot.
Operates: Sat. and Sun., May–Oct.; Christmas Trains in Dec.
Departures: Sat., 10:30 A.M., 1:30, 3:30 P.M.; Sun., 1:30, 3:30 P.M.
Duration: Round-trip, 1½ hours.
Fares: Adults, $6; seniors (62+), $5; children (2–12), $4
Features: Museum, gift shop.
Reservations: 800-755-2476

MY OLD KENTUCKY DINNER TRAIN
P.O. Box 279
Bardstown, KY 40004
502-348-7699

The train follows a 35-mile route through very scenic country-side, including Bernheim Forest, a private 13,000-acre reserve, crosses an old all-timber trestle, and also passes the historic Jim Beam Distillery.

Location:	Approximately 50 miles south of Louisville; depot on Route 31, 6 blocks from Town Square.
Operates:	Daily except Mon., Apr.–Dec.
Departures:	Tues.–Sat., 12 noon & 5 P.M.; Sun., 1:30 P.M.
Duration:	2 hours
Fares:	Lunch, $54.95 per person; dinner, $59.95 per person.
Features:	Gift shop in depot.
Reservations:	502-348-7300

Maryland

THE ENTERTRAINMENT LINE
P.O. Box 478
Union Bridge, MD 21791
410-875-2814

These excursion trains operate through some of the most scenic countryside in central Maryland, passing over several rivers and streams, through farms, orchards, wetlands, and wooded areas. The train follows a route once used during the Civil War to evacuate Union soldiers wounded at the Battle of Gettysburg. The Sunday afternoon excursion follows a 50-mile route to the top of the Catoctin Mountains, crossing over high bridges and passing Camp David en route. The company offers a wide variety of excursions, including trains featuring casual lunch and dinner buffets or dancing with a live deejay. There are also Santa trains, fall-color tour trains, carnival trains for youngsters, and trains for any number of other themes or special occasions. Please call for a complete list. Note, too, that trains may originate in either Westminster or Union Bridge, Maryland, so be sure to call and confirm departure location.

Location:	North from Baltimore on I-795 to US 140; exit at Route 27 and go west; look for Texaco station on left; depot is across the street.
Operates:	All year.
Departures:	Weekdays, 11 A.M.; weekends, 12 noon or 1 P.M.; Fri., 8 P.M.; Sat., 7 P.M.
Duration:	3 1/2 hours.
Fares:	Most range from $40 to $55 per person, although some are less. Substantial discounts for children.
Reservations:	800-553-3115

Massachusetts

CAPE COD SCENIC RAILROAD
252 Main Street
Hyannis, MA 02601
508-771-3788

The scenic ride begins and ends in Hyannis, with stops at the historic village of Sandwich and at the Cape Cod Canal. Diesel/electric locomotives haul passengers in classic coaches. Route takes the train through historic Cape Cod villages, past cranberry bogs, the Great Salt Marsh, and along Cape Cod Bay. A narrative is also provided. This railroad also operates a very nice Dinner Train (coat and tie required).

Location:	Depot is located in downtown Hyannis at Main and Center Streets.
Operates:	Scenic Train—weekends and holidays in May, daily (except Mon.), June–Oct. Dinner Train—daily (except Mon.) from mid-June through mid-Sept.; Wed., Fri., Sat., Sun. in spring and fall; weekends only in winter; does not operate in Jan.

Departures: Scenic Train—10 A.M., 12:30, 3:00, 6:30 P.M..
                  Dinner Train—6:30 P.M.
Duration: Scenic Train—2 hours. (Passengers may
                  leave train en route and return on later train.)
                  Dinner Train—3 hours.
Fares: Scenic Train—adult, $11.50; senior, $10.50;
                  child, $7.50. Dinner Train—$44 per person.
Reservations: 508-771-3788

Michigan

ADRIAN & BLISSFIELD RAIL ROAD COMPANY
P.O. Box 95
Blissfield, MI 49228
517-486-5979

From Blissfield, excursion trains travel over track of the Erie & Kalamazoo Railroad, which first began operations in 1836. Passing through rich farmland of southeastern Michigan, the train finally stops at Lenawee Junction, once a major rail stop, before returning to Blissfield. The company also operates a fine-dining dinner train, a murder mystery train, a ghost train, and snow trains.

Location: Take US Route 23 south from Ann Arbor or
               north from Toledo; take Exit 5 to US Route
               223 and go west 10 miles to Blissfield.
               Boarding site is on Route 223 at Depot
               Street.
Operates: Snow trains—Jan.–Apr., call for schedule.
               Excursion trains—Sat. and Sun. in May, June,
               Sept., Oct.; Tues., Thurs., Sat., Sun. in July
               and Aug.; Sun. only in Nov. Santa trains—
               Dec., call for schedule. Dinner train, Sat. and
               Sun. all year. Murder Mystery train—Fri. all
               year.

Departures: Excursion trains—2 P.M. Dinner trains—Sat.,
6 P.M.; Sun., 1:30 P.M. Murder Mystery
train—6 P.M. All other trains—call for departure times.

Duration: Excursion trains, 2 hours; dinner trains, 2½
hours; Murder Mystery train, 3 hours. All
other trains—call for information.

Fares: Excursion train—adult, $7.50; senior (60+)
$6.50; children (3–12), $4.50. Dinner train—
evening, $50.95; afternoon, $45.95. Murder
Mystery train—$57.95.

Reservations: 517-486-5979

COOPERSVILLE & MARNE RAILWAY
P.O. Box 55
Coopersville, MI 49404
616-949-4778

This scenic 13-mile ride is along one of Michigan's oldest
rail corridors in the middle of West Michigan, a premier
tourist destination. The route crosses two bridges, passes
through farmland and wooded areas, then follows
Interstate 96 for several miles. Several special trains are run
at special times during the year, including a Murder Mystery
Dinner Train.

Location: From Grand Rapids take I-96 west for 15
miles to either of the Coopersville exits;
follow signs to downtown.

Operates: July, Aug., Sept.— Sat.; Oct.— Sat. and Sun.,
Dec.—Sat. and Sun.

Departures: Vary according to date; call for details.

Duration: 1¼ hours

Fares: Adults, $7; seniors, $6; children (3–13), $4.
Murder Mystery Dinner Train, $75 per person.

Features: Gift shop

Reservations: 616-949-4778

KALAMAZOO, LAKE SHORE & CHICAGO RAILWAY
P.O. Box 178
Paw Paw, MI 49079
616-382-4244

The train takes passengers on a 13-mile round-trip through Michigan's wine country, passing through woods, wetlands, vineyards, and along the shore of Lake Cora. There's an optional stopover at Bonamego Tree Farm where you can picnic or hike until a later train comes along. In winter, Santa Trains provide a chance to cut your own Christmas tree.

Location: Take I-94 west from Kalamazoo to Exit 60; go ¼ mile north.

Operates: Weekends during May, June, and Sep.; plus Tues., Wed., Thurs. in July and Aug.; daily in Oct.; Santa trains operate between Thanksgiving and Christmas.

Departures: 11:30 A.M., 1;00, 2:30, 4 P.M.; Santa trains: 10 A.M., 1:30 P.M.

Duration: One way, 35 min., round-trip, 75 min.

Fares: Adult, $7; seniors (62+), $6; children (2–11), $3. Santa trains: adults, $19; children, $9; most trees, $25.

Features: Sandwiches and drinks available on the train.

Reservations: 616-382-4244

MICHIGAN STAR CLIPPER
Coe Rail Scenic Train
840 N. Pontiac Trail
Walled Lake, MI 48390
810-960-9440

This company has two very distinct operations: A three-hour scenic ride passes through some commercial sites, but features residential and wooded areas, plus wetlands, a bird sanctuary, lakes, and ponds. Equipment includes restored 1917 coaches from the Erie Lakawanna Railroad. The dinner train is made up of Pennsylvania Keystone cars, with two dining cars separated by a kitchen car. The food is rated 4-star and is served by folks decked out in formal attire. Male passengers are requested to wear coats and ties; ladies should dress comparably. Jeans or shorts are not acceptable. This is a special experience—the way it used to be in the Golden Age of fine rail dining and travel.

Location:	From I-96, take Exit 162 (Novi Road) and go north to 13 Mile Road; go left on Decker, left again on Maple (15 Mile Road), then right on Pontiac Trail for one block.
Operates:	Scenic Train—Apr.–Oct.; Dinner Train—year 'round.
Departures:	Scenic Train—Sun. at 1:00 and 2:30 P.M.; Dinner Train—Tues., Wed., Thurs., Sat. at 7:00 P.M.; Fri. at 7:30 P.M.; Sun. at 5 P.M.
Duration:	Scenic Train—1 hour; Dinner Train—3 hours.
Fares:	Scenic Train—adults, $6; seniors, 65+, $5; children, 2–10, $5. Dinner Train—$53.50 per person (additional $15 for special entertainment).
Features:	Scenic Train available for special charters, field trips, fall color tours; dinner train features murder mystery, musical review, and illusionist. Call for details and schedule.
Reservations:	810-960-9440

Nebraska

FREMONT & ELKHORN VALLEY RAILROAD
1835 N. Somers
Fremont, NE 68025
402-727-0615

This train is run by a local chapter of the National Railway Historical Society and operates 15 miles of former Chicago

& Northwestern track passing through the Platte and Elkhorn Valleys to Hooper, Nebraska. At one time, this track extended through Wyoming and into the Black Hills, prompting people to call it the Cowboy Line. Passengers ride in either former Chicago & Northwestern heavyweight coaches or in an air-conditioned streamlined coach once owned by the Milwaukee Road.

Location:	From Lincoln, enter Fremont on Highway 30 (Broad Street); left on 17th Street, right on Somers Avenue.
Operates:	Apr.–Dec.
Departures:	Apr., Nov., Dec.—Sun., 1:30 P.M.; May Oct.—Sat., noon and Sun., 2 P.M.
Duration:	One way, 1½ hours; round-trip, three hours.
Fares:	Adults, $10.75 reg. coach or $12.75 a/c coach; children (12 and under), $5.75 reg. coach or $6.75 a/c coach.
Features:	Museum, souvenir shop.
Reservations:	800-942-7245

Nevada

VIRGINIA & TRUCKEE RAILROAD CO.
P.O. Box 467
Virginia City, NV 89440
702-847-0380

Route follows the original right of way past some of the most famous Comstock gold and silver mines. Train is hauled by a steam locomotive. Passengers may ride in either open cars or enclosed caboose and may get off at midpoint.

Location:	Enter Virginia City on "C" Street (heading north from Carson City, south from Reno); turn downhill on Taylor Street, then right on "E" Street.

Operates: June–Sep.
Departures: Approx. every 50 minutes between 10:30 A.M. and 5:45 P.M.
Duration: Round-trip, 35 minutes.
Fares: Adults, $4; Children, $2; all-day passes, $8.
Features: Gift shop.
Reservations: 702-847-0380

New Hampshire

CONWAY SCENIC RAILROAD
P.O. Box 1947
North Conway, NH 03860
603-356-5251

An 11-mile route through Mt. Washington Valley, with passengers able to choose enclosed coaches, open-air cars or luxury seating in a restored 1898 Pullman parlor-observation car. Both diesel and steam-powered trains are available.

Location: US 302 to North Conway Village; Exit Route 16.
Operates: Early Apr.–late Dec.
Departures: 10 A.M., 12 noon, 2, 4 P.M. (Days and times of operation vary depending on time of year).
Duration: 1 hour
Fares: Adult—coach, $7.50; first class, $9.50. Children 4–12—coach, $5; first class, $7. Children under 4—coach, free; first class, $3.50.
Features: Dining-car seating available. Working railroad yard with turntable. Museum, gift shop, model railroad.
Reservations: 603-356-5251 (Dining-car reservations, ask for ext. 19.)

HOBO RAILROAD
P.O. Box 9
Lincoln, NH 03251
603-745-2135

Passengers travel in former New York Central coaches along the Pemigewassat River and through very scenic countryside in the White Mountains. A variety of wildlife is usually seen and the 15-mile trip is especially worthwhile during the fall color season. Depending on which trip is selected, optional lunch or dinner is served. The 7 P.M. train features a five-course fine-dining service in the Cafe Lafayette, a New York Central dining car originally built in 1924 and now completely restored. A number of special trains are also operated.

Location:	North on I-93 into White Mountains; take exit 32 to Kancamagus Hwy.
Operates:	Mid-Mar.–Dec.
Departures:	May 30–Oct. 31—11 A.M., 1, 3, 5, 7 P.M. daily. Schedule from mid-March to May 29 and from Nov. 1 to Dec. 31 depends on demand; call for details.
Fares:	Adults, $7; children, $4.50. Lunches, $5.95; Cafe Lafayette, $34.95 per person.
Features:	Hobo picnic lunch offered on most trains
Reservations:	603-745-2135 or 603-745-3500

WINNIPESAUKEE SCENIC RAILROAD
P.O. Box 9
Lincoln, NH 03251
603-745 2135

This train runs over former Boston & Maine track between the towns of Meredith and Lakeport and along the shore of Lake Winnipesaukee, the largest lake in the state. The scenery is delightful year-round, but spectacular during the fall colors. A dining car is available as an option for passengers during summer months.

Location: North of Laconia on US Route 3 to
               Meredith.
Operates: Daily from July 1–Labor Day; Irregular
               schedule in May and June, and from Labor
               Day–Oct.; call for details.
Departures: From Meredith—10:30 A.M., 12:30, 2:30, 4:30
               P.M. From Weirs—11 A.M., 12 noon, 1, 2, 3, 4,
               5 P.M.
Duration: 1 and 2 hour trips; Fall foliage trips, 3 hours.
Fares: 1 hour trip—adults, $6.50; children, $5.50.
               2-hour trip—adults, $7.50; children, $5.50.
               Food service additional.
Reservations: 603-745-2135 or 603-279-5253

New Jersey

MYSTERY EXPRESS
c/o Murder To Go, Inc.
92 Ridgedale Ave.
Florham Park, NJ 07932

Guests board the "Mystery Express" for drinks and appe-
tizers, dinner, dessert, and coffee. During the trip, as passengers relax and dine in restored vintage railroad cars, one
or more "murders" occur. The plot thickens, then unfolds
and—just before the train reaches its destination—is
solved.

Location: Directions are mailed to guests along with
               other information needed for each event.
Operates: Usually on Sat. in the spring and summer.
Duration: 3–4 hours, depending on the event, includ-
               ing dinner.
Fares: Approximately $90 per person, including
               food, drinks, and mystery adventure.
Reservations: 201-301-0562 (Information for spring/summer
               events available by April of each year.)

New Mexico

CUMBRES & TOLTEC SCENIC RAILROAD
P.O. Box 789
Chama, NM 87520
719-376-5483, 719-376-5493

Narrow-gauge trains, each hauled by steam locomotives, depart daily from both ends of this 64-mile route, meeting half-way at Osier, Colorado. Passengers have the option of returning to their point of origin or changing trains and continuing on to the opposite terminus with return provided by van. This railroad is considered one of the spectacular examples of mountain railroading in North America.

Location: Two boarding points—110 miles north of Santa Fe, New Mexico, on US 84; or 28 miles south of Alamosa, Colorado, on US 285

Operates: Memorial Day weekend–mid-Oct.

Departures: From Chama, New Mexico, 10:30 A.M.; from Antonito, Colorado, 10 A.M.

Duration: 6–8 hours, depending on choice of itineraries.

Fares: Chama or Antonito to Osier and return—adults, $32; children (11 and under), $16. Through trip, Chama–Antonito (one way, either direction—adults $50; children (11 and under), $26.

Features: Restaurant and gift shop at Osier; snack car on both trains.

Reservations: 505-756-2151

New York

NEW YORK & LAKE ERIE RAILROAD
P.O. Box 309
Gowanda, NY 14070
716-532-5716

From the Gowanda station, the train travels up a steep grade and through Old Stone Tunnel, which has been in use on the rail line since the 1860s. Continuing on historic Erie Railroad track through scenic rural countryside, the train passes through the towns of Dayton and Markhams Corners. The train stops at the South Dayton station before beginning its return trip. The railroad also operates the Blue Diamond Dinner Train and a Murder Mystery Dinner Train, both of which extend their runs beyond South Dayton to Cherry Creek.

Location: 35 miles south of Buffalo on Route 62; in Gowanda, turn east on Route 39 and go ¼ mile to depot.

Operates: Memorial Day weekend–last weekend in Oct.

Departures: Every Sat. and Sun., 1 P.M.; plus Sat., and Sun. in October, 3:30 P.M. and Wed. and Fri. in July and Aug., noon. Call for scheduled times for dinner trains and other special excursions.

Duration: 2½ hours

Fares: Adults, $8; seniors, $7.50; children (3–11), $4. Blue Diamond Dinner Train, $30–40 per person; Murder Mystery Dinner Train, $55–$65 per person.

Reservations: 716-532-5716

North Carolina

NORTH CAROLINA TRANSPORTATION MUSEUM
P.O. Box 165
Spencer, NC 28159
704-636-2889

Steam and diesel locomotives pull trains on a tour around this large complex, the Historic Spencer Shops, once Southern Railway's largest steam locomotive servicing facility. Included are a large roundhouse with turntable, and other accessory facilities—all operated under the jurisdiction of the State of North Carolina.

Location:	North from Charlotte on US 85, exit 79 (Andrew St.) toward Spencer, left on Salisbury Ave. (Route 29). Historic Spencer Shops on left.
Operates:	Daily (Closed on Mon., Nov. 1–Mar. 31)
Departures:	Schedule varies considerably during year. Call for details.
Duration:	Rail tour—50 minutes
Fares:	Diesel: adults, $3.50; seniors/children (3–12), $2.50. Steam: adults, $4; seniors/children (3–12), $3. Group rates available.
Features:	Museum includes many examples of other transportation modes.
Reservations:	704-636-2889 (Suggest calling in advance due to irregular schedule for train rides.)

Pennsylvania

BELLEFONTE HISTORICAL RAILROAD
Train Station
Bellafonte, PA 16823
814-355-0311

The railroad operates scheduled excursions and charters over more than 60 miles of track in Centre, Clinton, and Blair counties. Equipment used is self-propelled rail diesel cars. Scenic attractions include Bald Eagle Valley, Nittany Mountain, Sayers Dam, and Big Spring in Bellafonte. This trip is really exceptional during the fall with its colorful foliage. Wildlife is also abundant in the area.

Location:	Nine miles from State College (Penn State); from I-80, take Exit 24 south to Bellafonte; station is located just off High Street.
Operates:	Sat. and Sun., Memorial Day–Labor Day
Departures:	1, 2:30, 4 P.M.

Duration:	One way, 30–40 min., round-trip, 60–80 min.
Fares:	Adults, $5–7; children, $2–3.
Features:	Dinner trains and a Santa Claus Express operated periodically; call for details.
Reservations:	814-355-0311

GETTYSBURG RAILROAD
106 N. Washington St.
Gettysburg, PA 17325
717-334-6932

Passengers ride in enclosed coaches pulled by a Baldwin steam locomotive. A 16-mile ride goes through the first-day battlefield in Gettysburg and then on to Biglerville, Pennsylvania. A 50-mile Fall Foliage trip goes through Adams and Cumberland counties to Mt. Holly Springs, passing through wooded areas, mountains, and orchards. Special theme trains are operated during the year and include dinner trips, a Christmas train and, as would be expected, several different rides with Civil War themes.

Location:	One block west and one block north of Center Square in Gettysburg.
Operates:	Apr.–Oct., with several special trips in Dec.
Departures:	Days and times vary; call for details.
Duration:	Biglerville, 1½ hours; Mt. Holly Springs, 5 hours.
Fares:	Biglerville—adults, $7; seniors (65+), $6.50; children (3–12), $3.50. Mt. Holly Springs—adults, $16; seniors (65+), $15; children (3–12), $9.
Features:	Gift shop and snack bar.
Reservations:	717-334-6932 (Recommended for Mt. Holly Springs trip.)

MIDDLETOWN & HUMMELSTOWN RAILROAD
136 Brown St.
Middletown, PA 17057
717-944-4435

Passengers ride in vintage Pullman coaches during an 11-mile trip through wooded areas along the Swatara Creek. During the northbound portion of the trip, a narrator gives a brief history of the railroad and the Union Canal, pointing out historic landmarks including the remains of a canal lock, century-old lime kilns, an operating stone quarry, and Horse Thief Cave. On the return trip, there's a wonderful view of the Swatara Creek Valley as the train crosses a 35-foot high bridge. Passengers may leave the train to tour Indian Echo Caverns. Coaches are pulled by either diesel/electric or steam locomotives. The railroad also operates a dinner train.

Location:	From Pennsylvania Turnpike, take Exit 19; route 283 east 3 miles to Middletown (Hummelstown Exit); turn right at top of ramp, go 1 ½ miles and turn right on Main Street; go one block and turn left on Race Street; straight for 6 blocks to train tracks.
Operates:	May, June, Sept., Oct.—Sat. and Sun.; July and Aug.—Tues., Thurs., Sat., Sun.
Departures:	11 A.M., 1:00, 2:30 P.M. (4 P.M. train operates on Sat. and Sun.); dinner train departs at 6:30 P.M.
Duration:	Round-trip, 1 ¼ hours.
Fares:	Adults, $5.75; children (3–11), $2.75. With Echo Caverns tour—adults, $12.75; children, $6.25. Dinner Train—adults, $25; children, $18.50.
Features:	Gift shop on train, collection of streetcars and other rolling stock on premises.
Reservations:	717-944-4435

Utah

GOLDEN SPIKE NATIONAL HISTORIC SITE
P.O. Box 897
Brigham City, UT 84302
801-471-2209

Although train rides are not offered at this time, officials hope to begin doing so in the near future. The magnificent replica locomotives are operational. This listing has been included because of the great historical significance of the site.

Location: North of Salt Lake City on I-15, exit at Brigham City and go west on Rt. 83 to Lampo Junction; go left on Rt. 504; follow signs to Visitor Center.

Operates: Visitor Center open year 'round, except Thanksgiving, Christmas, and New Year's Day. Locomotives operational from approximately May 1–Sept. 30 and Dec. 29–31.

Schedule: Visitor Center: 8 A.M.–4:30 P.M. (Open to 6 P.M., Memorial Day–Labor Day). Steam locomotives operate 9:30 A.M. and 4 P.M. during May and Sept.; 10:30 A.M., 3:30 and 5 P.M. during June, July, and Aug.

Admission: $2 per adult or $4 per vehicle (whichever is less).

Reservations: Not required.

Washington

LAKE WHATCOM RAILWAY
P.O. Box 91
Acme, WA 98220
360-595-2218

Passengers ride in several restored and refurbished passenger cars dating back to a period between 1910 and 1926 and originally part of the Northern Pacific's rolling stock. The steam locomotive is typical of those that operated in the area during the first several decades of this century. After leaving Wickersham, the train heads into a tunnel, passes alongside Mirror Lake, then goes through a forest.

Location: North from Seattle on I-5; exit at Burlington and go east on Route 20 to the town of Sedro Woolley; then north for 10 miles on Route 9 to Wickersham.

Operates: Tues. and Sat., mid-June–August; plus some holidays. Departures: 11 A.M., 1 P.M.

Duration: Round-trip, 1½ hours.

Fares: Adults, $12, children (2–17), $6.

Features: Gift shop, coffee shop on train, handcar rides in summer.

Reservations: 360-595-2218

West Virginia

CASS SCENIC RAILROAD
Box 107
Cass, WV 24927
304-456-4300

This is an old logging railroad—or, more precisely, it's what's left of a much larger logging operation from the early 1900s. Passengers ride on original flatcars which have been refurbished and converted into coaches. The train passes through some very pretty wooded countryside, but the vintage Shay steam locomotives are what railfans come to see. These engines were originally designed to haul very heavy loads up steep grades and around tight curves, and this ride certainly gives them a chance to show what they can do. The route includes switchbacks and an almost unbelievable 11 percent grade, meaning an increase in altitude of 11 feet for every 100 feet of track. Putting that into perspective, the steepest grade on any main-line track in the country is 4.7 percent. The train stops at Whittaker Station, then continues to Bald Knob, a lookout over 4,800 feet above sea level. This railroad is the focal point of a state park, which offers other recreational opportunities and some quaint accommodations.

Location:	In eastern West Virginia between Dunmore and Green Bank; from US 219, exit on State road 66 and go east to Cass.
Operates:	End of May–Oct.
Departures:	Days and hours of operation vary; call for details.
Fares:	To Whittaker Station—adults, $9; children $5. To Bald Knob—adults $13; children, $7. Ticket does not guarantee a seat on the train, but does include admission to wildlife and historical museums.
Features:	Country store, museum, theater, overnight accommodations.
Reservations:	304-456-4300 or 800-225-5982

Wisconsin

NICOLET SCENIC RAIL
P.O. Box 310
Laona, WI 54541
715-674-6309

This train operates through the Nicolet National Forest, which lies south of the Michigan border and includes much of six Wisconsin counties. The normal 20-mile excursion passes through lovely countryside and stops for passengers to detrain in Wabeno. The 54-mile ride to Tipler runs during the height of the fall foliage and stops in Long Lake. As would be expected, it's a spectacular trip. Rail cars are from the post–World War II "streamliner" era, and include lounge and dining cars.

Location:	East of Rhinelander on US Route 8 at the intersection of Route 32.
Operates:	To Wabeno, mid-June–Aug.; to Tipler, mid-Sept.–first week of Oct.
Departures:	To Wabeno, 10:30 A.M.; to Tipler, 11:00 A.M.
Duration:	Round-trip to Wabeno, 3 hours; round-trip to Tipler, 5½ hours.
Fares:	Wabeno—adults, $11.50; seniors (60+), $10; children (3–12), $8; family (2 adults, 2 children), $33. Tipler—adults, $28; seniors, $25; children, $18.
Features:	Passengers may buy lunch in dining car or bring own food aboard.
Reservations:	800-752-1465

Canada

Alberta
HERITAGE PARK HISTORICAL VILLAGE
1900 Heritage Dr., S.W.
Calgary, Alberta T2V 2X3
403-259-1900

A great many restored buildings and numerous exhibits combine to recreate a typical settlement in western Canada from around the turn of the century. Many of the exhibits are railroad-oriented, including a number of restored rail cars of historical significance. Both streetcar and train rides are offered, the latter in coaches pulled by one of several steam locomotives.

Location:	Village is located in Calgary at intersection of Heritage Drive and 14th St., S.W.
Operates:	Daily from late-May–early Sept.; weekends and holidays, early Sept.–mid-Oct.
Departures:	Park opens 10 A.M.; train runs continuously.

Fares: Adults, $7.50; seniors (65+), $6.50; children
                (3–16), $4.50.
Reservations: None required.

FORT EDMONTON PARK
P.O. Box 2359
Edmonton, Alberta T5J 2R7
403-496-8787

More than 65 authentically recreated buildings depict life in
Edmonton from time of the fur trade in the mid-1800s
through the 1920s. Staff people in period costumes help to
provide a very realistic atmosphere. Train rides are offered,
with passengers riding in three coaches pulled by a restored
Baldwin steam locomotive built in 1919.

Location: Park is located in the southwestern part of
                town, where Whitemud Dr. crosses Fox Dr.
Operates: Daily, third week of May–Labor Day; Sun.
                only through Sept.
Departures: Continuous.
Fares: Adults, $6.25; seniors and youth (13–16),
                $4.75; children (6–12), $3; family, $18.
                (Includes park admission.)
Reservations: None required.

British Columbia
BC RAIL, LTD.
P.O. Box 8770
Vancouver, British Columbia V6B 4X6
604-631-3500

This is an 80-mile trip from Vancouver to Squamish, passing
along the shores of Howe Sound and through spectacular
mountains. The trip includes a 2-hour layover in Squamish,
which provides time for sightseeing and shopping. The consist includes a truly splendid steam locomotive, a maroon and
black *Royal Hudson* built in 1940, along with coaches and two
club cars.

Location: In Vancouver at 1311 West First St. at inter-
               section of Pemberton Ave.
Operates: June–mid-Sept.
Departures: Sun., Mon., Wed., holidays; 10 A.M.
Duration: 6 hours
Fares: Adults, $33.50; seniors and youths, $29.50;
               children, $9.50.
Reservations: 604-631-3500 (Required; recommend making
               well in advance by phone.)

ROCKY MOUNTAINEER
340 Brooksbank Ave., #104
North Vancouver, British Columbia V7J 2C1
800-665-7245

These trains operate in either direction between Vancouver
and Banff, Jasper, or Calgary. The Canadian Rockies provide
some of the most magnificent scenery in all of North
America, and wildlife sightings are numerous. The company
offers a wide variety of tour packages from two to 14 days.
They can originate from several points and all include at
least some transportation in very comfortable coaches of
the *Rocky Mountaineer.* The rail portions of the tours are all
in daylight and the packages include overnight stays in
hotels, plus continental breakfasts and lunches on board.
Schedule and prices vary considerably, so please call for an
information packet.

Operates: Roughly from mid-May–early Oct.
Reservations: 800-665-7245

Manitoba
PRAIRIE DOG CENTRAL
Vintage Locomotive Society, P.O. Box 33021
Winnipeg, Manitoba R3G 0W4
204-832-5259

Several interesting steam locomotives are on display here. One, built in the 1880s and operated by the Canadian Pacific until 1918, pulls passengers in restored wooden cars on a 36-mile round-trip to the town of Grosse Isle.

Location:	Departures are from the Canadian National's St. James Station at 1661 Portage Ave.
Operates:	June–Sept.
Departures:	11 A.M., 3 P.M.
Duration:	2 hours
Fares:	Adults, $13; seniors and youths (12–17), $11; children (2–11), $7. (Includes admission to exhibits.)
Reservations:	None required.

Ontario
SOUTH SIMCOE RAILWAY
P.O. Box 186
Tottenham, Ontario L0G 1W0
905-936-5815

This excursion train operates on an 8-mile circuit, and features a wonderful steam locomotive built for the Canadian Pacific Railroad in the 1880s. It pulls passenger cars originally built in the 1920s, most of which have recently been restored. Other locomotives and a variety of rolling stock are also on display.

Location:	Five minutes north of town on County Road 10.
Operates:	Sun., late May–first week of Oct.; some Mon. and Tues. Call for specific dates.
Departures:	10, 11 A.M.; 12 noon; 1, 2, 3, 4 P.M.
Duration:	50 minutes
Fares:	Adults, $7; seniors & students (12–18), $6; children (3–11), $3; family (2 adults, 3 children), $18.

Features: Railfan Day in early July; call for details of special events.

Reservations: None required.

Pro-Rail Associations

The common bond among the following organizations is that they have all been formed to support and promote rail transportation within their geographical areas. All would welcome a few more dues-paying members.

ALABAMA Association of Railroad Passengers
325 Skyland Blvd. East
Tuscaloosa, AL 35405

ARIZONA Rail Passenger Association
P.O. Box 7482
Phoenix, AZ 85011

ARKANSAS Association of Railroad Passengers
32 Fair Oaks
Conway, AR 72032

Train Riders' Association of CALIFORNIA
926 J St., #612
Sacramento, CA 95814

(COLORADO)
ColoRail
P.O. Box 480452
Denver, CO 80248

CONNECTICUT Association of Rail & Bus Users
P.O. Box 891
Meriden, CT 06450

(DELAWARE)
Delmarva Rail Passengers Association
P.O. Box 11102
Wilmington, DE 19850

FLORIDA Coalition of Rail Passengers
1000 W. Horatio Ave., #125
Tampa, FL 33606

GEORGIA Association of Railroad Passengers
P.O. Box 851
Decatur, GA 30031

ILLINOIS Association of Railroad Passengers
1609 E. Broadway
Monmouth, IL 61462

INDIANA Association of Railroad Passengers
5346 Chipwood Lane
Indianapolis, IN 46226

IOWA Association of Railroad Passengers
3349 Southgate Ct., SW, #108
Cedar Rapids, IA 52404

(KANSAS)
MISSOURI-KANSAS Rail Passengers Coalition
P.O. Box 411192
Kansas City, MO 64141

LOUISIANA Association of Railroad Passengers
P.O. Box 30353
New Orleans, LA 70190

(MAINE)
TrainRiders/Northeast
P.O. Box 4869. Downtown Station
Portland, ME 04112

(MARYLAND)
Delmarva Rail Passengers Association
P.O. Box 11102
Wilmington, DE 19850

(MASSACHUSETTS)
TrainRiders/Northeast
P.O. Box 4869. Downtown Station
Portland, ME 04112

MICHIGAN Association of Railroad Passengers
P.O. Box 351
St. Clair Shores, MI 48080

MISSOURI-KANSAS Rail Passengers Coalition
P.O. Box 411192
Kansas City, MO 64141

ProRail NEBRASKA
3915 Apple St.
Lincoln, NE 68503

(NEW HAMPSHIRE)
TrainRiders/Northeast
P.O. Box 4869. Downtown Station
Portland, ME 04112

NEW JERSEY Association of Railroad Passengers
P.O. Box 5475
Somerset, NJ 08875

NEW MEXICO Association of Railroad Passengers
416 Columbia Dr., SE
Albuquerque, NM 87106

(NEW YORK)
Empire State Passengers Association
RD 4, Fish Rd.
Mexico, NY 13114

(NORTH CAROLINA)
Carolinas Association for Passenger Trains
6003 Teaneck Pl.
Charlotte, NC 28215

OHIO Association of Railroad Passengers
479 Humiston Dr.
Bay Village, OH 44140

OKLAHOMA Passenger Rail Association
1120 S. 21st St.
Chickasha, OK 73018

OREGON Association of Railway Passengers
20585 SW Cheshire Ct.
Aloha, OR 97007

(PENNSYLVANIA)
Keystone Association of Railroad Passengers
P.O. Box 426
Harrisburg, PA 17108

(PHILADELPHIA AREA)
Delaware Valley Association of Railroad Passengers
P.O. Box 7505
Philadelphia, PA 19101

RHODE ISLAND Association of Railroad Passengers
P.O. Box 8645
Warwick, RI 02888

(SOUTH CAROLINA)
Carolinas Association for Passenger Trains
6003 Teaneck Pl.
Charlotte, NC 28215

TENNESSEE Association of Railroad Passengers
610 W. Due West Ave., #421
Madison, TN 37115

VIRGINIA Association of Railway Patrons
P.O. Box 867
Richmond, VA 23207

WASHINGTON Association of Railroad Passengers
Security Bldg., Rm. 418
203 E. 4th Ave.
Olympia, WA 98501

(WEST VIRGINIA)
Retain the Train
P.O. Box 1162
Huntington, WV 25714

WISCONSIN Association of Railroad Passengers
Pleasant Valley
Stoddard, WI 54658

And finally, remember the parent organization in Washington:

National Association of Railroad Passengers
900 2nd St., NE, #308
Washington, DC 20002

Glossary

air brake   The standard braking system used on both passenger and freight cars. Compressed air is used to hold the brake shoe away from the cars' wheels. When air pressure is reduced, the brakes are applied. This concept has an important impact on safety because, should anything go wrong with the system, the brakes are automatically applied. Every car on the train has its own brakes. The braking system for the entire train is controlled by the engineer in the locomotive. Often, when a train is backing into a station, the brakes are applied by the conductor, who operates a special valve in the vestibule of the last car (which, when backing, becomes the first car).

air signal   A separate air line runs the length of a passenger train which, when activated by a valve at the end of each car, beeps in the locomotive cab. The conductor can use this means to signal the engineer . . . *can,* but seldom does, since normal communications are carried out by hand-held radios.

alerter (also **deadman control**)   This device automatically applies the brakes and stops the train if the engineer should suddenly become incapacitated. If one of the train's controls (throttle, brake, whistle, etc.) isn't touched during a specific period of time (usually 20–30 seconds), a horn will sound inside the locomotive cab. The engineer then has 5 seconds to respond before the brakes are automatically applied.

articulated car   Two rail cars joined together to function as one unit, such as the articulated buffet cars operated by Amtrak on trains between New York and Florida. Passengers may move between the two cars without opening or closing doors, but the cars flex at the spot as the train rounds curves.

A-unit   There can be as many as four locomotives pulling a long freight train. This term refers to the first locomotive at the head of the train. Usually, it's the only one with an engineer. Also called the **lead unit.**

Automatic Train Stop System (also referred to as **ATS**)   If a train passes a signal calling for reduced speed without an electronic acknowledgment from the engineer, this system will stop the train automatically.

axle   The steel shaft on which the wheels of the rail car are mounted. Unlike most other wheeled vehicles, the wheels of a rail car are welded to the axle, which then revolves with the wheels. This is an extra safeguard to prevent the wheels from slipping off the rails, and it also transfers the weight of the car to the journal bearings.

axle generator   A small generator, run by the revolving axle, which provides electrical power for the specific car . . . lights or heat for a caboose, for example.

ballast   Coarse gravel or crushed rock used to form the roadbed on which tracks are laid.

blue flag   This signal (a flag is used during the day, a light after dark) displayed in front of and behind rail cars means that people are working on or under that equipment.

bogie   The European term for a rail car's wheel assembly, which is called a **truck** on this side of the Atlantic.

boxcar   This is what most of us call a "freight car," a completely closed car with sliding access doors on each side, used for any kind of general cargo that can't be exposed to the weather.

brake (*see* **air brake**)   There's also "dynamic braking," which uses the locomotive's traction motors to *produce* electricity instead of consuming it. If the locomotive is a pure electric, this power is fed back into the system through the overhead wire; if it's a diesel/electric, it's blown out through vents in the top of the locomotive. Either way, the process slows the locomotive. Dynamic braking will only slow a train gradually and, therefore, is used in much the same way a driver downshifts his car to control the speed when heading down a hill.

cab   A compartment in the locomotive where the crew sits and operates the train.

caboose   A car at the end of freight trains for train crew members. Most of us think the caboose is where crew members can rest or sleep, but its primary function is as a rolling observation post from which the train can be observed and potential problems spotted . . . overheated journal bearings ("hot boxes"), for example. Regrettably, cabooses are gradually giving way to automatic detectors at trackside which alert the crew to such problems.

cab ride   What you and I would probably give a month's pay for!

cafe car   This is sort of halfway between a dining car and a lounge car, with a small kitchen and seating area plus a lounge. Generally, cafe cars are used on small or short-haul trains.

catenary   The overhead system of wires and supports from which electric engines draw the power to operate.

coach   A rail car for carrying passengers. Normal configuration is rows of seats separated by a center aisle, with two seats on each side of the aisle.

coal car   An open-topped hopper or gondola car used for carrying coal. Many of us incorrectly used this term for a *tender,* the car placed immediately behind a steam locomotive from which coal was shoveled into the firebox.

conductor   The on-board person ultimately responsible for the operation of the train and for the rest of the train crew.

consist (pronounced CON-sist)   The total number of cars, including the locomotive, making up the entire train.

container   The box-like "intermodal containers" that are filled with various commodities and then loaded on flatcars, swung aboard ships by cranes, or hauled to their destination by flatbed trucks.

continuous welded rail   These are rails that are welded together in long sections. For rail passengers, welded rails mean a smoother, quieter ride, although a few travelers still claim to prefer the click-ety-clack of rails that are bolted together.

coupler   The device at each end of all rail cars used to hook cars together. The standard coupler works automatically when cars are connected but, for safety reasons, the uncoupling process must be done manually. (Once the cars have been coupled together, a yard worker *does* have to connect cables and hoses for electrical power and brakes.)

crossbuck   The traditional signal at railroad grade crossings, with flashing red lights and the crossed signs, forming a flattened "X" shape, usually saying "Railroad Crossing."

crossover   A track arrangement permitting a train to transfer from one track to another (usually parallel tracks).

cross tie   The wood or concrete structure to which the rails are fastened.

cupola (pronounced CUE-po-la)   The small observation dome on top of the caboose.

cut   The passageway cut through earth or rock through which the train passes. Also a **cut of cars,** referring to several rail cars, coupled together, which are moved from one train to another as a unit.

derailment   When the wheels of a car or locomotive come off the rail. While derailments are usually accidental, they're sometimes deliberately caused for safety reasons. Watch for small signs in rail yards that say "DERAIL." They mark a special section of track which will derail (in other words, stop) an unattended car that may be rolling toward a main track where a collision could occur.

diaphragm   The ribbed fabric shield stretched between passenger cars, protecting you from the weather as you pass from one car to another.

diesel-electric locomotive   This is the most common kind of locomotive and the one which most of us mistakenly refer to simply as a "diesel" engine. There is indeed a diesel motor—and a very powerful one, too—but it doesn't actually move the train in the same way, for instance, the diesel motor moves a bus. Instead, the diesel motor powers a generator which, in turn, produces electricity which powers the traction motors on each axle . . . and *that's* what moves the train.

dispatcher   The person who operates from a central location and is responsible for and directs the movements of all trains within a specific area.

dome   The round, raised opening on the top of a tanker car through which the car is filled. The dome also provides an area for the liquid in the tanker car to expand because of heat.

dome car   A passenger car with a glass-enclosed upper-level viewing area. A great place to ride!

driving wheel   Any of the locomotive's wheels that are turned by the engine to move the train.

electric locomotive   Any locomotive that is powered by electricity and which gets that electrical power directly from an outside source—that is, from an overhead wire (catenary) or from an electrified third rail.

engine   Although technically meaning the machinery which produces energy, in the context of this book the word "engine" is frequently used as a synonym for "locomotive."

engineer   This is the person who actually gets *paid* for sitting up there in the cab of that locomotive and driving it . . . something many of us are certain we'd do for free.

equipment   Engines and cars of all kinds. Anything that rolls along the tracks. Also referred to as **rolling stock**.

express train   A passenger train which operates with minimum delays, usually meaning it makes only a few stops on its route. An **express freight** operates in the same fashion, being routed from Point A to Point B as quickly as possible.

extra train   A train that does not appear on the published timetable. The airline equivalent is called an "extra section."

fireman   Except for special excursion trains powered by a restored steam locomotive, firemen are, alas, part of an earlier time. In the days of steam, the fireman was primarily responsible for keeping the firebox adequately fed with wood or coal. The second person in the locomotive cab is sometimes still referred to as the fireman, but on Amtrak trains that's given way to the more appropriate term, **assistant engineer**. The freight railroads are now using either that term or **co-engineer**.

first class   In North America, this almost always means sleeping-car accommodations, although both Amtrak and VIA Rail in Canada offer forms of upgraded coach class that are sometimes referred to as first class.

flag stop   A station, usually but not always included in time-tables, at which the train stops only in response to a signal.

flange   On the wheel of a rail car, this is the one-inch ridge on the inner rim of the wheel that keeps the train on the track.

flatcar   A railway freight car without tops or sides that is used for hauling materials that may be exposed to the weather.

flat spot   As the term implies, a spot on a wheel that has been flattened, usually from the wheel sliding along the rail. If there's such a wheel on your car, you'll probably be able to hear and feel it. (That's one more reason to try securing space near the center of the car.) This is not just a matter of comfort, however. Freight cars with flat spots on their wheels cause more fuel to be used and, if left unattended for too long, can turn into safety problems. Once spotted they're promptly taken out of service for repairs.

foamer   Railroad slang for a railfan; that is, someone so hooked on trains that he or she supposedly foams at the mouth when one appears. Not really derogatory . . . but not a compliment, either.

FRED   The automatic detector mounted on the rear of most trains to electronically alert train crews to any mechanical problems. It's an acronym for "Flashing Rear End Device." They get the job done, but have replaced the traditional cabooses on freight trains, which are sorely missed by most working railroad people. That helps explain why they generally translate the acronym as "F - - - - - - Rear End Device."

freight car   Any railway car used to transport almost anything: manufactured goods, fruits and vegetables, coal and other minerals, etc. The term does not apply to tanker cars.

frog   A special construction at the intersection of two tracks, permitting trains on one track to cross another track (as opposed to permitting a train to cross *from* one track *to* another). You can usually tell when you cross a frog from the clattering noise the wheels make.

fusee (Pronounced few-ZAY)   These are basically the same type of flares that police use to warn cars to slow down for a highway accident. They're used the same way by railroad people, dropped off the rear end of a slow-moving train to warn trains coming up from behind.

gandy dancer   Old-time railroad slang for anyone working on the tracks. The term comes from the brand name of the specialized track work tools made by the Gandy Manufacturing Company more than 100 years ago.

gauge (or **gage**)   In the railroad context, this refers to the distance between the rails, which, throughout North America, has been standardized at 4' 8½".

gondola car   A car with low sides and an open top for carrying just about anything that does not need protection from the weather.

grade   Refers to a change in elevation for a section of track. For example, a 2 percent grade means the track goes up (or down) a total of two feet over a distance of 100 feet.

grade crossing   A spot where a road crosses the train tracks at the same level (on the same grade).

green eye   Railroad slang for a clear signal, meaning the train may proceed at normal speed.

gross weight   The total allowed weight of a freight car and its contents. You'll see this with the appropriate numbers stenciled on the sides of most freight cars.

hand car   A small, four-wheeled vehicle, usually powered by a small gasoline engine, which carries workers and inspectors along the tracks.

head-end power   Electricity being provided to the entire train by a special generator located either in the engine or in an additional unit placed immediately behind the engine. Usually abbreviated HEP.

helper   Additional locomotives, usually unmanned and remote-controlled from the lead unit, which provide extra power to help the train over steep grades.

highball   A semi-slang term meaning a signal or a verbal instruction that authorizes the train to proceed at the maximum legal speed. The term originated from the old practice of hoisting a colored ball to the top of a signal pole to indicate a clear track ahead.

hopper car   These differ from gondola cars by having sloped sides and ends, permitting the contents to be dumped out through doors in the car's bottom. These cars carry bulk cargo, such as grain (in which case they're covered) or coal (in which case they're not).

hot box   A railroad term for an overheated journal bearing, a constant concern since, if unnoticed or unattended for too long, it can result in the failure of the axle on which it's mounted.

hot box detector   These are the devices which have finally put the caboose out of business. They're sensitive to heat and are placed at various locations along the main tracks. Overheated bearings (hot boxes) are noted and the crew is notified, either by a recorded announcement or by an automatic signal.

hump yard   A railroad yard in which various cars are separated into different trains. A switch engine pushes freight cars, singly or in small "cuts," over a hump—literally a high spot in the yard. Once over the hump, the engine separates from the cars, allowing them to roll slowly by themselves, drawn by gravity, down the long, slight incline, being switched as they go, to join the proper train.

journal bearing   If there's a critical part common to all rail cars, the journal bearing is it. There are two of these box-shaped bearings for each axle and, essentially, they bear the weight of the car. An overheated journal bearing is referred to as a hot box and, if unnoticed, can cause a serious breakdown.

lading   Another word for a freight car's load.

load limit   This is the maximum weight that a given car is permitted to carry. It's computed by subtracting the weight of the car, as it stands empty, from the maximum allowable gross weight. The load limit is stenciled on the side of every car.

locomotive Frequently referred to as "the engine" by most of us, this is the self-propelled machine that hauls the train. If there is more than one locomotive in the consist, the first is called the "A" or the "lead" unit. Additional unmanned locomotives are referred to as "B" units.

main line The tracks receiving regular, heavy use.

main track The track on which scheduled trains are operated.

Metroliner The electric-powered high-speed trains operated by Amtrak in the Northeast corridor, between New York City and Washington, D.C.

mile post (also **mile marker**) White posts with black numbers usually located at trackside that indicate the number of miles from that spot to or from a specific point. Sometimes these markers are signs fastened to metal posts by the track or attached to utility poles.

multiple unit This term refers to two or more locomotives coupled together to increase hauling capability. Such locomotives are all radio-controlled from the lead unit.

narrow gauge (see **gauge**) Any gauge that is less than the standard gauge of 4' 8½", although 36" is the most common. Narrow gauge tracks are usually used in areas where the terrain requires the curves to be too sharp for the longer, standard-gauge railroad cars.

observation car A passenger car specially designed to be the last car in a passenger train, featuring observation windows at the end of the car. These cars are usually fitted as lounge cars. VIA Rail Canada has several of these beauties and uses them on their long-distance trains.

pantograph This is the device that extends upward from the roof of an electric locomotive and presses against the overhead wire (catenary), collecting the electricity to power the locomotive.

parlor car   Really an outdated term, this was in effect a first-class coach car, used for short-haul daytime travel, with large revolving seats and other features not available in ordinary coaches. There was an extra fare for the additional luxury, of course.

piggyback cars   Railroad flatcars used for hauling semi-truck trailers.

rail   Made of rolled steel, a rail is usually 39 feet long. The cross section of a rail can best be described as having an upside-down capital "T" shape. All rails look basically the same, but the larger and heavier rails are used where high-speed and/or heavy trains operate. Smaller, lighter-weight rails are used in rail yards where traffic is less frequent and slower.

rapid transit   Any high-speed rail system used for moving people in urban areas.

red eye   Railroad slang for a red (stop) signal.

refrigerator car (or **reefer** in railroad slang)   An insulated, closed car with cooling equipment designed to keep its contents at a specific temperature. Many of these cars are also equipped with heaters to keep fresh produce from freezing during extra-cold winter weather.

rerailer   A device used to guide a car's wheels back onto the track after a derailment.

right of way   The strip of land on which a railroad track is laid.

rim   The outer circumference of the wheel on a railroad car or locomotive; the part of the wheel which comes in contact with the rail.

rock and roll   Railroad slang for excessive side-to-side movement of rail cars; caused by poor track conditions.

sander   A device, operated from the locomotive cab, that applies sand to the tracks in front of the driving wheels to prevent them from slipping; used going up steep grades or if ice or snow has covered the tracks.

siding   A track located adjacent to the main track onto which one train is diverted to allow another to pass.

signal   A mechanical or electronic device which communicates instructions to the train crew relating to the train's speed, usually in connection with other rail traffic or track conditions.

slide fence   These wire fences are placed along the track in mountainous areas. If they're knocked down by a rock or snowslide, signals are automatically triggered to warn trains of possible obstructions on the tracks.

snow fence   You'll see a lot of these along the tracks in the open prairies of the west. They disrupt the wind patterns and, if placed properly, keep snow from drifting on the tracks.

spur track   Unlike a siding, which is relatively short and is usually parallel to a main track, a spur can be of any length and runs off in another direction. Often spurs are what freight trains use to provide service to towns or manufacturing businesses located in the vicinity.

standard gauge   The standard distance between the rails on track throughout North America: 4' 8 1/2".

stock car   A car used for carrying livestock. Usually the same size and shape as a standard boxcar, but with slats on the sides for ventilation (which is needed!).

stopping distance   How far the train travels from the time brakes are applied until it comes to a stop. Examples: A 100-car freight train traveling at 30 miles per hour could require over a mile to come to a stop; an Amtrak passenger train traveling at 80 miles per hour has a stopping distance of about 4,000 feet.

Superliners   These are the bi-level cars used by Amtrak on its long-distance western routes . . . and a few eastern ones, too.

switch   A moving section of track, usually operated by remote control, which is used to transfer a train from one track to another.

switching locomotive (also called a **switcher**)   A locomotive used for moving individual cars or sections of a train from one track to another in a station or yard.

switchman   A railroad employee, also called a "yard brakeman," whose primary job is assisting in the moving of rail cars in a yard.

tank car   A railroad car used for transporting liquids.

terminal   More than just a station, this is by definition an important rail facility, where both passengers and freight are handled and where many other railroad activities are carried out.

third rail   An additional rail, installed parallel to the regular track, through which electric power is supplied to the locomotive. The electricity is collected through a metal "shoe" which slides along the third rail.

throttle   The knob or handle which is used to increase or decrease the amount of fuel (or electricity) going to the engine, with a corresponding effect on the train's speed.

tie   More commonly called a **cross tie,** these are the wood or concrete pieces which are embedded in gravel and to which the rails are fastened.

timetable   A published schedule detailing the movement of trains, both passenger and freight.

track   The entire structure over which trains operate, including rails, cross ties, and the various fastenings which hold it all together.

traction motor   Electricity, either taken from an overhead wire or generated by an on-board diesel motor, goes to the traction motors which, in turn, power one set of the locomotive's wheels. There are several such motors in each locomotive.

traffic control system   As with the airlines, this term refers to the system of signals, operated by railroad personnel, which controls the movements of trains.

train   One or more locomotives pulling one or more cars.

trainman   An on-board railroad employee who assists the conductor.

trainset   A train which is not assembled and disassembled, but functions as a complete unit over a long period of time . . . typically, a set number of cars with a locomotive at each end of the train (making it unnecessary to turn the entire train around at the end of its run). Trainsets of this type are operated by Amtrak along the Hudson River between New York City and Albany.

trolley   The overhead wire which provides electric power for railroads or transit systems. (Generally, "trolley" is used when speaking of light-rail systems such as urban trolley cars, while the term "catenary" is used in connection with intercity trains.)

truck   This is the entire wheel assembly at each end of a rail car: wheels, axles, bearings, brakes, suspension, frame . . . the whole works.

trunk line   Much more than a spur line, this term refers to a rail line that can extend over many miles.

turntable   A kind of "lazy susan" for trains, used to turn engines and cars around at rail terminals.

unit train   A train which carries only one commodity—coal, for instance—from Point A to Point B.

vestibule   The enclosed area at the end of each passenger car.

weigh bridge   The railroad equivalent of a weigh station along an interstate highway where officials check for overweight trucks.

welded rail   See continuous welded rail.

wheel base   The distance between the first and last axles on a rail car or locomotive.

wide gauge   Two meanings here: (1) a section of track which has spread wider than the standard 4' 8½", meaning there's potential for a derailment; and (2) a term to describe tracks built to gauges wider than the North American standard, as in Russia.

work train   A train that doesn't generate revenue for the railroad; one that takes workers to a spot where track is being repaired, for example.

yard   A rail center where, within a specific area, train consists are made up, cars are moved about, and, in general, railroad activity is carried out.

yard engine   A locomotive which is assigned to a yard and functions only within the yard area. Almost always synonymous with "switching locomotive."

yardmaster   The person in charge of all operations carried out within the yard. The nautical equivalent is the Harbor Master.

yard speed   The speed which will allow the locomotive to stop within a distance equal to half the range of vision.

yellow eye   Railroad slang for a yellow (or caution) signal.

More Information About Trains and Train Travel

There are a lot of books, magazines, and videos about trains out there. The trouble is, most of them have a very narrow focus—great for the hard-core railfan, but way beyond either the knowledge or the interest of ordinary folks who just like to ride trains and want to know a little more about them. With that in mind, here are some of the sources I discovered in compiling this book.

Books

Armstrong, John H. *The Railroad: What It Is, What It Does.* Simmons-Boardman Book, Inc., 1993.

Beebe, Lucius, and Clegg, Charles. *The Trains We Rode.* Promontory Press, 1993.

Ditlefsen, Charles E. *Those Magnificent Trains.* Cedco Publishing Company, 1994.

Faith, Nicholas. *The World the Railways Made.* Carroll & Graff Publishers Inc., 1990.

Kisor, Henry. *Zephyr: Tracking a Dream Across America.* Times Books, 1994.

Maiken, Peter T. *Night Trains: The Pullman System in the Golden Years of American Rail Travel.* Lakme Press, 1989.

Porterfield, James D. *Dining by Rail.* St. Martin's Press, 1993.

Railroad Facts, 1994 Edition. Association of American Railroads, 1994.

Railway Age's Comprehensive Railroad Dictionary. Simmons-Boardman Books Inc., 1992.

Reutter, Mark. *The Lost Promise of the American Railroad.* The Wilson Quarterly, Winter 1994.

Train Journeys of the World. Barnes & Noble Books, 1993.

Vranich, Joseph. *Supertrains: Solutions to America's Transportation Gridlock.* St. Martin's Press, 1991.

Whistles Across the Land. Cedco Publishing Company, 1993.

Wilner, Frank N. *The Amtrak Story.* Simmons-Boardman Books, Inc., 1994.

Periodicals

A great deal of information on this whole subject may be obtained every month from several magazines. These are the most prominent publications, although the latter two are aimed at the hard-core railfan audience.

International Railway Traveler, P.O. Box 3747, San Diego, CA 92163

Passenger Train Journal, Pentrex Inc., 2652 E. Walnut, Pasadena, CA 91107

Railfan & Railroad, Carstens Publications, P.O. Box 700, Newton, NJ 07860

Trains, Kalmbach Publishing, P.O. Box 162, Waukesha, WI 53187

Videos

Literally hundreds of videos are now available on the subject of trains and railroads although, once again, most are not intended for someone who is simply interested in train travel. I can suggest three sources for videos that have passenger train travel in their listings in addition to the narrow-focus material.

Green Frog Productions, 200 N. Cobb Parkway, Bldg. 100, Suite 138, Marietta, GA 30062

Pentrex, P.O. Box 94011, Pasadena, CA 91109

Revelation Audio-Visuals, 977 East Ave., Tallmadge, OH 44278

Now here are some specific recommendations for videos dealing with trains and train travel, all of which are generally available from video catalogs.

America by Rail, CounterTop Video/James Entertainment

The California Zephyr and *The Empire Builder,* Green Frog Productions

Great American Train Rides, Vols. I and II, Pentrex

The Great Canadian Train Ride, International Travel Films

The Iron Road, Peace River Films

Last Train Across Canada, Cleo 24 Inc.

Locomotion: The Amazing World of Trains, A&E Home Video

Index